BLACK-WHITE
RELATIONS
IN THE 1980s

BLACK-WHITE RELATIONS IN THE 1980s

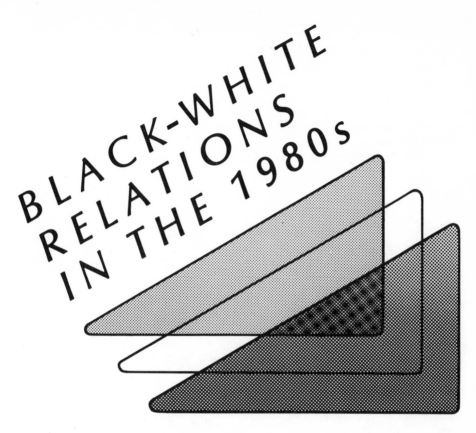

Toward a Long-Term Policy

Hubert M. Blalock, Jr.

PRAEGER PUBLISHERS
Praeger Special Studies

New York • London • Sydney • Toronto

Library of Congress Cataloging in Publication Data

Blalock, Hubert M
    Black-white relations in the 1980s.

    1. United States—Race relations.
2. Afro-Americans—Economic conditions.
3. Afro-Americans—Civil rights. I. Title.
E185.615.B555   301.45'1'0973   79-10224
ISBN   0-03-050461-9

PRAEGER PUBLISHERS, PRAEGER SPECIAL STUDIES
383 Madison Avenue, New York, N.Y., 10017, U.S.A.

Published in the United States of America in 1979
by Praeger Publishers,
A Division of Holt, Rinehart and Winston, CBS Inc.

9 038 987654321

Preface

IN SPITE OF ITS BREVITY, this book has taken me a very long time to write. It was begun during the period immediately after the "long hot summers" of the late 1960s and then set aside, reworked, set aside again, and finally put into print in its present form. Perhaps had I waited another five years the tone would have been different, but if so this is a reflection of the very rapid changes that are occurring in American race relations. Having moved to front and center stage a decade or so ago, black Americans are today in a peculiar position. Some have made it into the great middle class and even into white suburbia, whereas many others find themselves perilously close to becoming a permanent class of unemployed—suffering under the benign neglect of politicians of both parties, who are apparently engaged in a scramble to cut taxes and to reduce services of nearly all kinds.

There are both encouraging and discouraging signs at this particular moment. Some are results of long-term developments, whereas others would have been much less predictable a decade or so ago. Many of these will be discussed in the pages that follow, so there is no point in detailing them here. The basic message of the book needs to be emphasized at the outset, however. It is that intelligent policy must be planned on a long-range basis by persons who are removed from the immediate pressures and vagaries of the political process, and that without such a carefully conceived policy we run the grave risk of entering a downward spiral that, if once set in motion, could pose a very real threat to American democracy and civil liberties.

This rather alarmist assertion may seem overly pessimistic at a time of relative tranquility in relations between blacks and whites, as well as between whites and other minorities. But our own recent history should be an object lesson to those of us who had first-hand experiences involving campus and urban riots. Others may turn to the examples of the religious hatreds that have resulted in numerous lost lives in Northern Ireland and Lebanon, as well as the racial tensions that are at the boiling point in Rhodesia and South Africa. Certainly this is no time for complacency. Yet it is also not a time for panic or another series of half-baked, hurried social programs that are accompanied by false expectations of dramatic results. It is a time for reflection, planning and organization, and deliberate action.

Many of the proposals made in the remainder of this book are basically not new. What I do believe is somewhat different about this set of proposals is that, in making them, I have tried to emphasize that nearly every policy recommendation involves a set of dilemmas that needs to be squarely faced, and that usually there is no "obvious" solution that does not involve costs or risks as well as potential benefits. In this area, too, nearly every policy that one may propose is likely to involve conflicting principles that are each subscribed to by a substantial number of American citizens. Likewise a failure to act, or a tendency to vacillate among policies that are nearly opposite in their implications, will also have its costs. If we do not attempt to face each policy issue squarely but instead take the expedient way out, the long-term outcomes may be far more negative than the short-term benefits are positive.

Many persons have indirectly contributed ideas to this book, but since this is not intended as a scholarly work I have not attempted to supply the reader with lengthy lists of references that are readily available in textbooks in the field. I would, however, like to thank three persons who read and criticized a much earlier and very different version of this book, namely M. Richard Cramer, Albert J. McQueen, and John S. Reed. The fact that this version does differ considerably from that earlier one indicates that I have taken many of their remarks seriously. Obviously, however, none of them can be held responsible for the analysis and recommendations that I have made, some of which I recognize will be highly controversial. Finally, I would like to thank Alice Fowler, Beulah Reddaway, and Karen Wayenberg for typing the manuscript.

Contents

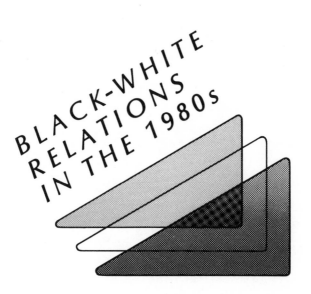

1

A Challenge to Liberalism: The Need for Long-Range Policy

THIS BOOK IS ADDRESSED TO PERSONS who consider themselves to be either liberals or moderates and who are genuinely concerned with relationships between whites and blacks, as well as between whites and other disadvantaged minorities. It is an account of how we can arrive at a well-integrated set of long-range policy guidelines to affect the events that will most likely shape our lives as well as those of our children and grandchildren.

White liberals have turned their attention away from race relations, though the reasons behind this shift are not completely obvious. Perhaps the vigorous civil rights movement of the 1960s, which involved substantial cooperation between blacks and whites, was merely another temporary faddish social movement that was impossible to sustain for any prolonged period of time. Other worthy causes have taken its place—anti-war protests, environmentalist and consumer movements, concern about governmental reforms, and the women's liberation movement with attendant interests in the ERA, abortion, homosexuality, and welfare reform. Perhaps these too will be relatively short-lived and replaced by other equally worthy liberal causes. One of the most important questions we shall need to address in the chapters that follow is that of how we can sustain a sufficient degree of interest in any important social issue long enough to come to grips with a whole series of stubborn problems that cannot be resolved quickly or cheaply. This basically requires a genuine program of action that must be planned and supported for periods of time that are measured in decades rather than years or terms of political office.

Another important reason why white liberals seem to have found other causes is that toward the end of the era of the civil rights movement considerable tension existed between many white participants and certain of the more militant and separatist-oriented blacks. In effect, the latter told the former to go home and mind their own business, or at least not to expect to play any leadership roles in the movement. Once the riots of the late 1960s began, it became faddish to write semipopular books that served primarily to increase the dissension or points of disagreement between black and white participants in the civil rights movement. These "tell it like it is" accounts of race relations tended to give an undue emphasis to themes of violence, hatred, and the failures of the liberal integrationist philosophy that dominated our thinking during the decades of the 1950s and 1960s. Not all of this literature was written by black separatists. Many of these books were authored by disillusioned white liberals as well as members of the so-called New Left. The flavor of most of these works was basically the same, as were many of the encounters that occurred between liberal whites and militant blacks of that period. Among academics, the same kinds of confrontations occurred, with white liberals being accused of both subtle and overt forms of racism.

These days of rather extreme tension between blacks and whites seem to have disappeared, though they may return at any moment. We shall not dwell upon them in the remainder of this book except to note how we may learn from them in terms of their implications for policy. They indicated rather dramatically that coalitions between parties with somewhat different interests and perspectives are often fragile and fraught with misunderstandings. One rather immediate effect of this conflict is that many white liberals appear to have lessened their efforts in connection with the race issue in favor of other issues in which they have more immediate interests. This is unfortunate from the standpoint of furthering the interests of minorities and in finding long-term solutions to problems involving racial and ethnic relations.

To design a realistic set of policy alternatives it is necessary to cope with three somewhat interrelated sets of issues, any one of which may create special problems or dilemmas that must be resolved before the policies can be implemented. First, there will always be diverse parties with competing sets of interests, priorities, and values, and having different kinds and amounts of resources to be used in any power confrontation that may develop over the policies in question. Second, even where there is general agreement over certain desired goals, whatever means that are developed to achieve these goals are likely to require one to take very difficult ethical positions with regard to societal values or norms that these means may violate. Often one must choose between conflicting principles in any given instance. That is, a means that is compatible with one principle may violate another, so that it is virtually impossible to achieve the desired objective without giving up something that is also valued. Third, it must be recognized that policies practically always involve a complex set of assumptions about the causal processes that are at work in a society, and we often lack the necessary empirical evidence to assess the validity of these assumptions prior to implementing the policy. Two persons who share the same interests and have exactly the same hierarchy of values may differ in terms of their beliefs about the best way to achieve these ends because one or both lack the necessary information to make an intelligent choice.

The first of these points—that any policy will encounter opposition based on vested interests—is so obvious that it deserves little further comment. Sometimes, however, policies are set forth without making an appraisal of the realities of power, with the result that false hopes are generated in the minds of those who underestimate the opposition. Double-barrelled policy recommendations that involve both a critique of existing programs and an intended cure often flounder on this point. For instance, if there is a simultaneous attack on traditional mental institutions coupled with a proposal that community mental-health centers be established in their place, as has occurred in the state of Washington, an economy-minded legislature may do away with the former while not providing adequate funds for the latter. If so, the half-implemented policy change may be far worse than none at all. More generally, the least controversial and cheapest set of recommendations will often be adopted, whereas perhaps the most fundamental and far-reaching ones will be sidetracked, particularly if they are at all costly. Such a compromise solution, based on the realities of power, may provide the seeds of later disillusionment and bitterness among the intended beneficiaries.

The second kind of problem, that of conflicting principles or values, creates many important dilemmas even within a reasonably homogeneous group. The issue of admissions quotas exemplified by the Supreme Court *Bakke* decision is an obvious instance. On the one hand, we have the principle of universalism that says that each individual is to be selected on the basis of his or her merits and by means of objectifiable criteria that are in effect "color blind." On the other hand, we have the principle that states that those who have suffered past discrimination should be compensated in some fashion, the simplest way being that of providing them with special advantages.

Any complex value system, such as the American Creed or the

Constitution and Bill of Rights, contains many different values that provide the basis for dilemmas of this sort. Therefore, we may fully expect that any particular set of interpreters of this constitution will differ according to the weights attached to these principles. If one set of nine Supreme Court justices comes down on one side of the fence, we must recognize that a slightly differently constituted Court may decide oppositely shortly afterward. In effect, there is no way of settling the issue without imposing some set of arbitrary weights on the valued principles and in reaching some sort of working compromise. Often this compromise will be consistent with the distribution of power that exists at that time. If the compromise is not consistent with the power distribution, pressures are likely to mount to change it. Each side will be able to invoke cherished rights and values to bolster its position. In many places in the subsequent chapters we shall need to confront value conflicts of this nature.

In connection with the third of these problem areas we merely need to note that we often do not know how best to proceed because of inadequate data, incorrect interpretations of previous facts, or faulty assumptions. Sometimes these assumptions are primarily due to hidden biases based on our own vested interests. On other occasions they are made simply because we must oversimplify a very complex reality and therefore fail to anticipate a sufficient number of contingencies that invalidate these assumptions. Whatever the reasons, we emphasize that all policy decisions must be based on at least some untested assumptions that are legitimately open to challenge.

All reasonably general policy recommendations must be tentative and not completely specific in at least two senses. First, such recommendations cannot be too detailed since they must always be tailored to time and place. The features of each situation will be unique to some degree and will also be continually changing. A policy recommendation worked out in too fine detail would therefore not fit all situations equally well and would undoubtedly prove unworkable in some. An overly rigid adherence to a policy of mandatory busing seems to be a case in point. Secondly, policy recommendations must be sufficiently flexible that they can be accommodated to new evidence, changing priorities among the several involved parties, and improved theories of social causation. In addition, of course, specific policies can best be worked out by persons who are intimately acquainted with the technicalities that are most relevant. Housing policies should be set by persons who are housing specialists and economic policies by labor economists and others who know the details of labor laws, the market situation, minority preferences, and so forth.

Nevertheless, if one becomes too engrossed in the immediate

details of specific policies it becomes difficult to see the forest because of the trees. There need to be more overview-type orientations to policy that attempt to set reasonably general priorities and guidelines. These considerations, in turn, depend in a very important way on overall priorities of the various subgroups within the society, a realistic appraisal of the distribution of power, and a balancing of short- versus long-range objectives.

In this book the focus will be on what I consider to be some of these larger issues and the very general policy implications they may have, rather than on the more fine-grained and detailed problems of implementation. In the first place, I am not enough of a specialist in any of these specific policy areas; in the second, any such detailed recommendations would rapidly become dated, almost before this book found its way into print. Such details do need to be hammered out and continually modified. But this is a much larger job that requires a division of labor among specialists. One of the general policy recommendations in this connection will be for the establishment of a national policy-oriented organization specializing in race and ethnic relations and operating completely independently of either political party. Such an organization would have the important functions of monitoring present practices and recommending and publicizing alternative policies of a coordinated nature.

AN OVERVIEW OF RECENT CHANGES IN BLACK-WHITE RELATIONS

Perhaps it is possible to specify rather general processes of change that majority-minority relationships tend to take. One such theory of change, which seems to be based primarily on the experiences of ethnic minorities in America is basically optimistic. It postulates a relatively smooth transition from an initial contact involving a certain degree of curiosity about strange customs, followed by a rather tense period during which the minority is used as a cheap source of labor and also during which a generation-gap within the minority produces considerable disorganization and crime. During this period the minority is segregated in the least desirable residential areas, but as some of its members gain status they are able to disperse into other areas. If there are several such minorities, one may follow the path of another, with that of the latest arrivals being smoothed by their predecessors. As a group becomes increasingly dispersed both occupationally and geographically, and as it loses its special linguistic and cultural characteristics, it also disappears as a distinct minority into the "Melting Pot" of

American minorities. Religious barriers to intermarriage may remain, but the minority is no longer considered a problem.

It is fashionable to point out that this kind of argument cannot be applied to blacks since their racial identity cannot be changed and since, perhaps with the exception of Chicanos and Puerto Ricans, there are no readily available minorities to follow them and take their place at the bottom of the occupational hierarchy. This thesis, too, is a bit oversimplified because it neglects the fact that there are racially distinct minorities, such as the Japanese-Americans, who seem to be well on their way toward disappearing as a minority problem in spite of the extreme hostility and discrimination they faced during and prior to World War II. But the reminder of a fundamental difference between black-white relationships and those involving the primarily white ethnic minorities in the United States provides a corrective to what may seem an overly optimistic thesis.

The only honest assessment of black-white relationships and our present social-science knowledge that one can make, I think, is that we cannot at this time predict the outcome with any degree of assurance. One major reason for this fact that deserves special emphasis is that timing is crucial in controlling many kinds of dynamic processes. If a sizable commitment of resources can be made before racial tension mounts to that of the late 1960s and before low-income blacks have become almost completely alienated, then the situation may be improved at a relatively steady pace. If we delay even as much as five or ten more years it may be too late. This is why the role of liberals and our ability to organize quickly and efficiently is of crucial importance.

From a historical perspective we are well aware of an increasing rate of change since 1940 in a number of important respects. Prior to World War II, changes in discrimination levels were by almost anyone's definition very slow as compared with present trends. With the exception of the efforts of the NAACP and National Urban League, both of which relied rather heavily on white supporters, the mobilization of blacks was at an extremely low level. World War II provided a stimulus for important occupational gains by blacks and their entry into a coalition with the industrial unions, particularly the UAW. It was anticipated that many of these gains would be lost after the war, as had occurred during the 1920s, but continued prosperity and an alert black leadership combined to prevent it. The urban and northward movement of large numbers of blacks did not abate as had occurred during the 1930s.

The decade of the 1950s was apparently one of rising expectations among the black middle classes, though we have little data to suggest any major mobilization of action on the part of the lower-class black masses. This was the heyday of a black leadership that would today be considered moderate but was at the time taken to be the extreme expression of radicalism, namely that centered in the NAACP. A series of important court cases, the most important of which was the 1954 *Brown* vs. *Board of Education* Supreme Court decision outlawing segregation in southern schools, were seen as major symbolic victories. At the time there were many warnings that these decisions alone would not bring other victories and that residential segregation and occupational inequalities were of more fundamental importance. There were enough signs that progress could be achieved through orderly legal process that a period of optimism among liberals followed.

In retrospect, it is obvious that we were lulled into a false sense of security that should be an object lesson. Some social scientists in the 1950s were sounding pessimistic notes merely to preserve balance in our thought. For example, it was noted that measures of residential segregation pointed to an absence of a correlation between levels of segregation and indicators of black-white economic inequalities, suggesting that a reduction of the latter inequalities alone would not be sufficient to achieve true integration. Furthermore, our data showed that the differentials between whites and blacks were somewhat greater in urban than rural areas, again suggesting that although absolute standards of blacks were indeed rising with the urbanward migration, blacks were not gaining ground relative to whites in these same areas. The hopeful signs outweighed the others, so that even those who examined the data carefully were cautiously optimistic.

The early 1960s were perhaps the golden era for the liberal because of the fact that, very suddenly it seemed, a grass-roots movement stressing nonviolent means and black-white cooperation developed where it was least expected—in the college sit-ins of North Carolina, in the Montgomery movement of Martin Luther King, Jr., and in Tallahassee, Florida. The themes of "We shall overcome" and "Black and white together" symbolized this protest, which gained rapid momentum in wiping out many important symbolic forms of segregation—bus seating arrangements, segregated recreational facilities, segregation in restaurants and hotels—and in challenging the white monopoly on voting within the South. It was undoubtedly during this period, rather than as a result of President Johnson's "Great Society" program, that black aspirations began to rise sharply and that "black power" became a reality. The politicians in Washington responded by passing meaningful civil rights legislation that was particularly directed toward the South.

In the early 1960s there were warnings by the same black leaders who gave impetus to the nonviolent protest movement that tension levels within the black ghettos were mounting, but these warnings were treated by most whites as mere opportunistic threats. The Black Muslim movement came to whites' attention, and it was known that violence was being espoused as a purely defensive weapon, but there was as yet little knowledge in the white community of the explosive situation developing in the black ghettos. Black leaders were pointing out in no uncertain terms, however, that the gains won by nonviolent protest and by civil rights legislation were not solving the basic issues of job discrimination, housing, residential segregation, and inadequate education. These would all require truly major outlays of financial resources and some fundamental changes in priorities.

A new era began with the Watts riot in Los Angeles during the summer of 1965 showing whites the extent of black rage and desperation as well as a liberal coalition's inability to influence the outcome of internal processes of the lower-class black ghetto. Programs of the "Great Society" were blamed for creating unrealistic expectations that had been building up long before. But these expectations were only unrealistic because of a stubborn refusal by a white-controlled society to allocate the proper resources to the problem. Thus was set in motion the debate that has not yet subsided and that promises to become even more heated. Must there be a truly major reallocation of resources and a change in white behavior, or is the basic problem one of an unreasonable minority that is misbehaving and not playing the game the way other minorities have done? The liberal of course favors the first interpretation, but it appears as though a majority of whites adhere to the second.

The basic threat that confronted us during the early 1970s was that of increasing polarization involving greater violence and intractability on both sides. The more "crime in the streets" and student unrest, the greater the mobilization of conservative forces, particularly the police. This extreme degree of tension has now subsided and, indeed, indifference and convenient ignorance on the part of whites are once more the prevailing pattern. It is not yet possible to tell which direction the so-called moderates will move, however, and this group certainly contains some of the most powerful economic forces within the nation, including representatives of business, banking, labor, education, religion, and government.

The major thesis of this book is that liberal forces must begin to organize in such a way as to develop the kind of rational program and methods of persuasion that will enable these moderates to see that the only sensible program possible under the circumstances is one that will, indeed, require a substantial commitment of energies and resources to the problem. Even the lip-service given to this point a decade ago has become a faint whisper with the rise of other liberal causes, including environmental issues and growing interest in the women's movement, the ERA, and problems of the aged. The mounting taxpayers' revolt and concern about inflation and energy have also dampened the liberal's enthusiasm for any program of basic reform that cannot be accomplished cheaply.

Without a substantial effort to develop a genuine policy oriented to improving the position of blacks and other disadvantaged minorities we may anticipate a growing degree of alienation among the lower-class minority population which may, in the 1980s, return us to a period of tension and violence that may be much more costly and prolonged than any we have previously witnessed. Yet, to be realistic, we must also anticipate a considerable opposition to any such program we may develop, not merely because it is costly but because of the conflicting interests among parties that it affects. We can either postpone further thinking about such policies, and await the consequences, or we can begin a concerted effort during the current period of relative calm.

THE NEED FOR COORDINATION AND PLANNING

The civil rights movement of the 1960s taught white liberals first-hand what blacks have known for a very long time: it is necessary to expend a major effort in order to achieve even minor gains. Progress is difficult to measure, especially in the short run, and when it does occur one can never be very sure exactly why. There are always many groups, including those most resistant to change, that are willing to take credit for any change that has already occurred, and the personal rewards we think we may have deserved have not been forthcoming.

Any liberal who has taken part in local action programs is familiar with this difficulty. I recall that it took three years of concerted effort during the 1950s to convince the administration of a major midwestern university that pictures of students should be left off application forms and that freshmen should be assigned roommates on a nonracial basis. (Now, two decades later, both pictures and racial assignments are demanded by minorities in many of these same settings!) A movement by a citizens' committee in that same community to achieve equal housing opportunities produced no noticeable results. A summer work-camp effort to achieve integration in a community center in another community produced only token integration that disappeared shortly afterward. A prolonged campaign to improve the lot of black nonacademic employees at a southern university with a liberal reputation resulted in only intangible gains.

There is also much inefficiency in this process. Many locally based action groups proceed by trial and error, with little knowledge of what has been attempted elsewhere. There are so many federal agencies and programs that only a full-time specialist can keep track of the resources that are, in fact, readily available. Thus a duplication of programs is almost inevitable, and there is little or no feedback of knowledge about successful and unsuccessful efforts. Nor has there been sufficient study of the apparent effects of different sorts of action programs under well-specified conditions. We have known for a long time that the situation is indeed complex, but we have not organized accordingly.

Long-range planning has never been a characteristic of the American political process, even in instances where there is a high degree of consensus on goals. Whenever even moderate amounts of dissent exist, the temptation has been to substitute vague promises for action and then to rely on crash programs designed to alleviate immediate crises and symptoms. This means that even well-intentioned promises cannot be believed, especially when these would involve a major commitment of economic resources.

The result is a series of minor efforts, each of which is intended to represent the beginnings of a large-scale program that never gets underway. As a partial resolution, laws protecting minority rights are passed, but these do not help reduce the basic economic inequalities, the deterioration of urban ghettos, or the crisis in education, all of which will require long-range commitments of large sums of money.

Nor have we even designed a well-integrated package of experimental programs that have been carefully evaluated by objective research. Such experimentation must slightly precede more ambitious programs and must also run concurrently with them. Each step should ideally lead logically to the next. If not, we must fully expect that crash programs of the sort initiated by the Johnson administration during the 1960s will fail. One cannot simply spend large sums of money for the purpose of conducting experimental programs without encouraging opportunism, sloppy research proposals, and half-baked ideas. This is true if for no other reason than that adequately trained personnel will not be available on such short notice, nor can careful plans be made without the benefit of much preliminary work. Therefore there is a desperate need for coordination of these activities by an organization that is not at the same time subject to the whims of the political process.

The liberal orientation in the field of race relations is basically one that requires a long-range perspective that is especially likely to be rejected by both black and white extremists. Whenever changes are slow in coming and continuous rather than dramatic, however, it is exceedingly difficult to evaluate their causes or even to monitor them carefully. For this reason, I would strongly endorse the argument that we need social indicators comparable in accuracy and comprehensiveness to those that exist as barometers of the economy. We need measures of residential segregation, income inequality, housing variables, and educational achievement that become public knowledge and that are reported on a regular basis. We must also be willing to accept the implications of these measures, rather than continually debating their quality or finding excuses for their failure to respond to particular programs. Once more, I would argue that such indicators be constructed and reported by an organization that is completely free from political pressures.

In the face of trends that may possibly favor extremism on the part of some whites and minority members and a general drift toward the political right by what may be the majority of white Americans, I believe that liberalism may lose its momentum without devices such as these. Equally important, our energies may be diverted into putting out the fires started by extremists, so that we shall find it increasingly difficult to reconstruct any long-range program from the ashes. If we do not move quickly and decisively, we may discover that no one will listen to us if and when another crisis period occurs.

2

Basic American Value Conflicts and Competing Ideologies

GUNNAR MYRDAL, IN HIS CLASSIC WORK, *An American Dilemma*, emphasized that white Americans have a deep sense of guilt because of the conflict between the American Creed, stressing the equality of opportunity, and existing discrimination against blacks.[1] Myrdal argued that whites have many ways of alleviating this guilt through rationalizations and convenient ignorance, but he also foresaw a vital force for change in this guilt mechanism. Doubtlessly such guilt has played a major role in motivating white liberals to action, particularly since it is becoming increasingly difficult to maintain a state of ignorance in the face of black militance and the attendant publicity.

Empirical research has shown much less apparent guilt than Myrdal implied. Of course the guilt may be so deep-seated and mixed with basic fear that it is completely repressed by many whites, but there is another rather simple explanation for this negative finding. The American Creed contains a very large number of important values, rather than just a few, and it is relatively easy to call upon whatever set of these values is convenient in order to justify one's behavior. I am not prejudiced when I move to a suburb to escape black immigration; I am merely protecting my family and exercising my basic right of freedom of movement. If I strive to provide the best possible education for my children while voting against a program designed to benefit children in another section of the community, I am once more being a dutiful parent and exercising my right to vote as a free individual. If I work hard and save my money, why should I favor a political plan that, in effect, gives some of my earnings to persons who refuse to accept a job commensurate with their natural abilities and training?

Given a multitude of important values and at least some degree of incompatibility among them, it obviously becomes impossible to arrive at a single ranking or hierarchical arrangement of these values that will satisfy everyone. This means that a simple principle such as that of the "greatest good for the greatest number" is inherently unworkable as a practical guide. The rankings we assign to each value will depend on our own vested interests, our position in the social structure, and the degree to which we take some of these values for granted while perceiving others to be threatened. Obviously, physical safety and the need to avoid starvation would be foremost in almost anyone's list, but most Americans have become so accustomed to taking these for granted that we tend to ignore them unless they are threatened. We cannot understand the motivations of those who, by force of circumstance, must place these values higher than those of individual freedom or democracy.

With these preliminary comments in mind, and recognizing the necessity of analyzing our value conflicts in much greater detail than is possible in this short work, let us merely list with brief comment some of the values that appear basic in American society.[2] These will be grouped under the headings of economic, political, and social values for the sake of convenience. All are familiar, of course, though the political-legal values have been most clearly specified as basic rights and embodied in the American Constitution and Bill of Rights.

ECONOMIC VALUES

Equality of Opportunity. This very prominent value in American ideology is ambiguous in an important respect that bears directly on minority relations. It does not, of course, imply that all persons should have the same status or equal rewards but merely that they be given an equal probability of succeeding in the footrace. Does this mean exact equality, or equality apart from differences in biological givens, such as sex and innate intelligence? Does it imply that advantages of parents should not be passed on to their children, which of course means that the disadvantages of other parents will likewise not be passed along? If one allows for the biological inheritance of abilities or for the fact that parents will naturally act so as to prepare their children for adulthood, then one can never expect full equality of opportunity. And without good measures of biologically inherited traits and of the effectiveness of early socialization, one cannot measure the degree of true equality by simply noting the degree to which children's occupations (or educations, incomes, health) fail to be predictable from those of their parents. In short, opportunity is a vague word.

Rewarding Achievements. It is a fundamental assumption of a capitalist system that good performance must be more highly rewarded than mediocre or poor performances. In American society most such rewards are material, but clearly not completely so. It is believed that without such differential rewards there would be insufficient incentives to achieve socially important goals. We recognize, however, that any existing set of rewards depends upon a priority system that may only in part be in the best interests of the society at large. It may be dominated by considerations of maximum benefit for the elite or by criteria determined by short-run interests of the populace (for example, much larger salaries paid to movie stars and athletes than to scientists and school teachers).[3] Inherent strains in any society, including American, develop over the allocation of rewards to different occupations, and there is no purely logical way of making these decisions. How much should a coal miner receive for extremely dangerous work as compared with a lawyer?

Maximizing Efficiency of Production. Since real per capita income in the final analysis depends upon efficiency of production, our economy depends upon our ability to find ways to improve this efficiency even at the expense of short-run costs in certain sectors of the economy as well as some temporary unemployment. This efficient use of manpower requires continual retraining and an educational system that places a high premium on flexibility in the use of new skills. Those unable to adapt to the necessary changes will be most likely to join the ranks of the unemployed. Personnel policies that result in rigidities at the expense of innovation are to be avoided.

Free Enterprise. The economic system best suited to achieving the goal of maximizing efficiency is assumed to be that of free enterprise involving the competition of large numbers of actors, no one of whom can monopolize the market. As is recognized, the growth of corporate giants as well as various devices aimed at regulating truly free competition have forced a revision in this idealized economic system, but nevertheless there is sufficient lip-service to the ideal that it remains a basic American value. The small business represents the epitome of its expression.

Maximizing Opportunities for One's Children. Although nepotism is a nasty word, parents are expected to place a high value on helping their children to succeed. This includes making sacrifices for their education, supporting community institutions designed to assist one's children, and supplementing their formal education in every possible way consistent with one's standard of living. Mothers, in particular, are expected to enrich their preschool children and to educate themselves with this purpose in mind. As implied above, this familistic value, in practice, conflicts with the value of equality of opportunity, a fact that was noted by sociologists long before programs such as Head Start brought it forcefully to our attention.

Protection of the Unsuccessful and Incapable. Those who fail in the footrace, as well as the aged, the ill, and the mentally incapacitated, must be protected and must be supported at some minimal economic level.[4] Ideally, this should be done by the individual's own family, but if necessary by the state. The support by the state should not be at too high a level, however, if persons are to be rewarded according to their performance. Families that are not in a position to support their own dependents should be somewhat discredited. A good breadwinner is one who refuses outside economic support for his or her dependents and who makes every effort to manage on one's own. This American value places the greatest strain on the lower classes in general, and lower-class minorities in particular. As implied, the incompatibilities with other values make it extremely difficult to arrive at any consensus on the proper level of support for the unemployed, the aged, the ill, and other categories of persons unwilling or unable to make a full contribution to the economy. They also lead to heated debates over the degree to which many such persons really need public support.

Private Property. Individuals have the right to protect, buy, and sell private property in accord with their wishes and resources, subject only to reasonable restrictions that are uniformly applied and that are necessary only for the protection of individuals' rights. Thus one must tolerate a certain amount of zoning, for example, prohibiting one from establishing a house of prostitution or a hamburger stand in an expensive residential area. At issue, of course, are such questions as the right of a white owner to refuse to sell or to do business with blacks or that of a white voluntary association to refuse the use of its facilities to blacks.

POLITICAL-LEGAL VALUES

Majority Rule. Each eligible citizen should receive one vote equal in weight to that of every other citizen. Although he or she is to be encouraged to use this vote, a citizen should not be forced to go to the polls. Votes should not be bought and sold nor subject to any form of control other than attempts to influence by persuasion. The mechanisms of the secret ballot and supervised ballot-counting are necessary to assure that the election has been honest. If there is evidence of dishonesty there must be corrective mechanisms. Unless there is such evidence, however, all parties must abide by the principle of majority rule.

As is widely recognized, many opportunities exist in practice to deviate from the ideal. It is sometimes difficult to distinguish between genuine persuasion, seduction of voters by deception, the purchase of votes, and actual intimidation. There are many possible reasons why registered voters may not vote. Ambiguities regarding eligibility rules frequently arise. Correlates of race (such as literacy) may be used to affect the relative numbers of registered voters. Gerrymandering and disproportional representation may also result in violation of the one-person, one-vote principle.

Freedom of Speech, Religion, Press, and Physical Movement. Controversies over freedom of speech and the exact limitations implied are sufficiently obvious that they deserve no further comment. The right to move about in physical space is so often taken for granted by whites that it has escaped our detailed attention, at least until the concern about "safety in the streets" became paramount. This freedom has long been of crucial importance to blacks, however, who find themselves physically segregated as a result of a system of private property and rules permitting the use and sale of this property. Does the right of movement in physical space include only the right to the use of public lands? If so, there is a vested interest on the part of whites in restricting the amount of truly public land in favor of private facilities that may be used on a discriminatory basis.

Legal Equality. All citizens are to receive equal treatment by the courts, law-enforcement agents, and all public agencies, including those dispensing economic or medical assistance. But it is obvious that laws may be made discriminatory by providing for differential punishments (and rewards) for behaviors characteristic of specific groups. Thus the sentence for a $50 theft from a pawnshop may be greater than that for a million-dollar collusion between officers of two companies operating in restraint of free competition. Equally obvious is the fact that the levels of services (for example, legal aid) may be manipulated quite legitimately in the democratic political process. In the interest of economic efficiency these levels may be set so low that, in effect, the poor or members of a disadvantaged minority may be the only ones who suffer.

Personal Security and Protection of Private Property. All individuals, including corporations, are entitled to impartial protection by public officials and, if necessary, may resort to their own means if adequate public protection is unavailable. This important American value is very much in the forefront today and requires little comment. At issue are questions of the degree of protection that can and should be given by public officials, the actual impartiality of this protection and its abuses, and the range of options that are legitimately open to individuals under the heading of "self protection," including protection from illegal acts by law-enforcement officers themselves. What proportion of a nation's scarce resources should be diverted from productive uses into this "service" function?

The Minimization of Internal Conflict. Though this value is not specifically embodied in the Constitution or Bill of Rights, it is obvious from the number of conflict-reducing mechanisms in the Constitution that this is absolutely essential in American ideology. Too much internal conflict—external conflict is another matter—threatens the very democratic process by weakening adherence to the rules of the game. Conflict not only poses threats to the personal safety of individuals and to guarantees of legal equality, but by polarizing society, it also threatens to destroy many kinds of delicate balances of power such as that between the executive, legislative, and judiciary branches of government.[5] Minorities and other interest groups who find themselves consistently outvoted and subject to discrimination are nevertheless supposed to work within the system, relying on persuasion rather than force or extra-legal tactics of any kind. It is this rejection of conflict as a means that has been recently challenged on the grounds that it is hypocritical, since "legitimate" means of violence are under the control of the white majority that has often seen fit to use them whenever convenient.

Federalism and Decentralization of Power. Insofar as possible, decision-making powers should be given to local communities and to states, rather than being concentrated in Washington. Likewise, major centers of power such as large labor unions and industries, coalitions among financial elites, and very large voluntary organizations such as the two principal political parties are suspect and must be subjected to controls. Multiple centers of power based on divergent interests are assumed preferable to single centers. This important value often conflicts with that of achieving maximum efficiency, but it is seen as necessary in protecting the political and economic rights of individuals. In practice, of course, each major interest group strives to increase its own power at the expense of others, so that the degree of alarm expressed over concentration of power depends on one's position with respect to the policies of those groups that are perceived to be in the best position to gain this power.

SOCIAL VALUES

Integrity of Family and Other Primary Groups. The nuclear family consisting of mother, father, and their preadult children is the ideal norm in which reasonable deviations may occur. Children are expected to leave their parents' home when they marry, or even if they remain single, and to have the right to decide where to reside and with which other family units they wish to associate. Proper socialization requires that each child belong not only to a family but also to peer groups that are primarily of his or her own choosing.

This process is facilitated by relatively stable neighborhoods made up of reasonably homogeneous family groupings. In the case of adults, one's choice of friends and primary groups should be completely free. This implies a mutual choice pattern that is devoid of any pressures to associate with those whom one does not like. This means that one must be free to change neighborhoods and group memberships in accord with his or her resources to do so. Much more debatable is the position that this, in turn, gives one the right to exclude "undesirable" persons from one's neighborhood or primary-group memberships.

Integrity of Voluntary Organizations. By the same token, individuals have the right to form larger voluntary organizations for the purpose of influencing political processes, for economic reasons, or for purely social purposes. They also have the right to determine the membership and policies of these organizations, but they may not interfere with the rights of others. In particular, they have the right to exclude minority group members from organizations that are purely social. The notion that minorities may also be excluded from political and economic organizations, such as political parties or labor unions, no longer seems acceptable to the majority of Americans.

VALUES AND INTEREST GROUPS

Many alternative lists of basic American values could be constructed, and I would certainly not wish to claim that the items above are exhaustive. They should be sufficient, however, to indicate that there are many important values that are likely to be at stake in any power struggle between opposing groups and that each side is likely to stress that set of values that it perceives to be most threatened. This is not merely because of opportunism, the need to motivate its members, and win coalition partners, though this is part of the story. It is also due to the fact that certain values are being threatened and may be relatively less secure than others that are taken for granted.

Opposing groups will see their opponents' neglect of some values as involving hypocrisy, opportunism, and an attempt to preserve vested interests, and to some extent they will be correct. The essential point is that a multiplicity of important values permits a considerable amount of flexibility in the choice of sacred symbols and slogans, as well as legitimate claims that one's opponents are genuine threats to one's security. "Americanism" (or almost any other kind of "ism") means very different things to various parties, and unless we keep this in mind we shall grossly oversimplify the total picture.

During the late 1960s, for example, many whites felt threatened by what they perceived to be a black uprising and by liberal efforts to appease black militants by offering promises that, to them, violated important American values. Why should "they" receive handouts when "we" have to work hard for a living? Why should we pay taxes to support "socialism"? Liberals are thought to be soft on criminals but not at all concerned about protecting the victims. White conservatives may claim that white liberals are letting blacks take over and ruin our cities and then expect the government to bail them out financially. They see blacks invading "their" neighborhoods. They also see liberals insisting on busing thereby destroying neighborhood schools.

It is tempting to pass these claims off as mere rationalizations. After all, what is so sacred about "neighborhood schools," which we all know have generally been neglected by parents until they were threatened? We must realize that in terms of the way contemporary events are being viewed, however, certain values are perceived as being threatened, and it is not only the demagogue who is capable of pointing this out. Many American values have never been achievable by blacks, but these are often the very same values that whites, particularly the white middle-classes, take for granted: legal rights, voting privileges, equality of economic opportunity, personal safety, and the right of freedom of movement. By the same token, many black militants and even white liberals fail to see why these whites now feel threatened. Perhaps we have poked so much fun at certain of these values that we cannot understand that others may take them seriously. But they do, and this is a political reality we must face.

Obviously the basic problem is to obtain rights for a small minority sufficiently rapidly to satisfy all but the most unreasonable of its members, while at the same time not threatening other values held sacred by the majority of white Americans. The general role that the liberal must play in this process would appear to require a high degree of objectivity, an ability to assess accurately the priorities and sensitivities of each party, and a definite plan by which objectives can be achieved roughly in the order of their priorities to blacks. Put this way, it becomes obvious that the task is much more complex and difficult than has usually been claimed by those who advance relatively simplistic solutions.

PRIORITIES, VALUES, AND WORKING THEORIES

The problem of establishing a clearcut set of policy priorities is one that is being given a considerable amount of lip-service, but in the field of race relations the subject has yet to receive really careful attention. Whenever there is a genuine lack of consensus on a subject, there is often an accompanying conspiracy of silence, the assumption being that it is perhaps better to work on day-to-day crises than to tackle the really difficult, more basic issues. Along with this kind of short-run and supposedly pragmatic approach, we often have major ideological disputes that remain so abstract and illusive that they, too, seem to inhibit a detailed consideration of the basic issues of disagreement. This combination of very delimited programs and overly theoretic ideological disputes seems to characterize present-day race relations. It is definitely not a healthy state of affairs from the standpoint of taking concrete steps toward achieving a higher degree of genuine consensus.

There is much more to the problem of establishing priorities than this, however. Even if there were a complete consensus on values and objectives, priorities would also depend upon the nature of one's "working theories" or assumptions about the nature of the causal processes that affect various outcomes. Thus, suppose that all Americans really desired that all individuals be given truly equal opportunities. It does not follow that there would also be agreement on the specific means by which such equality could be achieved. For example, some persons believe that complete integration of the races would be necessary to achieve this objective. Others may believe that equal, though segregated, educational opportunities would be sufficient. A few may even believe that true equality of opportunity requires the destruction of the family system as we presently know it, since most parents attempt to pass along to their own children whatever privileges they have achieved. In short, priorities depend upon one's assessment of means as well as ends, and often there is considerable disagreement, as well as scientific ignorance, about the relative advantages and costs of alternative means.

Given the fact that reality is too complex to be comprehended by the human mind and that simplifications become absolutely essential, we develop ideologies or belief systems that help us to make these simplifications. Among all of the potential values or goals for which we might possibly strive, only a few are singled out explicitly in these ideologies. Such belief systems also provide relatively simplistic theories about social causation that typically suggest that certain means will be much more efficient than others. Ideologies also rule out other means as being unethical or inappropriate. Where several goals or values might appear to be contradictory, in the sense that the achievement of one would inhibit the achievement of the others, ideologies often have the function of making these incompatibilities seem easily resolved.

Ideological systems also tend to exaggerate inconsistencies in rival systems, so that those who have been persuaded by the ideology in question will be able to resist rival systems by resorting to simplistic explanations of why the alternative system cannot possibly work. Americans are of course very much aware of such oversimplifications in communist ideologies, being perhaps much less aware of comparable oversimplifications in their own ideologies. This merely means, of course, that the ideology is working in the sense that it is effective in shutting out competitive belief systems.

All working theories are oversimplified, however, and this means a number of important things. First, they are not likely to be accepted by those persons who have a vested interest in rejecting them or whose interests are apparently better served by some rival set of beliefs. Conflicts of interest that involve basic economic or political issues thus often become confounded with ideological disputes, with each side desperately clinging to its own simplified working theories and rejecting those of the opposing side. For example, the economic and political struggle between the United States and the Soviet Union is often seen as primarily an ideological duel between communism and capitalism, though it is much more difficult to see Soviet-Chinese rivalry in these terms.

Secondly, oversimplified working theories usually lead to oversimplified action programs that fail because they have not taken a sufficient number of factors into consideration. The very simple assumption among many liberals that integration will solve the race problem is merely one illustration. Another is the simplistic theory that the demise of capitalism will eliminate racial discrimination and prejudice. A third is the conservative belief that discrimination will end once a minority has learned to conform and to compete on equal terms with the majority, or that "time" is all that is needed to reduce discrimination.

Very few educated persons now subscribe to such highly simplistic working theories. But in the case of race relations their rejection has tended to lead either in the direction of vacillation and inaction or to a form of eclecticism that has resulted in what might be termed a policy of "a little bit of everything." In effect, this means basically no working theory at all. Perhaps it is more correct to say that each of us has his or her own private working theory, but we are insufficiently sure of ourselves and adopt the expedient policy of bending in whatever direction the wind happens to be blowing. If blacks demand integration, then give them a little bit. If they want separatism, give them this too. If they want jobs and shout loudly enough, let them have a token number. Give them some relief money too. But if the white backlash is sufficiently strong, then hold the line. The recent history of mandatory busing illustrates this kind of "policy" all too well.

If we are willing to admit that reality is highly complex and that we do not know very much about the basic causes of prejudice and discrimination, or even about the priorities of the most important actors on the scene, then it seems clear that the rational course of action is to seek more information. Decision making always must be made in the face of uncertainties, but with respect to economic decisions, at least, it becomes desirable to invest certain resources so as to obtain the necessary information to reduce these uncertainties.

In the case of race relations and other controversial areas, however, the lack of genuine consensus on goals has resulted in a failure to invest such resources. In place of objective data and systematically developed theories, the efforts to reduce such uncertainties have taken the form of oversimplified ideologies purporting to explain what needs to be done in easily-understood terms. Thus it comes to be believed that there is no real need for experts or technical specialists who are sufficiently informed to be able to deal with complexities of this nature. In effect, the complexities are denied. The request for further research or additional information is seen as a hoax or clever excuse for inaction. It is thought that the answers are already obvious.

Of course working theories differ with respect to complexity, as do ideologies, and there are usually several versions of each ideological system depending on the educational level and intellectual sophistication of the intended audience. Generally speaking, the most simplistic belief systems have least appeal to highly educated groups, and for this reason we tend to find that extremist positions in either direction are less likely to be endorsed by these persons. Education can be either broadly or narrowly based, however, and it is quite possible for persons who have received very narrow technical training to have major blindspots with respect to ideological systems. Such intellectual blinders may be deliberately encouraged by those who control the educational process, as for example in totalitarian societies.

In the United States, however, there has been a tendency for breadth and depth to be positively correlated, so that, as a general rule, doctors, lawyers, scientists, and businessmen are more likely to be well read and ideologically sophisticated than are carpenters, plumbers, farmers, and machine operators. But even where they, themselves, may not believe highly simplistic ideological systems, educated elites may have vested interests in supporting those who are most proficient in espousing them. Thus they may contribute to the campaign coffers of a George Wallace or a Ronald Reagan while not believing their proposed solutions are realistic. By the same token, highly educated liberals may tend to support militant black extremists whose vastly oversimplified arguments do not make sense to them, but who are thought to be highly provocative and sufficiently dramatic to provide otherwise apathetic white audiences with a series of jolts and dramatic indictments.

Therefore, it is not possible to describe racial ideologies in such a way as to do them justice, either in terms of their content, or their sponsors and intended audiences. Especially among the intellectual groups, such belief systems are likely to be interlinked with ideological systems that integrate a much broader spectrum of issues. Thus liberalism encompasses not only a set of orientations toward racial and ethnic minorities, but also toward the poor in general, toward the role of the United States in international relations, and so forth. The radicalism of the white New Left and certain of the more highly educated black militants is concerned with such matters as U.S. imperialism, Maoism and world revolution, and the unity of the third world countries.

Our own discussion of such ideologies, however, must be focused more narrowly on the topic of black-white relations in the United States and cannot deal with the question of the overall consistency of such ideologies or their appeals to other elements of the United States or world populations. The best we can do is to attempt to identify a few of the themes and working hypotheses of three ideological systems: the liberal, the conservative, and the radical. Our purpose in doing so is to emphasize that each orientation not only stresses a different set of priorities or goals but also makes a different set of assumptions about the causal processes that are operative.

THE LIBERAL IDEOLOGY

The values that are emphasized most strongly by American liberals are those of equal opportunity, sympathy for the underdog and the universal guaranteeing of certain minimal standards of living, and the protection of civil liberties. Liberals also give a high priority to the preservation of order and the reduction of overt conflict. Although there is general adherence to the principles of free competition and the notion that the successful should be more highly rewarded than the unsuccessful, liberals tend to believe that even the losers should be given a reasonable slice of the pie and thereby protected from an overly competitive economic system. Since they perceive economic power to be highly concentrated in the hands of financial and industrial elites, liberals generally believe that the only major force that can counteract this concentration of power is that of big government made sensitive to the voice of the voter. Therefore, liberals have tended to favor the expansion of federal powers at the expense of both local governments and big business, and they have been equally concerned that all classes of citizens achieve strength through the ballot. Liberals have also tended to favor the growth of groups capable of organizing this vote so as to apply pressure by legal means.

In terms of black-white relations, one of the major working assumptions especially characteristic of white liberals is that blacks (and other minorities) are not really in control of their own destinies. Virtually all a minority's behavior can be explained as being a reaction to prejudice and discrimination by whites, and thus it is white racism that is basically responsible for all inequalities that exist between blacks and whites. Blacks are not to be held responsible for their actions. If they commit crimes, it is the system that is basically at fault. If they do poorly in school, this is a mere reflection of segregation. Therefore, it is thought that virtually all changes must be made by whites. White liberals must lead the way, both by changing whites' beliefs and practices and by affecting those of blacks as well.

Integration, which will be discussed more extensively in the next chapter, is believed to be of fundamental importance in changing race relation patterns, and residential desegregation is the key to other forms of integration. (Very recently, however, this goal of residential desegregation has been modified and partly replaced by educational integration.) It is integration that will change basic attitudes, rather than vice versa as many conservatives claim. Therefore, it is very important to achieve integration even before hostile attitudes have been reduced, and this may mean that such integration must be enforced by governmental action. If possible, this should be through positive inducements, since these are more likely to lead to positive acceptance. But if necessary, negative sanctions may need to be employed to assure this integration. If so, these should be linked with firm and explicit policies that indicate that there will be no vacillation and no toleration of violent responses. Once integration has been accepted, it is assumed that the basis will have been laid for friendly and natural interaction between the races.

Another working assumption of liberals has been that most white Americans (outside of the South) do not have deep-seated prejudices that cannot be modified rather easily, once integration has become the law of the land. There are, however, certain kinds of people who are thought to be primarily responsible for racial discrimination. These include most southern whites, leaders of the Republican Party, and many persons who are in "gatekeeper" occupations that block black access to various occupations and residential areas. These gatekeepers include realtors, bankers, personnel officers, and top policy makers in big business. There is divided opinion among liberals as to the position of labor leaders in this regard, with many of the liberal-intellectuals believing that the predominantly white trade-unionist leaders ought to be included in this group of gatekeepers. Liberals recognize an important role played by economic vested interests of white members of the blue-collar class, particularly in times of depression, but have tended to give relatively more weight to the potential common interests between white and black workers than to the cleavages between them.

To the degree that guilt serves as one of the motivating factors in the white liberal orientation, there tends to be a self-serving ingredient that reinforces the ideological position that whites must point the way for blacks, that whites have the obligation to assist those blacks who are actively attempting to integrate, and that these particular blacks are to be defined as leaders and spokesmen for their fellow blacks. Above all else, blacks are never to be criticized or faulted for failure to achieve or to organize as a group. By the same token, however, those whites who are attempting to aid the process of integration should also not be criticized by blacks. Both groups are operating against very strong forces of inertia and both need each other. But because the initiative must rest with them, whites will find themselves having to take leadership positions, though where possible they should turn over official positions to blacks. One of the basic themes, here, is that of interracial harmony and cooperation as the primary "educational" mechanism that will ultimately make integration work.

Perhaps partly because of the operation of a guilt mechanism there is often an accompanying "holier than thou" attitude toward those whites who do not share this liberal orientation. This includes the tendency to interpret conservative explanations as "mere rationalizations" and as indicators of an underlying prejudice. Liberal intellectuals, especially, feel hostility toward anyone challenging the working assumption that minorities are not to be held accountable for their own behavior. Virtually all inequalities between the races can be attributed either directly or indirectly to discrimination, and the measurement of discrimination can therefore be equated with the measurement of inequality. If there are educational differences, then this is due to discrimination somewhere along the line. The same is true with occupational inequalities, income differentials, and so forth.

Prior to the mid 1960s there was an extensive belief among educated liberals that urbanization and industrialization would reduce prejudice and discrimination. This was based on the assumption that urbanization produces a broadening of horizons and, at least in America, is accompanied by improved education and opportunities for more extensive interracial contacts among near-equals. Although the South was blamed for racial extremism, it was thought that urbanization and the diversification of agriculture in that region, plus the resulting migration of blacks to the urban North, would tend to weaken the influence of the racial demagogue and open up the South to the two-party system. The result would be a growing influence of liberals within Congress and the passage of effective legislation that would diminish the power of the economic elites who controlled the job markets and financial affairs of the country.

Another fundamental assumption of liberals has been that progress is much more steady and probable if it can be achieved by peaceful and legitimate means, rather than through actual or threatened violence. Liberals do differ with respect to the degree to which they endorse rather simplistic beliefs in the brotherhood of man and the notion that prejudice is primarily a problem of misunderstandings and inadequate education. But in general, liberals and conservatives share the belief that it is necessary to preserve a high degree of consensus in order to achieve racial equality. This, in turn, has meant that liberals have tended to see integration as a relatively long-range goal. Because integration is also perceived as absolutely necessary to achieve equality, efforts to achieve short-term goals at the expense of integration have been strongly resisted. Thus liberals have assumed that it is far better to work slowly toward residential desegregation than to accept segregated though improved facilities. The combined stress on integration and peaceful means has therefore implied a need for long-range planning, as well as an emphasis on immediate gains of a more tangible nature.

Finally, the rather marginal or intermediate position of white liberals vis-á-vis the general white population, on the one hand, and blacks on the other, has perhaps reinforced the argument that gains must be achieved by a process of bargaining, compromise, and coalition formation. This, in turn, has meant a need to appeal to many whites who would label themselves moderates rather than liberals. This necessity has required liberals to play down the notion of overt power and conflict of interest, to deny any possible truth to Marxist analyses of capitalistic systems, and possibly even to overlook many kinds of impersonal factors that were producing unfavorable trends.

Issues therefore have tended to be seen in moralistic terms, as a struggle of right against wrong, rather than as involving factors such as changes in labor force demands, the geographic redistribution of the population, and the piling up of black migrants in the urban centers. For the most part, liberals have until recently tended not to pay much attention to policy recommendations involving these rather impersonal economic factors. Likewise, factors such as the competition between blacks and the increasing numbers of white women who have been entering the labor force have tended to be ignored, as have the effects of high birthrates among lower-class black women. One important factor that has received considerable attention among liberal intellectuals is that of the exodus of whites to the suburbs and the resulting decrease in the tax base of the central cities. But the possible impact of school desegregation policies, for example, on such suburban movements has tended to be neglected until recently.

THE CONSERVATIVE IDEOLOGY

Just as there are many variations on the liberal theme, there are also a number of different brands of conservatism. In particular, there is the conservatism of elites who tend to believe that the entire system is proper as it stands. There are also more particular conservative ideological themes that may be strongly endorsed by non-elite groups in their relationships with other lower-status groups. Thus in the case of race relations one often finds that members of a majority group who have generally low status, and who may in other respects be anti-elitist, may take an extremely conservative stance in relation to minorities with which they are in potential competition.

Such persons may waver in their positions, at one time attempting to form a coalition with the minority and at others forming the major source of support for racist demagogues. The populist movement in the South immediately prior to the turn of the century is an obvious case in point. But much the same tendency existed among the populist radicals of the West Coast, who turned their hostility toward the Chinese immigrants then being exploited as a cheap source of labor. In one sense these movements were not conservative, but in a second sense they were. The intent was to return to a system in which such competitors would no longer be an economic threat.

Here we shall focus on more elitist brands of conservatism, with the recognition that there will be certain aspects of conservative ideologies that will readily appeal to other groups and that may be specifically directed to non-elites. Any ideological system, to be effective, must be sufficiently flexible and vague to appeal to diverse audiences and to offer something to everyone—except, of course, to those elements of the population who happen to serve as scapegoats. In the case of liberal ideologies the scapegoats generally are the elites and the gatekeepers of those institutions seen to be standing in the way of progress. In the case of conservative ideologies there are apt to be two kinds of scapegoats: those at the bottom of the heap, and those liberal-intellectuals and "outside agitators" who are perceived to be stirring up trouble among the former group. The real enemy of the conservative, however, is the second group of "trouble-makers," since it is assumed that without the aid of such persons those at the bottom would accept their position as either justified or inevitable. Much of the conservative ideology is of course aimed at convincing the lower classes that the system is basically fair, natural, inevitable, or God-ordained.

In the elitist version of conservative ideology the assumption is made that the social system itself is working very smoothly and fairly, so that those who are at or near the bottom are in these positions as a result of their own personal failures, inabilities, or unfavorable attitudes toward work, saving, or any form of planning for the future. Furthermore, such persons will never really benefit from ameliorative programs designed primarily to redistribute goods and services. Along with this belief in the ineptness of the lower classes and certain minority groups usually goes a corresponding belief that these persons are relatively happy as they are, being basically content with living on a day-to-day basis without the responsibilities of those who must accept leadership roles.

Whenever there are signs of malcontent or rebellion on the part of these persons, conservatives readily assume that outside agitators have been at work. If the rebellion seems widespread and spontaneous, there is the immediate suspicion of a conspiracy, most likely one that has been infiltrated by communists. Those radical-liberals who encourage such open rebellions may mean well, but they are assumed to be playing into the hands of agitators and communists. Neither liberals nor radicals really have the true interests of the lower classes or (here) blacks at heart, nor do they understand their real needs. They are merely using them to further their own political ends.

Since the system itself is assumed not at fault and would otherwise work smoothly, there is no need for governmental interference. Such interference with the natural workings of a competitive system will only lower efficiency and thereby adversely affect everyone's level of living, including those at the bottom of the ladder. The unemployed are in this position because they are unwilling to work for wages commensurate with their skills. Any effort to reward them for this failure, either through direct payments or through a more general redistribution of income will either encourage them to demand higher wages and thus drive them out of the labor market altogether or to expect continued "handouts." The best way to help these people is to expand the economy and to stimulate the growth of business. In this way, the benefits will trickle down from those at the top to those at the bottom.

Power should be given to those who know how to run the social and economic system most efficiently and smoothly, since these persons can be trusted to develop policies that are at the same time fiscally responsible and also of benefit to all citizens. In America, although there has admittedly been some discrimination against blacks, the competitive system is more open and fair than anywhere else in the world. The amount of "racism" has definitely been exaggerated, and almost any black can now rise to the top just as easily as can whites. Blacks have a vested interest in claiming that racism is responsible for most of their difficulties, and of course they also want more than their fair share of power and political offices. Although such misperceptions and demands may be understandable, if we give in to them we will, in effect, be undermining the competitive system.

Segregation is thought to be a very natural social mechanism through which persons who have little in common with each other can readily avoid one another and thus reduce tension. It is not confined to race and is a very reasonable outcome of the competitive process. Those who can afford to do so will tend to live in the most desirable neighborhoods and utilize the more expensive services. Although there may be envy on the part of those who cannot afford these things, persons are generally most comfortable living and associating with others who are roughly in their own station in life. The same applies to racial and ethnic minorities. Generally, Jews tend to prefer other Jews, blacks other blacks, Catholics other Catholics, and so forth. Gradually such patterns of segregation may break down as the ethnic groups become more similar, but any artificial attempt to speed up the process will only fail. Certainly, most of the Supreme Court decisions aimed at forcing school desegregation are misguided. In fact, many conservatives believe that blacks themselves are just as opposed to mandatory busing as are most whites. This is assumed to be true because it represents a premature attempt to force a mixing of the races and also to force black children to compete on equal terms with whites when they are not prepared to do so.

Conservative ideologies have differed with respect to the presumed reasons for class and racial differences. At one time they were thought to be divinely ordained. Others have taken them as being biologically determined. Neither of these explanations is currently in vogue among American conservatives, who have adopted a more flexible version that holds out some promise for the ultimate rise in relative status of blacks and other disadvantaged minorities. It is thought to be more a matter of early socialization and family patterns that are basically not subject to any form of policy control, other than "teaching these people how to work, study, and plan ahead." This must be done through a very gradual process of education. At the same time, however, there remains a convenient ignorance and lack of concern over precisely how this is to be achieved or how the necessary funds are to be raised. Certainly the process will take at least several more generations.

Every ideological system must also be capable of warding off attack from opponents and therefore usually contains a number of very flexible elements as well as vague slogans on which it can rely. "Education" is one of these in the case of conservative ideology. Another is "time." This mysterious time, it seems, can take care of most anything if only it is given a chance. But if it is artificially sped up then failure is almost inevitable, as there is bound to be "trouble" from the "others." Another seemingly plausible device is to rely very heavily on the exceptions that "prove the rule," while being suspicious of statistics that usually tell a more complete story. For example, since there are a number of blacks who have in fact succeeded, it becomes important to display these persons as conspicuously as possible and to discount the failures of the much larger numbers as merely indicating personal shortcomings or an inability to take advantage of existing opportunities.

THE RADICAL IDEOLOGY

Both liberals and conservatives, at least in the contemporary American scene, have tended to play down the role of conflict and violence. Not only is conflict undesirable but it is also thought to be ineffective in achieving important goals within the social system—though paradoxically violence may be glorified and encouraged as an instrument in international relations, provided that it can be rationalized as "defensive." Radical ideology gives a much more predominant role to conflict, violence, and power as instruments of control. A major thesis is that elites have always used these mechanisms as the ultimate bases of their power and that violence has been far more common historically than conservatives and liberals are usually prepared to admit.

Since incidents of violence are extremely easy to document, radical literature usually takes full advantage of such acts to emphasize the point. The argument is that both conservatives and liberals are hypocrites if they decry violence and conflict as tools of the oppressed, while at the same time condoning them when used as mechanisms of control. In order to emphasize this hypocrisy, derogatory epithets are given to the agents of this violence. Police are called "pigs" and are seen as an occupying army within the ghetto. Acts that conservatives perceive as heroic attempts to preserve law and order are depicted in the radical literature as "murders" and "genocide."

Contemporary versions of radical ideology, then, see conflict and violence as being more important than accommodation and cooperation. Recognizing the inequality of power for what it is, however, they stress the selective use of violence as a countermeasure, primarily to wear down the patience of the "enemy" and to serve notice that violence on the part of the elites will be met with swift retaliation. The aim is to use the threat of violence to extract concessions in the power struggle. Since the "haves" will strongly desire to preserve peace and tranquility in order to enjoy their benefits, they will be prepared to pay a price to maintain law and order. It is assumed that they will lack the will to clamp down completely or to apply really extreme sanctions. Thus a premium is placed upon a kind of "war of nerves" as a mechanism for obtaining a genuine bargaining position.

Economic and political powers are seen to go hand in hand and to be highly concentrated. Those who control the means of production and the flow of capital can also control the political parties. Again, there is always sufficient evidence or at least strong suggestions of this close working relationship that a conspiracy theory becomes highly plausible. Economic and political elites are seen to be not only very small and close-knit but also of uniform intention in relation to the poor and underprivileged. Exceptions, such as a Roosevelt, a Harriman, or a Kennedy, are explained away as being rather naive "lackeys" of the establishment, being used to "dupe" the masses.

Even these so-called liberals are thought to have close ties with the military establishment, a belief that is reinforced by the fact that supposedly liberal Democrats have tended to support large military budgets, C.I.A. plots, and the Vietnam war with every bit the same enthusiasm as the most conservative members of Congress. Periodic exposes of F.B.I. or Pentagon documents tend to support these conspiracy theories and reinforce the belief among radicals that there is basically no difference between conservative and liberal policies when it comes to those who would pose a major threat to the smooth-running "system."

According to radical ideology as it pertains to present-day race relations in America, liberals are merely being used by those who are desperately trying to stall the inevitable revolution of the black masses and other disadvantaged groups. These liberals are deliberately holding out false promises in the form of apparently grandiose programs that are never adequately financed. These programs have promised to give some decision-making power to the "people," but when the latter have demanded genuine power they have discovered the true nature of the hypocrisy.

Actually, radicals believe, there has never been any intention of giving up either political or economic power. Instead, the effort has been to coopt a few blacks and other minority members, to label them as "leaders," and to encourage them to persuade other members of their group to work within the system. Since these so-called "leaders" represent a major challenge to those who are attempting to obtain real power rather than token representation, they must be attacked by any means possible. One form of attack to which they are especially vulnerable is ridicule. If they can be labeled as traitors, dupes, or opportunists their influence can be counteracted. Since these persons are themselves either unscrupulous or naive in the extreme, they should be depicted as such and their programs should be discredited.

Radical ideology also contains its fair share of vague programs and slogans. The "system" must be destroyed and the "establishment" overturned. Just what this system is, or what would replace it, is never made clear. Nor is the establishment clearly delineated. Sometimes it is a small ruling elite; at other times it seems to refer to nearly the entire middle class. Nor are the means for achieving these very general objectives clearly specified.

Merely because programs and slogans are vague does not mean that they are unimportant, however. The very vagueness and general-ity implied often makes it possible to appeal to diverse elements of the population. But by the same token this tends to play into the hands of opposing extremist groups. If "black power" is a vague term, it is also a very threatening one to the white conservative, who can make equally effective use of it in appealing to white fears. Calls to "overthrow the establishment" may have the same effect, particularly when no one quite knows just who is and is not a member of that establishment.

SOME IMPLICATIONS

The above very sketchy account of liberal, conservative, and radical ideologies was not intended to do full justice to any of them or to their numerous variations. It should be sufficient, however, to emphasize the major point that priorities depend not only upon one's hierarchy of values but also on working theories that selectively organize facts and beliefs into relatively simplified explanations of reality. Even if we were all given exactly the same set of facts and had precisely the same ends, it does not follow that our priorities would be the same unless our working theories were also identical. Furthermore, since practically all working theories contain assumptions that cannot be tested as well as deliberately unanalyzed ambiguities, to say nothing of a selective use of available facts, there is wide discretion possible for even the most intellectually honest of persons. For the vast majority of us this, in effect, means that we are free to pick and choose according to our own vested interests and personal preferences.

A careful collection and dissemination of facts may, perhaps, be of some use in attempting to arrive at a more general consensus. In the first place, there are many persons—particularly the young—who are not fully committed to any particular ideology or set of working theories. If accurate factual information is made available to these persons, and if one or another ideology or working theory seems more satisfactory in accounting for these facts than others, then it may prove successful in winning new adherents. In this open competition among belief systems, the pressure of facts and uncommitted audiences may combine to force revisions and clarifications that may result in much more complex working theories than our present very simplified versions.

It would be a mistake to hold out too much hope that facts, alone, will resolve such difficulties. In the past, ideological systems have generally proved capable of sufficient flexibility to accommodate themselves quite readily to almost any inconvenient facts. In the final analysis one may always fall back upon the absurd doctrine that "exceptions prove the rule." Given a highly complex real world in which there are multiple causes of most any phenomenon, it is very easy to select out as "most significant" that subset which seems most compatible with one's own working theory or ideology.

In addition to facts, then, consensus requires a genuine agreement to consider all working theories as highly tentative, to press toward clarification of all concepts, variables, slogans, and implicit assumptions, and to combine the most realistic features of each working theory into a single more comprehensive explanation. It is undoubtedly asking too much of extreme partisans to attempt to work toward such a consensus, and it is also unrealistic to ignore the important vested interests that are involved. But the task does not seem completely hopeless as a long-range strategy and seems to be one that liberal-inclined scholars and practitioners can begin to accomplish. Liberal working theories stand in an intermediate position with respect to conservative and radical ideologies and, at least in principle, are sufficiently broad to be able to encompass features of other explanations. In particular, these theories will have to be modified so as to give much greater attention to the importance of power and violence as well as to the autonomous behavior of minorities, both in terms of their political organization and their partial responsibility for controlling those deviant behaviors found objectionable by other groups in the society.

Thus liberal working theories have the potential advantage of being sufficiently broad to include elements from the right and from the left. But this very broadness has its attendant disadvantages, as we have already implied. Broad theories are often diffuse ones, with much room for slippage and vagueness. Furthermore, they are difficult to comprehend and are not likely to be very appealing during crises when quick and easy "solutions" are being demanded. They are most likely to be attractive to educated persons and to those who think more readily in terms of long-run solutions than immediate day-to-day needs. At the very least, these theories must themselves incorporate the fact that one of the powerful driving forces on both sides will be the demand for immediate and practical programs that promise short-term gains. This means, for example, programs that help to provide satisfying jobs for the unemployed and housing for the poor.

Although liberal ideology stands a reasonable chance of being modified so as to appeal to a relatively broad base of the American public, when applied to race relations it suffers a major disadvantage as compared with either conservatism or radicalism. Conservatism appeals directly to vested interests of white Americans through an emphasis on the need to cut taxes, to knock out welfare programs, to control inflation rather than reducing unemployment, and (above all else, apparently) to preserve segregated schools and residential areas. Likewise, radicalism appeals directly to lower-class blacks and other minorities through its emphasis on conspiracies among elites, economic exploitation, and control through violence.

Economic liberalism, it is true, has had an important appeal to the vested interests of the working classes. Liberalism as applied to race relations has not had this same appeal, however, except insofar as it has been able to convince blue-collar whites that their interests are best served through a coalition with black labor. Certainly, racial liberalism has had only a negligible appeal to white manual laborers in both the North and the South. For the most part, racial liberalism has had its major appeal among the more educated elements of the white and black population.

It should also be pointed out that many white liberals, as individuals, rarely have major vested interests in liberal policies of any specific type. Many are liberals out of a sense of guilt or because they see inconsistencies between the American Creed and reality. They are the kinds of Americans who, apparently, Gunnar Myrdal imagined as characterizing a much larger segment of the population. Most such liberals would not stand to lose economically or even politically if blacks suddenly were to face greater discrimination. Furthermore, there are many liberal causes that may attract one's attention and to which one may switch in the event that the cause of race relations seems lost. In fact, a number of blacks during the late 1960s felt that white college youth were beginning to neglect them in favor of the anti-war movement. The present interest in ecology and population control, to say nothing of women's liberation, also seems to be distracting attention of white liberals away from blacks and other minorities.

This is not to say that these other causes are not important ones and that liberals are not sincere. It merely indicates that there are numerous causes in a highly imperfect world that may attract one's attention. Sometimes, as for example in the case of women's liberation, these other causes are also in line with important vested interests. Some of these other causes may be aligned with racial liberalism, but often they are tangential at least in the view of most blacks. Such seems to be the case with respect to the recent ecology movement that has had little appeal among blacks, perhaps for this very reason.

Because of this availability of alternative possibilities, white liberals are especially likely to modify their positions and lose interest in race relations if they are actively challenged by black separatists and told, in effect, to mind their own business. The late Malcolm X confessed, with some regret, how he had once treated a young white college girl who had asked what she could do to help blacks. His reply, "Nothing!," reduced her to tears and, we might surmise, may well have turned her in some direction other than race relations. Demands by certain black students and black sociologists that only blacks and other minorities are qualified to teach and do research in the area of race relations may similarly turn these social scientists to the study of other phenomena, since they have plenty of available options.

I cannot see any realistic resolution to this kind of difficulty other than for liberals with interests in race relations to form a more closely-knit community and, in effect, to act as a mutual reinforcement society capable of providing its own rewards or incentives. This is why I see the formation of an autonomous organization of liberals, focused specifically on the subject of race relations, as a necessary prerequisite for maintaining momentum and for developing a coherent ideology, working theory, and concrete set of short- and long-range priorities.

NOTES

1. Gunnar Myrdal, *An American Dilemma* (New York: Harper and Brothers, 1944), chapters 1 and 2.

2. For a much more extensive discussion of these values see Seymour M. Lipset, *The First New Nation* (New York: Basic Books, 1963).

3. See Gerhard E. Lenski, *Power and Privilege* (New York: McGraw-Hill, 1966).

4. Comparable protective devices in many normal occupations are discussed by William J. Goode, "The Protection of the Inept," *American Sociological Review* 32 (1967):5–19.

5. Anthony Downs, in *An Economic Theory of Democracy* (New York: Harper and Row, 1957), argues that democracy is difficult to sustain in the presence of prolonged polarization.

3

Integration Versus Segregation: Is There a Resolution?

NO RACIAL ISSUES ARE AS HEATED AND POTENTIALLY EXPLOSIVE as those that involve the question of integration versus segregation. At the present time *the* issue in the United States is that of so-called "mandatory busing." A short while ago in the South the issue was school desegregation. In all regions the specter of possible invasion of predominantly white residential areas by blacks has raised the emotional issue of residential integration and the threat of lowered property values. The sit-ins, eat-ins, lie-ins, and protest marches of the early 1960s were directed at many forms of symbolic segregation—in buses, lunch counters, waiting rooms, and rest rooms. All of these issues, in their day, have been explosive ones because they have directly involved the basic question of the nature of the *contacts* between the races.

What, then, does the term "integration" mean to most Americans? It has obviously become a loaded word and one that is practically always associated with liberal policies. Integration has generally been denounced by many southern spokesmen, though much less so today than even a decade ago. Many whites seem to give a kind of lip-service approval to the notion, but in most specific instances close to home they have found it easy to rationalize their opposition in terms of other basic values, such as those of individual rights to privacy, the protection of property values, or the support of "neighborhood schools," which have suddenly become a highly treasured American value. Integration is now also being opposed by some blacks, who see it as a device to control or coopt the black middle class at the expense of the poor and as an attempt to prolong black dependence and lowered self-esteem. Clearly, many Americans are either ambivalent or openly hostile to the idea of integration. But are we all talking about the same thing when we use the word? To some extent we are, but there are several different shades of meaning that need to be identified before we proceed.

In the extreme, integration may mean to some Americans complete biological amalgamation through extensive intermarriage, so that the end result would be the complete disappearance of blacks (or other minorities) as a visible group. Since there are approximately eight whites for every black person in the United States, and since many blacks already have some white ancestry, it is clear that the resulting race mixture would involve only a slight darkening of the average white and a considerable whitening of all blacks. Obviously, such a complete amalgamation is a very long way off. Racial intermarriage in the United States, though perhaps a dramatic event, is extremely rare and has shown no signs of increasing over the past four decades. Miscegenation between white males and black females was, of course, quite common during slavery but has apparently now diminished to negligible proportions. It would thus, undoubtedly, take several centuries and perhaps even a half millenium for such amalgamation to resolve America's race problem. Most of us find it difficult to think this far ahead.

Perhaps a much more common meaning for the term "integration" is the one we shall use in the remainder of this book. Integration is conceived in terms of *participation* or *interaction* and is the polar opposite of complete separation. If there were complete separation this would mean no contact between any members of different races. All blacks would live within the ghetto, go to school there, work there, and recreate and die there without having had any contact with whites. It would be the extreme form of what is referred to as apartheid in South Africa. At the opposite pole, there would be complete integration if whites and blacks were mixed (in all activities) completely randomly so that, apart from sampling fluctuations, there would be approximately 12 percent blacks in every neighborhood, school classroom, occupation, political office, and social club. Between these two extremes of complete separation and random mixing there are of course many intermediate possibilities, and this obviously means that integration-separation varies by degrees and should be discussed in these terms.

An obvious correlate of this fact is that changes in degree of integration occur at different paces, so that if we look at the picture at any given point in time we will find that degree of integration will vary according to the nature of the contact involved. As a very general rule we find that there is a much higher degree of integration in situations that (1) involve very superficial contacts (such as shopping in supermarkets); (2) are more or less required through a division of labor (as in some types of occupations); or (3) do not depend highly on residential location. The major question, of course, is that of the causes of these varying degrees of integration and differing rates of change. We shall return to this question shortly.

There is also a third meaning to integration which is much less common, but which sometimes gets confounded with the extent of interaction or participation. This is the notion of the degree to which two (or more) groups are culturally similar. The counterpart, in some sense, to the notion of separation is that of "cultural pluralism" by which is usually meant the groups may possess sharply distinctive cultures while possibly interacting rather extensively with each other. At the other extreme, the groups may lose their separate cultural identities through borrowing and diffusion so that it becomes impossible to identify any distinctive characteristics, other than perhaps historical ones that have lost all practical importance.

In the case of black-white relations there has been a debate among intellectuals as to whether blacks (after emancipation) have ever possessed a sufficiently distinct subculture that they might be classed as an ethnic group as well as a racial group.[1] Clearly, Japanese- and Chinese-Americans are both racial and ethnic groups. Black Americans do not possess a distinct language, however, though there are several black dialects and numerous expressions that are shared in only a minimal way with whites. There are only a few direct African cultural holdovers, but efforts are currently being made to revive selective aspects of African cultures. Once more, cultural distinctiveness is a matter of degree, and there are differing rates of change depending on the class level of the minority group members and the kind of cultural element (for example, linguistic, familial, or economic) that is involved.

A major practical question is whether physical separation and cultural pluralism must always go together. Put another way, if a racial or ethnic group becomes totally integrated in the larger American society—that is, totally intermixed in the interactive sense—does this necessarily imply that it will lose its cultural identity? In the context of black-white relationships the question is being put this way by black separatists opposed to integration: Doesn't integration require us to imitate whites and to despise ourselves in the process? The suggestion is that blacks cannot develop self-respect and distinctive patterns of behavior unless they voluntarily segregate themselves from whites.

The implication of these remarks is that physical separation and cultural pluralism are not necessarily perfectly correlated but that there is a strong tendency for them to go hand in hand. How, then, could an ethnic or racial group maintain its cultural identity while still striving for integration in the sense of full participation? One possibility is for it to hide its cultural distinctiveness from view. For instance an ethnic group can maintain considerable pride in its heritage through a process of family socialization, independent study of a foreign language, travel to the "home" country, and so forth.

This is not always easy to do, however, since it is both time-consuming and expensive. How can Japanese-American parents motivate their children to learn Japanese, to read ethnic newspapers and books, and to study their history of settlement in this country? If the children are totally mixed in with white Americans, they are more than likely to view their parents' pride as corny and as detrimental to their own interests. If they could be sent to segregated schools and made to interact primarily with other Japanese-American children, the process would be made much simpler. This would require at least a degree of physical separation, however. It is difficult to hide ethnic cultural traits without at the same time either giving the impression that they are somehow inferior or superior or that they must be kept from view because of latent hostilities with other groups.

A second alternative would be to emphasize selectively only the most innocuous and acceptable features of the subculture, while ignoring the rest. This tends to be a very common and perhaps sensible resolution. Thus the Japanese-American family that artfully cultivates its garden so as to provide the atmosphere of the old country is not likely to lose status in a middle-class American neighborhood, nor is the Italian who loves opera and art, nor the European who enjoys an ethnic cuisine. A problem that blacks face in this respect, however, is that if whites do not show a genuine respect for the accomplishments of members of their race—and few whites in fact do—this particular solution is not a viable one. If these accomplishments are highly selective, they immediately lead to patronizing stereotypes such as those of the black athlete, entertainer, or musician. Cultural contributions of which blacks should feel genuinely proud, such as those of spiritual music and New Orleans jazz, may then become symbols of subordination and inferiority rather than the reverse.

Many American ethnic groups have been able to transmit a pride in their respective subcultures by emphasizing hostilities with groups that are not really relevant for their day-to-day interaction with other Americans. Thus Irish may hate the English, Poles hate the Germans and Russians, and Jews hate Arabs without this having any real impact on their minority-group status in this country. They may take pride in past battles and heroes and retain an active interest in current international issues without identifying the rest of the American public as their enemies.

Blacks are not in this situation. It is difficult to imagine any black parent attempting to create race loyalty without pointing to past heroes of the antislavery movement, without emphasizing the atrocities of the slave trade, and without pointing to more recent struggles that have been engaged in by race heroes. Joe Louis and, later, Mohammed Ali become vivid symbols of a form of legitimated aggression against whites, just as martyred black leaders become symbols of illegitimate aggression against blacks. For the white man in America is and always has been the enemy! The development of racial pride, in this instance, becomes very difficult if not impossible without a corresponding emphasis on hatred or hostility toward white Americans. If blacks turn their attention to the African continent, they reach the same conclusions, except that the culprit is the white man in general and not just the American.

In most instances true integration seems to require a very high degree of acceptance on the part of both the dominant and subordinate groups. This involves a kind of informal working agreement that in exchange for a movement from subordinate to egalitarian status the minority will give up its distinctive identity, at least insofar as any traits defined as noxious by the majority are visible to it. Presumably, the majority will also borrow a certain number of minority cultural traits and characteristics. An alternative possibility that is theoretically possible—though difficult to imagine as anything more than a temporary expedient—would involve the assignment of strict quotas to the respective groups. With only two major groups involved, such a system is at least theoretically workable even in the long run. But with many groups it would seem to be totally unmanageable except in a highly static society with minimal geographic and social mobility.

At present we are witnessing the institution of both formal and informal quota systems in terms of entrance into college and professional schools, the teaching profession, labor union apprenticeships, and office holding in professional and political organizations. One rationale behind such quota systems is that they are necessary in order to give the minority a foot in the door to equal participation and that they may be relaxed once the competitive position of the minority has been sufficiently improved. It is at least theoretically possible that a degree of integration could be maintained by such quota systems, even in the absense of a complete acceptance by either party or strict competitive equality. This question of quotas will be discussed in the next chapter.

We have emphasized that both integration and cultural pluralism are matters of degree and that different aspects of culture and different types of integrated activities are likely to change at varying rates. When we add to this the fact that integration, per se, is not the primary goal that is espoused by many blacks—who emphasize that they want dignity and self-respect more than integration—we see that timing may be a crucial matter. If certain types of integration could be quickly achieved, and if such integration in fact enhanced the black person's self-respect, then there would be less apparent need for cultural pluralism and pride based on a form of black racism. If some relatively unimportant forms of integration are achieved while others are denied, however, and if these experiences with partial integration prove to be more irritating and ego-threatening than enhancing to blacks, then one would naturally expect tendencies to retreat to a separatist and pluralistic solution.

Thus a study of the dynamics of the temporal and causal sequences becomes necessary. Which kinds of changes are most likely to take place first, are least likely to be resisted by whites, and are most important to blacks? Are there certain kinds of integration that are necessary before others can take place? What factors are likely to speed up or to impede changes? Assuming such questions can be answered, what are the implications for strategy? Clearly, these are empirical questions that might be answered with adequate research.

At present the debate is taking the following form. The liberal position, grossly oversimplified, has been, and still is, that integration in each aspect tends to reinforce integration in every other aspect. The more blacks and whites who work together on the job, the more readily they will accept residential integration, and vice versa. Residential integration is perhaps the key to most other types since so many activities take place near the home. If, for example, blacks and whites lived in the same neighborhoods there would be no need for mandatory busing. They would tend to eat at the same restaurants, belong to the same churches, and join the same organizations. They would also engage in neighboring and—that ultimate threat to the white segregationist—their children would begin to date and even marry each other.

The whole liberal argument basically rests on the assumption that there would be minimal conflict and that the bulk of the contacts would be among persons with roughly equal statuses, so that the black participants would not always come off second best. In the extreme form this thesis takes the "brotherly love" assumption far too seriously, ignoring all vested interests in maintaining status differences and competitive advantages that whites presently have. In the less naive form, the argument is that these basic changes will occur only very gradually with lots of hard knocks along the way, with the knocks, of course, occurring primarily to the blacks.

The liberal assumption has also been that once given an inequality of economic resources between whites and blacks, which in turn is based on an inequality of power, then the greater the degree of segregation the greater the degree of inequality of services, facilities, training, and opportunities in general. The argument has been that whites who control the purse strings will not be willing to provide equal quality goods and services to blacks unless they are forced to do so. Especially when these services are dependent upon economic resources that are locally based, as in the case of central cities of large metropolitan areas, it is not at all likely that blacks will receive their proportionate share. This is true because those leaders who are subject to partial control by the black community will not be in a position to bargain for a larger slice of the total pie. A case in point, of course, is the major financial difficulty that most large cities are now experiencing. They are unable to convince small city and rural-dominated legislatures, governors, or suburban whites that their relative share should be increased. In fact, they find themselves providing valuable services to commuters and visitors without adequate compensation even for these services, to say nothing of services to their own citizens.

In the face of this dilemma and the recognition that residential segregation cannot be eliminated quickly enough, the liberal position has been that economic resources must be distributed from a central source that is more sensitive to the needs of the black population. This has of course meant Washington and has raised the specter of socialism and a concentration of power in the hands of the central government. Thus, given the unequal distribution of power and economic resources between whites and blacks, the attempted resolution has led to a value conflict between egalitarian norms, on the one hand, and those aspects of the American Creed that favor decentralization and fear of big government, on the other. Furthermore, it has raised for the liberal the possibility that this centralized power may be used against the black as well as in his or her favor. The fear, here, is that extremist reactions by blacks may create a law and order obsession and a white backlash that will result in repressive legislation. The liberal political strategy has, in effect, depended on black voters holding a balance of power that will induce both major political parties to make concessions. But this, in turn, requires that the white vote remains approximately evenly split.

This set of liberal assumptions and strategy has generally been shared by both white and black leaders. It is an approach that has relied heavily on the notion that integration requires a relatively low level of conflict, though the threat of conflict may well be used as a bargaining tool. The basic idea is that, in any complex society, there will be numerous potential bases of conflict because there are diverse kinds of people and conflicts of interests. Thus, there are class, sex, age, political, occupational, regional, and racial differences, any of which may become the focal point of conflicts.

The argument is that if these categories criss-cross each other—that is, if they are only very weakly intercorrelated—then it is much less likely that relatively permanent and sharp lines of cleavage will develop. Obviously, age and sex cleavages cross-cut each other, as do sex and class lines. Although age is somewhat correlated with status positions, younger persons always have the expectation of rising in status as time passes. Racial lines are not likely to be linked with either age or sex differences, though of course young blacks may disagree with their elders concerning desirable strategies. But class and race are likely to be associated, particularly in localized areas. Integration is seen as a means of reducing the association between class and race, thereby reducing the probability of a major cleavage. The problem, or course, is that conflict is created by the *act* of attempting to reduce this correlation by raising the relative status of blacks through integration.

At least some liberals have also tended to take a relatively long-range perspective on the matter, arguing that the overall goal should not be jeopardized by more immediate gains involving segregated facilities. Blacks should hold out for integrated swimming facilities rather than accept segregated and usually inferior ones. This outlook has particularly influenced public housing policies in recent years. The argument has been that no new units should be constructed in segregated areas, or in areas so close to ghetto boundaries that the new units are likely to become completely segregated as a result of out-migration of whites. The implication, of course, has been that blacks can afford to wait for integrated facilities and that they will recognize their long-run interests in doing so. The assumption has also been that the proper governmental policies, both in terms of incentives and negative sanctions, can bring about such integration relatively quickly and that, after a brief period of opposition, the integrated facilities will be accepted by both groups.

Another assumption—which has, in fact, been supported by a reasonable amount of empirical evidence—has been that the degree of white resistance will be a function of their perceptions of the intentions of those who are setting and implementing policy. In particular, if policy is stated explicitly and enforced uniformly and fairly, there is less likely to be resistance to desegregation. If the policy-makers waver, however, or if they state very general guidelines but make no effort to enforce them, then they will leave the impression that they do not really favor them and that they are merely putting on a show for the benefit of the minority. Minority members will of course perceive the situation in much the same way. Those persons who appear to be setting policies, or serving as gatekeepers of discrimination, are then subjected to pressures from both sides, since they are perceived to be either sitting on the fence or hypocritically trying to satisfy both sides at once. The implication, more generally, is that if the power of both sides is approximately equal, or if one side's strength of determination seems to wax and wane, then the overall amount of overt conflict is likely to be high.

These assumptions and the basic strategy of integration they imply are now being challenged from both sides, whereas previously they have been overtly opposed only by white conservatives. The black separatist position, stated most baldly, is that the integrationist approach is nothing but a hypocritical trick to keep blacks under subjugation through appeals to potential black leaders to desert the masses and look to their own selfish goals. Accordingly, the thesis is that those blacks who accept integration as a goal are going to be continually frustrated because they will never be really accepted by whites, though they may be patronized and eagerly used as token representatives of their race. But worse, they will find it necessary to imitate whites, to reject their fellow blacks, and generally accept white images of blacks. In the process they will develop deep-seated ambivalences toward both groups, toward competitive relationships with whites, and toward themselves.

A form of conspiracy theory is used to portray the white liberal as in league with conservatives—this in spite of the obvious disagreements that have existed among whites over racial policy. Some who do not see the matter as one of conspiracy tend to perceive the liberal as merely being used by other whites, who have never intended to accept more than a token degree of integration. Or liberals are seen as patronizing and totally unable to view the matter from the perspective of the masses of poor blacks. The liberal emphasis on delayed gratification and the necessity of taking the long-term perspective is a case in point. "Of course," say the black separatists, "these whites are willing to sacrifice the immediate needs of blacks for the 'cause' of integration. What do these whites know about poverty, overcrowding, and all of the day-to-day insults we face? Only other blacks can understand, and those blacks who have accepted the white-man's goal of integration are trying their best to hide the ugly reality from their own view."

Given white racism, the argument continues, blacks can only achieve a sense of dignity and self-respect through their own efforts, within a segregated environment free from contacts with whites, and by developing a power base that makes possible genuine coalitions within which black partners can bargain from a position of strength, not weakness.

The danger of white backlash is discounted by such separatists for several reasons. First, it is claimed that blacks should not care how whites react; there is certainly no need to attempt to please whites. Second, white opposition is thought to be already nearly at its maximum. Third, even if a white counterreaction should result in extremist action, the present situation is more intolerable than overt conflict. This third position is not uniformly endorsed by black separatists, however, since many recognize the nature of the odds against blacks should an extreme form of conflict develop. But such extreme reactions are thought to be very unlikely, and their threat is taken to be a form of bluff.

Those blacks and whites who have attempted to reconcile these positions while basically retaining the ultimate goal of integration—and a good many black civil rights leaders and white social scientists are included in this category—have for a number of years warned of some of the dilemmas and apparent inconsistencies involved. Black integrationists, especially, have warned that white liberals have tended to underestimate the extreme degree of alienation, despair, and hatred that exists among the black lower classes, particularly those in the urban slums. Separatist leaders such as Malcolm X, too, warned of these potentially explosive and divisive tendencies, but they did not really become visible to most whites until after Watts and the long, hot summers that followed.

Most social scientists, in turn, warned that white resistance to integration was not likely to melt away, since it rested on important vested interests in terms of economic and status gains. The Swedish economist Gunnar Myrdal pointed out thirty-five years ago, for example, that in spite of lip-service to the contrary, Americans have had a long history of basic distrust for the law and a corresponding tendency to pass unenforceable legislation without proper forethought.[2] He has been proven correct numerous times in the recent past.

Social scientists have also pointed to a number of basic economic and demographic trends that have not resulted directly from discriminatory policies but that are tending to work against both integration and the process of equalization of black and white resources. One of these major trends has been the rapid and large-scale migration of rural southern blacks into both northern and southern cities. Though these migrants had been previously segregated in numerous ways, their contacts with whites in many of these small communities had been more extensive than they were to be in the large metropolis. Furthermore, though most of these blacks experienced absolute gains in levels of living, many perceived that they were actually losing ground relative to the whites around them. Even if the migrants themselves did not experience it this way, their children did.

The second major trend has been in the nature of the labor force. Farmhands and unskilled labor have become less and less important to the economy through automation; white craft unions have maintained a tight hold on the skilled labor market, and a major expansion has occurred in the white-collar occupations. Furthermore, white women have been able to outcompete with black men for these latter positions, and the percentage of women in the labor force has been steadily increasing. We shall discuss these important economic trends in a later chapter. The main point in this connection is that there have been many impersonal economic forces that have counterbalanced much of the work of liberal integrationists. As a result, these efforts appear hypocritical to those who either have not been aware of their effects or who have deliberately chosen to ignore them.

I assume that there is general consensus on at least this point. Much will depend upon the speed at which various types of integration can be achieved, as well as the degree to which integration is accepted by the dominant white group. Thus a rational program aimed at achieving integration, in the face of white opposition and a high degree of skepticism among blacks, depends upon an accurate assessment of both black and white priorities. In 1944 Gunnar Myrdal postulated that there is both a black and a white ordering of preferences and that these are, roughly speaking, in inverse orders.[3] At the top of the white hierarchy is the bar against intermarriage and a resistance to social mixing with blacks. These goals, claimed Myrdal, are at the very bottom of the black preference hierarchy. Blacks are most interested in good jobs, adequate housing, quality education, and certain basic legal rights.

Though this "rank-order of discriminations" hypothesis has not received empirical support in all of its detail, at least the above-cited preferences have been found to exist. In particular, there have been literally hundreds of studies that have made use of what are called social-distance scales that clearly indicate that whites are least willing to marry blacks, somewhat more willing to invite them into their homes, still more willing to have them living not too far away or holding down the same jobs, and least resistant to relatively impersonal kinds of contact situations. Almost all black spokesmen assert that blacks *are* most interested in jobs, adequate housing, quality education, and the basic economic and medical necessities, and that they are least interested in close social mixing and interracial marriage. Issues such as that of interracial schools apparently fall in intermediate positions in both hierarchies.

Another kind of fact seems well established. If interracial contacts are to lead in the direction of genuine integration that also involves acceptance of the contact by both groups, the contacts must involve persons of approximately equal status. In the old South, where an elaborate racial division of labor required extensive contacts among persons of very unequal statuses, white Southerners insisted on a rigid racial etiquette that clearly emphasized the status differential. This involved specified terms of address and deferential behavior, the careful regulation of contacts between white women and black men, and a host of symbolic forms of segregation (e.g., separate waiting rooms and drinking fountains) that served the purpose of drawing a sharp line between the two groups in spite of their extensive contact. These patterns of etiquette were extremely irksome to blacks, who were thereby continually reminded of their lower status. "Integration" of this sort will be totally unacceptable to most blacks. But many black experiences with integration in the North have been almost equally unacceptable because of somewhat more subtle patterns involving patronizing stances by those whites with whom they have had contact.

Obviously, then, integration is a relatively slow process, though it can certainly be sped up. Those blacks who attempt to live and work among whites also find that there is considerable variation among white responses, ranging from genuine acceptance, to uneasy attempts to bridge the gap, to patronizing and paternalistic responses, to outright hostility and snobbery. We need to emphasize repeatedly, however, that this does not imply a conspiracy or hypocrisy on the part of all whites. It merely means a wide range of positions and responses exist that cannot be expected to give way to uniform genuine acceptance until several generations have become accustomed to the process.

Many blacks, if not the overwhelming majority, will not be able to accept this kind of treatment and will rightly say that there is no reason why they should have to do so. For this very reason it is absolutely essential, if the long-range objective is to be met, that those relatively small number of blacks who are willing to undergo this experience should be compensated in other ways. And it is also essential—though whites can have little to say about this—that these blacks also be more readily accepted by blacks who have elected to follow the separatist route. They cannot be ridiculed by separatists as "oreos" (black on the outside, white on the inside) without this creating an even greater ambivalence toward both groups.

WHAT ARE SOME POLICY IMPLICATIONS?

Is it possible to play it both ways and maintain progress toward integration while allowing for separatism? If integration and separation are opposite poles of the same continuum, then it would seem as though we are being pulled in both directions. Indeed in some cases we are, as for example when the NAACP is pushing for mandatory busing, the achievement of which immediately brings denunciations from other black organizations, including CORE, a formerly integrationist group. Because some blacks may be able to move toward integration while others are more oriented toward separation, however, it becomes possible to achieve at least a much higher degree of integration than we presently have. Also, of course, there are many areas or domains in which interracial contact takes place, so that it is possible for blacks to interact with whites in some settings (e.g., on the job) while retreating to the more comfortable segregated atmosphere of the home and community for relaxation. Such a compromise position will not please the strict separatists, nor is it the best possible resolution for those who believe that any movement away from integration will be to the disadvantage of both groups.

The long-range interests of the group may not coincide with the short-run interests and needs of its individual members. This may be the case with respect to integration. If all blacks and liberal whites were to work wholeheartedly for integration, and if the black participants were willing to make the very real personal sacrifices that this would entail, then I believe a substantial amount of overall integration could be achieved within two or three decades given recent trends. This is not going to happen, however, and it is unreasonable for white liberals to expect such a high degree of self-control, discomfort, and personal sacrifice on the part of the majority of blacks. Most blacks want to achieve self-respect now, and they also want higher quality facilities and better opportunities now in preference to integration later. Their point of view is quite rational. Why trade off immediate gains for some long-range objectives that are by no means guaranteed and that depend on the good-will of whites whom they cannot trust? Moving toward integration requires a good deal more faith in the future than most lower-class blacks can be expected to have in terms of their own experiences and the actual historical record.

It seems clear that immediate personal goals cannot be sacrificed in the bargain, and this means a return to an emphasis on improving the quality of living within the ghetto, with the full recognition that the majority of blacks will not take major steps toward genuine integration within the next several decades. Hopefully, however, they will be developing competitive skills, self-respect, and organizational tools so that larger and larger proportions will be able to take this step with a minimum of difficulty when they choose to do so.

At the same time, however, we must continue to provide every opportunity to those blacks who wish to make the transition. This means finding more white-collar positions, breaking the craft-union barriers, and opening up predominantly white suburban schools to blacks. It also means that small pockets of blacks should be encouraged to settle in the white suburbs and that small-scale public housing units should also be constructed in these areas. As a general principle, it would seem wise to move as rationally as possible in the direction of breaking up the largest segregated units in favor of smaller ones.

Thus, instead of all-black colleges it would seem preferable to encourage black-studies programs in predominantly white schools, and to permit segregated dormitories or other housing units for those blacks who might otherwise prefer an all-black campus. Similarly, if it were possible to break up the concentrated black ghettos in our largest metropolitan centers it would seem advisable to encourage resettlement in much smaller units in the suburban fringes or in smaller neighboring cities. Such policies will be strongly resisted by the local white inhabitants and some black politicians, however. Settlement in sparsely populated areas would be a conceivable alternative, an example being Floyd McKissick's "Soul City" in North Carolina, though it appears as though the relatively few efforts to establish such new communities have been failures.

This is of course a return to voluntary types of integration that basically depend upon the self-selection of those white and black participants who are most likely to develop compatible interests. Contacts between mutually hostile groups do not help the cause of integration unless the hostility can rather quickly be brought under control. Clearly, the introduction of poorly educated and openly hostile black students into formerly all-white schools has had disastrous results even where the predominant white attitude has been one of "tolerance" accompanied by a degree of patronization. The difficulty with strictly voluntary arrangements, however, is that they often touch only a small fraction of the members of each group and therefore represent only a token form of integration that is mainly beneficial only to the participants.

If such experiments are to be anything more than a holding operation, ways must be found to provide positive incentives to the participants so as to increase their numbers. Though perhaps politically difficult, this can be done by devices such as charging lower rents in the case of housing units, lower interest rates and downpayments in the case of homes, and offering better and cheaper educational opportunities in the case of schools and colleges. Thus, those who choose to integrate will be rewarded in a tangible way for making the effort. To the degree that such programs can be planned and publicized in advance, enjoy bipartisan support, and be seen as long-term rather than experimental in nature, they should become increasingly popular among members of both groups. The younger generation, especially, can be expected to take advantage of them.

These proposals would probably not be strongly resisted by most whites except in two crucial respects—whenever they would hit close to home (say, near one's own neighborhood), and whenever the financial costs were perceived to be too great. Neither of these difficulties is insurmountable, though they do set limits on both the magnitude of scale and the pace with which such programs could be instituted. There will also be opposition from black separatists. Their fear would be not only that this is one more token gesture, but would also tend to siphon off the very blacks who are most needed within the ghetto. Therefore, to be effective, integration proposals of this sort must be combined with other programs designed to strengthen ghetto programs. The essential point is that individual blacks should be given a genuine choice among alternatives, each of which is positively rewarded in some way.

Does integration tend to reduce efforts to achieve other objectives and would programs such as these tend only to divide still further the black community? First, I see no solid evidence that those blacks who have opted for integration have taken a back seat in terms of their interests in the cause of race relations. Certain militant separatists have decried the fact that only a small minority of black intellectuals and middle-class members have taken an active part and that their efforts have tended to be both sporadic and addressed to needs of their own class. The same criticism has been leveled at white liberals. But just how active and effective are the black separatists? The truth is that it is generally only a small fraction of any category of persons who become actively involved in sustained efforts. Even Malcolm X was plagued during his last few years by the complaint that he and his followers merely talked and criticized those blacks who were actively taking integrationist positions.[4] It is plausible to assume that, if properly motivated and rewarded, there will be a sufficient number of persons who will be willing to work actively within the ghetto, while others are serving the cause of integration through personal example and continued efforts to reduce white resistance.

It is exceedingly difficult for whites to appreciate fully the physical and psychological barriers that are faced by blacks who wish to integrate. Not only do they face the opposition and insults of whites, but they are also practically always under pressure from their own group. For example, in the public schools there have been many instances where black adolescents have had to confide to their white friends that they were afraid to interact with them for fear of reprisals and that they hoped they could understand if they found it necessary to reject them in public encounters. One can imagine the dilemmas faced by black parents who might prefer to send their children to an integrated school in a predominantly white neighborhood, but who would be worried about the treatment the children might receive on their return each day to the ghetto. In effect, these children would be living in two distinct worlds, both of which would be hostile in different ways.

Obviously, then, those blacks who wish to integrate cannot be encouraged to do so without their being given the opportunity to remove themselves from the ghetto. Yet many such blacks will be highly ambivalent about making such a move unless they perceive that there are others who are also doing so and that their paths are being smoothed in tangible ways. One mechanism for accomplishing this would be through relatively small and widely scattered public housing units or inexpensive apartment complexes that contain a number of whites and perhaps eight or ten black families that can rely on each other for mutual psychic support. For the most part, those black families that are most likely to wish to avail themselves of such opportunities will be middle-class oriented although perhaps objectively poor. They will therefore conform reasonably well to middle-class behavioral expectations.

There is most certainly one major area in which integration must advance at a steady pace—the occupational sphere. There is another, education, where we must at least be able to provide integrated opportunities for all blacks who desire them. A completely segregated occupational structure seems out of the question unless a separate black nation is formed. Even in the Union of South Africa occupational apartheid has proven completely unworkable, as should be obvious given the desire of whites to preserve their status superiority. Complete separation would require a complete duplication of economies, and it is difficult to imagine such a state of affairs without a truly major overhaul of the national economy. Moreover, if such an overhauling were to occur it would undoubtedly result in a much worse situation for blacks. A relatively small number of blacks can, of course, be employed within the ghetto, and recommendations concerning expanded opportunities of this nature will be made in later chapters. Clearly, however, a much higher percentage of blacks will need to work in integrated settings than are likely to move into integrated neighborhoods or join integrated social organizations.

This implies that the main thrust of the integrationist movement, for some time to come, can be in the occupational sphere. The question will be considered in greater detail later, but in general terms the principle as well as the practice of labor-force integration has been gaining ground rather steadily since the early 1940s. Because of the absolute expansion of the white-collar labor force and the relative decline of farm and unskilled labor, whites have improved their occupational statuses relatively more rapidly than have blacks. But the rigid racial barriers to many of the professions are now being broken down. As we shall discuss later, however, there are still certain occupations that stand in the way of black advance, particularly those involving skilled blue-collar trades that are tightly controlled through union apprenticeship policies. One of the next major integrationist moves must be in the direction of breaking down this stranglehold on positions that are at the top of the blue-collar hierarchy and near the threshold of white-collar occupations.

The integration of a minority into various kinds of activities could conceivably be achieved if members of the dominant group were sufficiently altruistic to open up all such activities to the minority. But this would be expecting too much. At best, blacks can hope for such altruism on the part of only a small fraction of the white population and indifference on the part of the rest. Nor would such altruism really help to resolve the problem of the black person's self respect. Obviously, then, blacks must depend upon various types of resources if integration is to be achieved and if it is to be emotionally satisfying to blacks as well as whites. In effect, blacks must have something to exchange in order to maintain interaction on an equal-status level. And they must have the leverage to induce whites to give up their present advantaged positions.

I have distinguished elsewhere between two major kinds of resources, competitive and pressure resources.[5] Competitive resources generally attach to individuals and involve positive kinds of rewards that these individuals can exchange for other advantages. The most obvious kinds of competitive resources are those we associate with education and occupational skills that make it possible for the individual to compete successfully in the labor market. Money is another important competitive resource that enables the individual to buy his or her way into many kinds of situations, including residential areas as well as social clubs. Other types of competitive resources are commonly discussed in terms of personality traits: self-respect, confidence, determination and perseverance, reliability, integrity, trustworthiness, and so forth. Still others involve the personal attractiveness dimension: physical attractiveness, "personality," friendliness, popularity, or notoriety. The possession of these and other kinds of competitive resources by the individual basically gives him or her something to offer the other party.

Pressure resources, on the other hand, generally involve the ability to punish the other party for not behaving in a desired fashion. In the context of minority relations these resources have typically involved organized efforts by blacks (or other minorities) to apply pressure on discriminatory parties through legal sanctions, boycotts, or unfavorable publicity. These pressure resources have been very effective in forcing discriminatory employers and unions to hire at least a token number or even a quota of black workers. They have also provided the individual minority employee or member of an organization an effective mechanism to air grievances through the threat of exposing the group to outside pressure.

Pressure resources tend to require repeated or continuous application, or at least the threat of action. Therefore they require a high degree of mobilization on the part of either the minority itself or some agent acting on its behalf. The basic reason for this is that the power involved is what French and Raven have referred to as "punishment power," which does not provide positive incentives for rewarding individual minority members.[6] More often than not, this form of power is resented unless compensated by other more positive forms. Thus we would expect that the insistence on black quotas in an occupation may be a wise strategy as a temporary mechanism to give the minority an opportunity to prove itself. But if, after a reasonable period of time, those blacks who have entered under such quota systems are not able to compete on equal terms, then resistance to such quotas and the pressure policies that underlie them can be expected to stiffen.

Clearly, then, a minority or any category of individuals must rely on improving its competitive resources. Black integrationists and separatists, as well as white liberals, seem well agreed on two important kinds of competitive resources, educational and occupational skills. They are also agreed, in principle, on the need to improve self-respect, motivation, and self-reliance. But there is much less agreement as to how these skills and personality traits can best be attained, whether through integrated or segregated schools, for example. There also seems to be disagreement among blacks concerning certain other traits that whites would consider to be competitive resources. Should blacks emphasize punctuality, neatness, and respect for their (usually white) supervisors? Or are these merely traits that are symbolic of white middle-class culture? And how about personality traits that would make black neighbors attractive to whites in a middle-class setting— physical cleanliness, an interest in the maintenance of neighborhood aesthetic standards, and the repression of overt acts of hostility? These characteristics are competitive resources and, in fact, it is the perceived lack of such traits that provides one of the most convenient white rationalizations for excluding blacks from their neighborhoods and organizations.

Let us illustrate this point concretely by examining the kinds of resources that are presently needed by blacks in order to break down patterns of residential segregation. First, pressure resources have been needed to force certain gatekeepers of residential segregation—particularly realtors and financial institutions—from actively preventing blacks from using those competitive resources they have. Pressure resources have also been used to obtain the necessary legislation to force landlords and owners not to refuse to rent or sell to blacks, though the enforcement of such legislation has been very uneven and virtually impossible in the case of owners of single units.

Second, it is necessary for individual black families to have the financial resources to qualify for mortgage loans or to purchase their homes outright, and this has of course implied that only relatively small percentages of blacks could even hope to join the suburban movement of whites. This illustrates the obvious point that certain resources cannot be obtained without others and that there will inevitably be time-lags between the attainment of various objectives. Thus one cannot obtain the necessary accumulation of cash and meet mortgage requirements without having a well-paying job, without having had the opportunity to obtain the necessary schooling, and without having had the motivation and opportunity to save regularly.

The above resources are not sufficient to break down the pattern of residential segregation, though they may provide the opportunity to obtain better quality housing. Unless whites can be induced to remain in an area being "invaded" by blacks, the result will simply be a replacement of whites by blacks, creating another segregated area. This is precisely the process of minority-group succession that American cities have been undergoing for at least a century, with the added factor that an inmigration of blacks is much more visible and apparently threatening than an inmigration of other white ethnic groups. Given the prejudices against them that place them in a handicapped position, blacks must have compensatory competitive resources that make them especially attractive as neighbors, and in particular they must somehow or other be able to overcome existing negative stereotypes. Either this or the possibility of retreat must be cut off for whites or at least made financially costly. But these latter alternative possibilities only make the threat of inmigration all the more serious and the resistance all the more pronounced.

What kinds of competitive resources would be needed? Novelty or prestige value is one. If token numbers of blacks were thought desirable in order to "prove" the quality of the neighborhood, this might lead to increased acceptance of the first few black neighbors. Such a pattern, if it even exists anywhere except in a few ultra-liberal communities, is usually more than counterbalanced by the threat of a loss in property values. If blacks had the reputation of being unusually good gardeners, "ultra" middle class in their behavior, or as making unique cultural contributions to the community, these factors might also contribute to their acceptance. This is not the case, however. The very opposite types of stereotypes in fact exist, though they are gradually changing in a more favorable direction. Several decades of successful integration of the public schools, coupled with increasing occupational integration, may gradually reduce these negative stereotypes to the point where black competitive resources are sufficient to achieve the genuine acceptance needed to reduce white exodus to negligible proportions.

DANGERS OF EXTREME SEPARATISM

We have been more or less assuming that separatist tendencies among both blacks and whites will be effectively counterbalanced by integrationist movements, with the result that both processes will be at work for some time to come. But what if the forces of separatism were to become so strong that relatively extreme forms of segregation were to result? What other outcomes would be likely to accompany this and what would a stable segregationist system look like? In attempting to answer these questions let us make one very reasonable assumption: that whites will continue to possess, at the very least, approximately 90 percent of the economic resources of the nation and political control over national and state policies, though not necessarily city politics.

One of the basic assumptions of the liberal-integrationist position has been that white apathy is one of the major determinants of the present situation. Militant blacks of both persuasions, the separatist and integrationist, have assumed that it is necessary to dramatize the situation and to shock the white populace out of this attitude of indifference, what Myrdal referred to as "convenient ignorance." The integrationist assumption is that indifference can be partly overcome as a result of close contact through which individuals of both races learn to see each other as individuals rather than as members of opposing groups.

It has also been assumed that whenever the degree of racial mixture is increased it becomes much more difficult to withhold resources from the other group. Thus it may not be true that sitting beside white children makes any real difference in the performance-level of black children, but it does assure them that they will have the same teachers, be in classes of the same size, and have the same programs as whites. In the ghetto, they could be given much lower-quality facilities without the white population really caring much about it. One of the "shocks" to many liberal white Southerners that resulted from school integration, for example, was that schools that had been thought to be adequate for black students were seen to be ill equipped for their own children. Segregation obviously facilitates the psychological process of hiding inequalities from view.

Some militant black separatists of the late 1960s did not seem to have faced up to this obvious fact. They took for granted that they would be provided with the necessary resources to build up a segregated system competitive with that in the larger white society. In the realm of black business enterprises, it was pointed out long ago by E. Franklin Frazier, among others, that such businesses are far too small-scale to afford any realistic chance of survival as major competitors of the large white enterprises.[7] Many, for example, are basically confined to providing services for which there is a special (segregated) clientele: black funeral parlors, beauticians and barber shops, pool halls, and the like.

Although such types of marginal businesses could very will be augmented by black-controlled cooperative grocery chains, lending institutions, and other businesses, these latter would need to receive special advantages in order to compete successfully with their much larger white-owned counterparts unless the latter were totally excluded from the black community. Where would this support come from, if not from federal loans and grants? This is not to say that some increase in black business earnings cannot be achieved, but it does imply that one cannot hope for miracles in this respect.

In order to counteract the tendency for whites to be indifferent to high black unemployment rates, poor schools, dilapidated housing, and so forth—none of which is really visible to whites because of the high degree of segregation—blacks often must find ways to dramatize their situation and obtain the necessary leverage to take corrective steps. How can one dramatize things to people who cannot or do not see them for themselves? The most obvious possibility is through violence or the threat of violence. Dramatic talk and literary efforts may help, but these tend only to reach the white liberal.

The other avenue is through the political process, a slow and torturous route that carries no more guarantees than does the promise of integration. As we have already noted, and as is perfectly obvious, this political leverage basically presupposes a divided white electorate. It also presupposes a judicial system and personnel that are basically in sympathy with blacks and that consistently act in their interests. These conditions were, in fact, obtained over the past thirty years, but they are by no means guaranteed, as evidenced by recent decisions of the Nixon Supreme Court. They have been part and parcel of the integrationist movement and could very well subside with it.

The principal danger inherent in the separatist movement is therefore that it will even further increase white indifference. Dramatic actions by blacks will be required to obtain the necessary resources to operate segregated institutions in such a manner as to make them truly competitive. But if these acts were to become increasingly dramatic, white indifference might turn into something much more frightening. What might begin as minor skirmishes between black extremists and police could become open race wars in which police are actively encouraged to do even greater violence to the black ghetto, and where increasing numbers of white vigilantes decide to take the law into their own hands. We are presently seeing just such a situation in Northern Ireland, where there are practically no racial distinctions of any note but where religious hatreds have once more become combined with class interests in a highly explosive situation. Once such a conflagration begins, incident feeds on incident, and it is extremely difficult to hold back an accelerating pattern of conflict.

Integration, of course, does not assure us that intergroup conflict will steadily decline. The case of Nazi Germany is a far too vivid one to permit such naive optimism. But a racially distinct group that is physically separate in numerous isolated urban centers would be a particularly vulnerable scapegoat in times of crisis. To be sure, bands of black extremists could conduct guerrilla warfare in these nerve centers of America and could create a nightmarish situation for whites. But one cannot be too certain that restraint would be the response. After all, the situation in Vietnam reminds us that people who are basically indifferent to those of another race or culture can also be indifferent to their mass slaughter and can easily rationalize aggression on behalf of numerous high-sounding principles. Extreme violence now seems so unlikely that the mere mention of its possibility immediately brings on powerful defenses. But many things happened in the decade of the 1960s that should make us realize that it *can* happen here!

A Separate Nation?

The Marcus Garvey movement of the 1920s based its considerable appeal to blacks on the possibility that they might form their own nation somewhere in Africa. The plan was, of course, almost doomed to fail at the time if only because it was inadequately financed and lacked the support of the black middle class. This possibility was again raised by the Black Muslim movement, though once more, no specific plans were seriously considered, or at least made public. It is apparently also true today that there is no general consensus among separatists as to the advisability or feasibility of such an "ultimate" solution. Clearly, relatively few black Americans would find the notion of resettlement in Africa a viable solution. This also says nothing about the diverse African reactions to such a mass migration. What about the possibility of carving up the United States and forming a black nation from perhaps a ninth or tenth of this territory? Such an idea is indeed almost unimaginable to most of us, but so is that of protracted guerrilla warfare.

It would at least seem to make sense to attempt to study this type of resolution as rationally as possible and to evaluate it as one of several potential solutions. I believe that if this were done seriously enough we would decisively reject it but that the result of such a careful look would be a wholesome one. Let us briefly examine what some of the major issues and problems would seem to be, putting aside for the moment the whole problem of national pride and the implications for the international position in the larger world community. These considerations, incidentally, might not turn out to be the really crucial ones in a rational decision-making process because I suspect that the effects of partition might be just as positive as negative with respect to national power and prestige. Certainly, if protracted guerrilla warfare were to break out, the results of such an outcome would seem to be far more harmful to the nation than outright partition.

First, a number of geographic criteria would need to be considered. Blacks would have to be given a single contiguous territory of approximately a ninth the area of continental United States. The temptation of whites would be to try to pass off the most marginal lands to blacks in much the same way that American Indians have been successively displaced into areas that are sparsely populated and either virtual deserts or relatively unproductive forest lands. Such territory would of course not be acceptable to blacks. Also, it would make no sense for a black nation to be formed in such a way that it would be completely surrounded by the remainder of the United States and thus totally landlocked.

For all practical purposes these criteria alone would seem to limit the possibilities to something like the following: (1) California, Arizona, and Nevada; (2) Washington, Oregon, and Idaho; (3) Florida, Georgia, Alabama, South Carolina, and either North Carolina or Mississippi; (4) Texas, Oklahoma, Arkansas, and Louisiana; or (5) New England, New York, and New Jersey. Each of these possible units would provide the new black nation with at least two major seaports and several major cities. Each would also provide a reasonably diversified economy, including the opportunity for tourism.

As soon as one even begins to *name* the present states that might become a part of such a black nation, emotional issues come to the forefront. What white citizens of these states would want to leave? "Why should our region be selected?" they would ask. How many blacks in the nonselected regions would be willing to relocate? The resulting political debate—if we can even imagine it taking place—would un-doubtedly be heated in the extreme. Realistically, the possibility of the northeastern states would have to be ruled out since this is obviously a major nerve center of the United States, California might have to be ruled out for much the same reason. The Pacific Northwest would be a very feasible region except for the fact that it presently contains so few blacks that the logistics and costs of relocation would be staggering. The Southeast and Southwest are much more viable alternatives from that standpoint. And of course there are *other* minorities to be considered, particularly the large numbers of Chicanos and American Indians in the Southwest. Would these minorities be given a choice as to which nation they preferred? No doubt they would also press for separatism under these conditions. We might then be faced with the issue of further partition. One could well imagine a kind of loosely-knit "American Commonwealth" modeled somewhat along the lines of the British example.

Assuming some degree of consensus could be reached concerning territorial boundaries—a not-very-likely outcome in itself—one of the most immediate problems would be that of relocation. Persons desiring to move would need to be compensated for their homes and property, given adequate transportation allowances, and assisted in their efforts to resettle in other areas. Undoubtedly there would be housing short-ages in some areas and surpluses in others, though this would seem to be one of the least difficult problems to resolve. It would mean, however, that resettlement would not take place overnight. Perhaps as much as a full decade would be required. Certain types of persons, particularly the elderly and the rural, would be most upset by the process, and allowances would have to be made to compensate such groups more than others. Many Americans are very much accustomed to moving about, however, and once the emotionalism had subsided, most should be able to make this kind of adjustment rather easily.

The economic dislocations, however, would be much more difficult to handle. To the degree that persons' occupations depend on regional characteristics—as for example coal mining, oil drilling, shipping, steel and other heavy industries, and farming—the resulting dislocations would be serious indeed. The degree of advanced planning required to relocate workers according to their skills, to shift banking and commer-cial headquarters about, and to adjust the economy of the newly-formed black nation to the skill-levels of the present black labor force would be far greater than anything United States governments have ever attempted. Also, it would be necessary to work out procedures for compensating businesses whose facilities were vacated or converted to other purposes and whose managements and even ownership would gradually become black controlled. Economic aid programs for the new nation would also have to be planned in advance and bipartisan commitments made for at least a decade of assistance designed specifically to help the new nation get on its feet.

Given our technical knowhow and a sufficient commitment to the task, these and other kinds of problems could be solved. The dislocations and individual hardships created would be real ones for many persons, but it can be argued that similar dislocations and hardships presently exist and are especially likely to affect disadvantaged minority members. The question, then, would boil down to whether the more advantaged white population would be willing to consider this possibility at all seriously.

Under present circumstances I am virtually certain that it would not. Too many sacred values would be at stake, including the territorial integrity of the United States, national pride, a concern for national security, and (though never mentioned) a number of vested interests in present patterns of segregation and inequality. Furthermore, it would be unrealistic to assume a high enough degree of commitment to give up nonmarginal territory and to invest economic resources to a sufficient degree to enable the new nation to overcome an initial dependent status. And what president and political party would ever want to be held responsible by later generations, to say nothing of present opponents, for having divided up the country?

It seems much more realistic to assume that whites and blacks would consider this extreme form of separation only in absolute desperation, after having undergone a very prolonged period of turmoil. After perhaps twenty years of guerrilla warfare such as may go on in Northern Ireland, the formation of a separate nation might be seen as a last resort. If the new nation were formed under such conditions, however, the outcome would be far different from the one we have just imagined. Blacks would undoubtedly be offered the most marginal territory and might be forced to accept out of sheer exhaustion. The two nations would become lasting enemies, with the new nation undoubtedly turning to the third world, or whatever other alliances exist at the time, in order to protect itself from its dominating white neighbor. Its economic position would be exceedingly weak, as would its ability to improve the levels of living of its black citizens. The split would undoubtedly also be taken as a sign of weakness by the outside world, and a protracted form of guerrilla warfare would have made this assessment a valid one. Separation under these terms would hardly be to the advantage of either blacks or whites, nor can one imagine that it could possibly be carried out with the desirable advanced planning.

Since it seems more likely that this extreme form of separation would result from protracted hostilities than from rational planning and cooperation, it does not appear to be a viable solution. Nevertheless, I think the issue should be raised for serious discussion and debate in order to see what kinds of reactions are encountered. It is possible, though not likely, that such open discussion might produce a much higher degree of consensus and willingness to bargain than presently seems to be the case. Perhaps more important, by opening up this possibility of complete separation for careful thought we are likely to see many more complications than are presently apparent. In the process, the debate may serve to make the alternative of complete integration much more attractive. Or it may make it possible to find more satisfactory intermediate positions.

The heading of this section, "Dangers of Extreme Separatism," is perhaps misleading in one important respect. Extreme separatism may not constitute a danger provided that there is a high degree of consensus and that the process of getting there does not involve a protracted struggle. Given the lack of consensus that presently exists, the vested interests of both parties, and a balance of power that overwhelmingly favors the white majority, I cannot imagine that a separatist movement among blacks can have any result other than that of increasing these antagonisms and worsening the situation for blacks and whites alike. Under the circumstances, extreme separatism or black nationalism appears to be a utopian goal that cannot be achieved. But it certainly seems worthwhile to explore the question sufficiently to prove this assumption incorrect.

NOTES

1. For example, an earlier debate concerning the importance of blacks' African heritage between Frazier and Herskovits was later revived in discussions of the black family by Glazer and Moynihan and by Billingsley. See Melville Herskovits, *The Myth of the Negro Past* (New York: Harper, 1941); E. Franklin Frazier, *The Negro in the United States* (New York: Macmillan, 1958); Nathan Glazer and Daniel P. Moynihan, *Beyond the Melting Pot* (Cambridge: MIT Press, 1963); and Andrew Billingsley, *Black Families in White America* (Englewood Cliffs, N.J.: Prentice-Hall, 1968).

2. Gunnar Myrdal, *An American Dilemma* (New York: Harper, 1944), Chap. 1.

3. Ibid., Chap. 3.

4. Malcolm X and Alex Haley, *The Autobiography of Malcolm X* (New York: Grove Press, 1965).

5. H. M. Blalock, *Toward A Theory of Minority Group Relations* (New York: Wiley, 1967), Chap. 4.

6. John R. P. French and Bertrand Raven, "The Bases of Social Power," in *Studies in Social Power*, ed. Dorwin Cartwright, (Ann Arbor: University of Michigan Press, 1959), Chap. 9.

7. E. Franklin Frazier, *Black Bourgeoisie* (Glencoe, Ill.: Free Press, 1957).

4

Quotas, Double Standards, and Affirmative Action

ISSUES RELATING TO AFFIRMATIVE ACTION, reverse discrimination, and goals and quotas are deeply dividing the liberal community, as evidenced by the diversity of positions taken in connection with the celebrated *Bakke* decision by the U.S. Supreme Court. Should minorities and women be given special consideration in competitive situations because of presumed prior handicaps and/or past discrimination? The American public seems generally agreed that they should not, if we may believe the public opinion polls that show over 80 percent opposed to such differential treatment.

The issues in question are highly complex and not to be put to a simple vote if minority rights are to be protected. Yet, it is evident that individual members of the majority also have rights. Is it fair, for example, to admit a black candidate into a medical school in preference to a white who has higher qualifications (in terms of criteria currently in use) and who in no way can be held responsible for previous discrimination against the minority? Clearly, there are conflicting moral principles as well as practical expediencies that are involved, and therefore it is no wonder that the issues have divided us. It is also obvious that any judicial decision made by nine Supreme Court justices cannot be considered to be the final word on the matter, though it will of course have a major impact on policy.

Universalism and open competition are very important ingredients of the American Creed. This means that the most desirable positions are supposed to be awarded to the best qualified persons, regardless of race, ethnic or class background, sex, or even age. Yet we find empirically that the supposedly open competitive system in the United States does not result in a random distribution of occupants by race, age, or sex. The most prestigeful and powerful occupations are held primarily by older white males. Until very recently, minorities were grossly underrepresented in the top-ranked colleges and universities that serve as feeders into these upper-level occupational slots. We still find that blacks and certain other minorities—though not all minorities—tend to do less well on supposedly objective tests that were specifically designed to replace much more subjective criteria that, in earlier days, resulted in a disproportionate acceptance of sons and daughters of wealthy alumni or prominent citizens.

The reasons for these outcomes are not at all simple, but once again we tend to find simplistic answers that reflect whatever working theories and vested interests one happens to have. One such working theory minimizes the significance of imperfections in the system and relies heavily on the assumption that blacks and other minorities are simply not equipped to compete on approximately equal terms, either because of innate or biological inferiority or (the more common position) because they have been improperly trained and motivated.

At the opposite extreme, another working theory assumes that universalism and the use of "objective" tests to screen potential candidates are subterfuges to cover up the vested interests of the dominant group. Somewhere in between are those who believe that universalism has been only partially applied in practice and that the system is out of whack because strictly competitive criteria are being applied to those who have been given unequal resources. It is as though one runner has been given a head start over his or her opponent, with the observer witnessing only the last lap of the footrace.

The position of most liberals has been that existing inequalities between the races can be traced either directly or indirectly to discrimination. Mindful that racial or ethnic quotas have in the past been used against minority members—as for example quota systems used by private colleges to hold down the number of Jewish students—liberals have, at least until recently, tended to be highly suspicious of quota systems of any kind. The emphasis has been on replacing personalistic criteria with standardized evaluation procedures such as civil service examinations and standardized college entrance tests. It has been argued that racial, religious, and ethnic identities should be removed from the applicants' records insofar as possible. The assumption has been that knowledge of such characteristics on the part of screening agents would be used to establish racial quotas to the disadvantage of minority members. The emphasis, then, has been on replacing personal biases and vague evaluative criteria (such as "personality," "promise," and "potential") with objective performance scores in standardized settings.

Until recently the underlying assumption of most liberals was that universalistic criteria must be improved so as to make the competitive process more fair. The rules of the game must be clarified and the processes for deciding on the winners and losers must be objectified and made visible to the public, so that the honesty of the judges can be verified and these decision makers held accountable for their actions. The assumption has also been made that the application of universalistic standards all along the line, beginning with the entrance of the child into the public school system and continuing through adult life, will gradually reduce the inequalities between the races. It has been recognized that such a process will take considerable time and that universalistic criteria will be resisted, with varying degrees of success, at each of the crucial points in the footrace. The hope has been that impartially enforced rules will come to be accepted by all parties as the best possible means of achieving both genuine integration and a high degree of equality of opportunity between the races, if not among all individual members of each group.

Obviously the system has not produced these results, at least not rapidly enough to satisfy many blacks, other minorities, and liberal whites, who have recently challenged its workings in a number of important respects. As already indicated, a less than universalistic system applied to a person near the beginning of a career, say as he or she enters grade school, means that this person may be handicapped throughout life. Universalistic criteria applied at later stages, say as a student enters college or competes for a job, then merely tend to reinforce existing inequalities. Furthermore, a person's motivation and training are very much influenced by his or her perception of future opportunities, so that the resources that a particular generation brings into the competitive arena are partly determined by past practices and the results of previous footraces.

Therefore the system perpetuates itself through a kind of self-selective mechanism. In some few cases it may work to the disadvantage of whites. For example, black children see many successful black athletes and few black bankers. They train for careers in professional sports, develop the needed skills, and are then able to outcompete the white youth who have been preparing for other careers. A lag of as much as fifteen or twenty years may be involved. If all of a sudden blacks were to find excellent opportunities in science and industry, and poorer ones in athletics, it would be exceedingly difficult to reverse overnight the supply of candidates in these two very different kinds of professions.

Thus the universalistic ideal is a long-term goal that, in the best of our realistic alternative worlds, would involve many short-run dislocations and inequalities. Furthermore the goal is easily subverted owing to the elusive nature of many evaluative criteria. Ideally, candidates should be selected on the basis of their potential by getting them to perform in situations that are similar and therefore predictive to the tasks that they will later be expected to perform. One very good criterion for predicting how a student will perform next year is his or her performance this year. We make the assumption that the conditions will remain much the same as in the past. Therefore performance in high school is a good predictor of work in college, particularly if the competitors have all been exposed to similar environments, say the same high school or schools with similar standards.

Professional athletes are selected by watching them play in college or in minor leagues and with remarkably good success. The selection of a new employee requires much more guesswork however, since he or she has not been exposed to a previous environment that was very similar to the expected one. Should grades in college be used to predict this performance? Should all grades be considered or just the grades in particular courses? What other criteria are deemed relevant? Are these latter criteria easily objectified, or do they require the judgment of a skilled interviewer? How is the candidate's interest and motivation to be judged? If the candidate is a female, should it be assumed that she will only be a temporary member of the labor force and therefore a high risk?

Even where universalistic criteria can be invoked, there may be honest disagreements as to their adequacy in predicting later performance. This means that it is possible to select the most convenient criteria and ignore others. Often, convenience is a matter of cost or time saving. Thus an employer may rely on high school or college grades, or tests given in school, rather than a battery of tests the employer may devise. It is also possible deliberately to select criteria that are highly correlated with racial characteristics, and this means that suspicions will be aroused even if the criteria selected happen to be the most satisfactory ones for other purposes.

Thus performance on standardized college entrance examinations is known to be correlated with race, with blacks doing more poorly on the average than whites. Does this imply that they are "racist" criteria and should be replaced? If so, by what? Must the criteria ultimately selected be completely uncorrelated with race? Does the existence of racial inequalities in performance levels automatically imply that the criteria are racist?

One way to produce equality between the races is to insist on strict universalism all along the line, and to wait sufficiently long for blacks to catch up. But, as we have just argued, this strategy is difficult to enforce and does not provide short-run solutions. A second strategy is to apply racial quotas in such a way that blacks compete with other blacks, and whites with whites, with both groups being evaluated according to the same objective criteria.* This might involve, for example, dividing the pool of competitors into two separate groups, giving them the same tests, and selecting the best performers from each group so as to produce a ratio of approximately eight or nine whites to one black. In effect, this would amount to giving members of the one or the other group a fixed number of handicap points because of race.

A third possibility is to reject all criteria that differentiate between the races, if necessary blurring standards in such a way that selection becomes based on a totally different set of criteria. Still a fourth alternative that may sometimes be appropriate is to alter organizational goals so as to make minority-related characteristics legitimate ones in the screening process.

Most of our discussion in the remainder of this chapter will be focused on a series of delicate questions involving the second and third of these alternatives, namely the use of double versus blurred standards and the related topic of minority quotas. Before considering these issues, however, it seems necessary to comment briefly on the first and fourth alternatives.

There is probably a high degree of consensus among all persuasions of liberals that, in the ideal, the first alternative strategy of improving minority resources is both necessary and desirable in the long run. It was also the strategy that was most seriously put forth in the late 1960s in President Johnson's Great Society program. By setting up Head Start, the Job Corps, and other federal programs it was thought that blacks and other disadvantaged minorities could be given just enough compensatory education and training advantages that they could overcome initial handicaps and rather quickly find themselves competing on equal terms with whites. If so, a careful monitoring of discriminatory policies of school officials, employers, financial institutions, and other

---

*The Department of Health, Education and Welfare and others have attempted to distinguish between rigid quotas and goals which are less rigid and, presumably, more temporary. In order to emphasize that both are basically quota systems I shall not make explicit reference to goals but shall discuss later in the chapter the matters of rigidity and duration of quotas.

gatekeepers was thought to be sufficient to markedly reduce racial inequalities.

It has now become clear that, if this first strategy is ever to work successfully, it will be extremely costly and will require a prolonged effort. Therefore other more controversial strategies have been developed as alternatives or supplements. Undoubtedly, however, the intention has been and still is to see to it that this effort to improve minority competitive resources is continued and not undermined by these alternatives. It could be, however, that an insistence on other affirmative action programs might undermine this first alternative strategy. At least there are some who would argue that, for example, if overly rigid minority quotas become institutionalized, this may create a dual system of incentives and performance criteria that only perpetuate performance differentials between the races. We shall return to this matter later in the chapter.

The fourth strategy mentioned above has been seriously proposed by the Carnegie Council on Policy Studies in Higher Education in connection with entrance into training programs involving occupations that have a major service function, as for example law, dentistry, and medicine.[1] In brief, it can legitimately be claimed that medical, dental, and law schools ought to consider as one of their important objectives the training of professionals who can be expected to service certain needed populations, as for example ghettoized minorities. Since very few white doctors, dentists, and lawyers are attracted to these areas, and since it may be argued that they are also less capable of developing close relationships with minority clients, medical and law schools should very deliberately change their priorities and emphasize, as important *goals*, the training of minority personnel. The same might be argued in the case of police, social workers, auxiliary medical personnel, and other occupational groups that have direct contact with the minority community. If such goals were given higher priority, then larger numbers of minority trainees could be selected on the strictly universalistic grounds that they will provide better services to these citizens.

I think there is much to be said for this position, especially in connection with crucial services such as those provided by police, doctors and nurses, lawyers, and social workers. The Carnegie Council also points out that screening committees in such professional schools in effect serve as gatekeepers who may, if not monitored, basically affect the life chances of minority citizens whom the professions are intended to service. This is in contrast, say, to engineers, mathematicians, accountants, or basketball players whose "service" function is highly indirect and certainly not crucial to the minority community. Thus it would make little sense to ask mathematicians or even engineers to modify their goal hierarchies, as these related to professional performance, though of course affirmative action appeals might be directed to them on other grounds. Therefore an emphasis on this fourth alternative seems limited to a relatively small number of occupations, albeit important ones to the minority community.

BLURRED VERSUS DOUBLE STANDARDS

Before turning to the important question of the desirability of establishing either rigid quotas or somewhat more flexible "goals" for hiring or promoting certain percentages of minorities (or women), let us first consider the related matter of the kinds of selection standards that may be employed to evaluate candidates. It is obvious that if a minority's competitive position is exactly equal to that of the dominant group, then approximately the same proportion of minority and majority members will be selected for each occupation. This assumes, of course, that the criteria being used in the selection process are not biased, that they are uniformly applied, and that the applicant pools are not self-selected in some way. For example, it assumes that qualified minority members are interested in applying and in fact do so in the appropriate numbers.

Whenever inequalities are found to result from a complex selection process we can be assured that something has been responsible for them, but there may be considerable debate about the precise mechanisms involved. Because of the obvious impossibility of monitoring this selection *process* in careful detail, it becomes tempting to monitor it in terms of *outcome* criteria, as for example the percentages actually hired during a given time period. Whether these outcomes be specified in terms of rigid quotas or more flexible targets or goals, it is also clear that there must be some changes made in the selection process. Perhaps they should involve a more vigorous effort to induce eligible minorities to apply for the position or to undergo the necessary preliminary training. But they may also require some modification of the screening criteria. The two most obvious possibilities in this connection are the second and third alternative strategies referred to above, namely the institution of a double standard or the blurring of those standards that happen to differentiate between minority and majority applicants.

Let me illustrate the difference between these two strategies by referring to selection processes with which I am familiar, namely the selection of candidates to graduate school. When candidates are reasonably numerous and not known personally to the selectors, and when it is too expensive to bring them to campus for personal interviews, the criteria for selection usually boil down to a combination of the following: (1) the student's academic record, generally a quantified grade-point average; (2) scores on standardized tests such as the Graduate Record Examination; (3) a judgment of the quality of the college attended; (4) personal letters of recommendation; (5) statements by the student concerning his or her professional objectives; and (6) miscellaneous materials, such as term papers, that may have been included with the application. The first two criteria are easily quantified; the third is partly a matter of judgment but is reasonably objective; the fourth is wide open to interpretation and rarely distinguishes among candidates because letters are uniformly in praise of the applicant; and the fifth and sixth are exceedingly difficult to evaluate. The usual result is that the first two criteria tend to dominate the others, with the third also being a consideration.

Scores on the Graduate Record Examination are known to give the advantage to whites over blacks. Presumably, they have been designed to measure skills that will be useful in graduate work, particularly quantitative or mathematical reasoning and verbal skills and reasoning ability. Whether they measure true abilities or learned skills is more dubious, but they do tend to predict reasonably well performance in graduate school. This is not surprising, of course, since the tests measure performance in examination situations not at all unlike those that the students will later have to face. Should these test scores be discarded because they discriminate against blacks?

The earlier liberal response was to apply strictly universalistic criteria and to ignore the applicant's race altogether. Given the educational handicaps blacks faced, this meant in practice that only a handful were admitted into most graduate programs. There are two other alternatives. The first is to discard the scores altogether, relying on the remaining criteria of evaluation. The second is to retain the scores but to admit a certain quota of blacks by selecting blacks with the highest scores but considering them in a separate pool of candidates from the white pool. This second alternative results in a double standard unless both pools have the same mean scores. The first often results in a kind of blurred standard. Let us see why this is the case.

If the Graduate Record Examination scores are deleted, the next objective criterion becomes grade point average in college. But recently, grades in college have also come under attack as being discriminatory and "punitive." Some teachers, particularly from the younger generation, take the stance that grades inhibit true learning and that therefore it is wise to remove this barrier by either giving A's (and some B's) to all students, or by using a so-called pass-fail system. The latter generally reverts to a pass only system since very few students actually fail under this system. The result is an overall uplifting of grades for everyone, except, of course, for those who would have received A grades under a stricter grading system. Such a setup eases the life of the instructor who is not faced with making fine or unpopular distinctions. It likewise reduces the overall failure rate and works to the benefit of those whose performance level would otherwise be marginal. It also makes grades a much less useful criterion for selection into graduate school (or employment) because nearly all applicants have exceptionally high grades. In effect, it increases the measurement error involved since slight differences in grade point averages could be due to any number of irrelevant factors, including idiosyncrasies of a few professors, a temporary illness of the student, or a few missed questions on particular examinations. In effect, course work in college becomes much less easy to evaluate and this second criterion likewise becomes a blurred one.

The quality of educational institutions has also always been difficult to evaluate. How does a B average at Harvard compare with an A- average at a secondary state institution? If the Harvard faculty assume that they have obtained such a select group that nearly all of their students deserve high grades, then their own grades are likely to be inflated, though this may not be known to the person doing the selecting. (What the Harvard professors may not realize is that the blurring of standards in high schools and prep schools may be affecting this same selectivity on which they are counting to assess their own students!) Even assuming away this problem, we recognize that there are differences in quality among institutions of higher learning. If black applicants come primarily from state colleges or segregated institutions in the South, however, selection on the basis of school quality becomes suspect as a racist device, and the tendency is to assume away such a difference. Thus a B+ average at Harvard becomes equivalent to a B+ average at any other institution, and another evaluative distinction has become blurred. One is left with a handful of letters of recommendation for each candidate and a few other miscellaneous bits of information.

Obviously, such extreme blurring of standards has not yet occurred, and it is still possible to make reasonably accurate assessments of candidates. To the degree that the most discriminating criteria are replaced by those that do not differentiate among candidates, however, the greater the opportunity for extraneous factors to enter in. This is precisely why liberals have urged the adoption of objective and quantifiable measures because of a fear that subjective criteria would be used against minorities. Paradoxically, the pressure now is to remove such criteria whenever they may be used to differentiate among candidates in favor of members of the more privileged groups.

Let us move away from this particular illustration to the more general issue. Pressures to blur evaluation standards seem to result from a combination of two working assumptions. The first is that any criterion that distinguishes empirically between the races is ipso facto discriminatory or "racist" in nature. Even a test that has been constructed so as to tap mathematical reasoning ability—which is certainly not a white culture trait—is considered racist in nature if the average scores for blacks are lower than those for whites. The second assumption is that a frank acknowledgment of these differences and the use of a double standard are also racist and reflect a patronizing stance on the part of whites. Instead of recognizing existing differences in performance levels and working to reduce the gap, the attempt is made to wipe them out immediately by simply claiming that they do not exist. The performance differences are considered only apparent because they have resulted from biased measurement procedures that give the advantage to whites. Poor measurement is made to substitute for a host of factors that are the fundamental causes of the differences.

A blurring of standards results in immediate gains for both those involved in the screening process and for those applicants whose performance levels would have been below average. In the long run it is difficult to see how such a blurring of standards can work to most people's real advantage. If all students' college transcripts look very much the same—nearly all A's with a sprinkling of B's and a very occasional C—then how will the best students be rewarded? How will the medical and law schools select among their numerous applicants? Perhaps they can raise their fees and use this as a self-selection device, but this will hardly work to the advantage of minorities unless the latter are given special scholarships at the expense of the lower- and middle-class white population. How will a student go about rationally planning his or her program when it is apparent that an almost all A record will be mandatory, but where certain desirable courses are taught by tough-minded professors? Most probably, he or she will decide to take the "gut" courses or to opt for "pass-fail" courses in the most difficult subjects. And if persons are selected into medical schools on such a basis, and if few flunk out, how will this affect the public confidence in the quality of medical training? In effect, a blurring of standards will result in an inability to predict future performance and to reward past performance.

Standards of evaluation are not likely to become equally blurred at the same rate, and this will have important implications for recruitment into various professions. Certainly, performance standards are not becoming blurred in the arena of professional sports. In fact, new measures of performance are being constructed every day, and talent scouts are being employed in increasing numbers to make as accurate assessments as possible. This is made increasingly easy by nationwide coverage of sports activities, national press ratings of teams, and nationally based systems for making comparisons among athletes. It is difficult to imagine a more objectifiable and competitive occupation, and blacks are of course benefitting by this tendency toward universalism. Among the intellectual professions, mathematical and technical skills also seem more easily evaluated than verbal and social skills. That is, students can be more easily differentiated on mathematics examinations than on those on which they are required to write essays. This means that the truly superior athletes and mathematicians are more readily identified than are the best sales persons, executives, poets, and mothers.

The fact that standards are unequally blurred seems to have certain important implications for motivating individuals and their self-selection into different occupations. For one thing, we would expect that individuals capable of performing extremely well in certain tasks will be most attracted to those fields for which they can be most readily rewarded and recognized. Of course this need not be the case in some ideal utopian society, but it is a good working assumption in the case of a highly mobile society such as our own. This would mean that those occupations that retain highly selective criteria will be those that attract the most qualified applicants and repulse the least qualified. Those that utilize blurred standards will tend to attract the mediocre ones.

If this is true, then persons already in high positions in very competitive fields, who are secure enough to stand the pressure of competition, will have a vested interest in preserving the good name of their profession and will tend to insist on criteria that differentiate. Those who are attempting to enter these professions, however, and whose performance levels are below standard, will have a vested interest in substituting blurred standards for those that differentiate. To some extent, at least, the current struggle over criteria for evaluation between youth and their elders can be interpreted in this light. The higher the prestige of the occupation, and the more selective the performance criteria, the greater the proportion of relatively unqualified candidates who would like to be let in under a new set of guidelines.

Occupations also differ with respect to the need to discriminate among applicants who have demonstrated a certain minimum level of competence, however high. We refer to many persons as technicians when their job requirements call for the possession of certain skills, but where further skills beyond these levels are not really needed. The implication is that once the individual has picked up these skills (say those of a dental technician, a plumber, or a typist) he or she is more or less interchangeable with others who also possess these skills. This is in sharp contrast with, say, the skills of a scholar, a corporation executive, or a U.S. Senator. It is presumed that it is possible to devise screening instruments that can assess whether or not the candidate possesses these necessary minimum skills. If so, the choice among eligible persons can proceed according to other characteristics such as date of application, age and sex, minority group status, or willingness to work for a particular wage or salary.

In these occupations it would make little sense to blur the standards of selection, though they might be lowered or raised according to supply and demand conditions. Persons having truly exceptional scores or other qualifications may be hired in the hope that they will move on to other positions, though sometimes they are looked upon with suspicion as being overly qualified for a technician's position. A blurring of standards in other occupations might very well improve the average level of qualifications of such technicians by augmenting their ranks with persons whose qualifications for these other occupations might not be as readily recognized. Presumably this would make relatively little difference in the quality of services rendered. In contrast, if unqualified applicants were let into these technical occupations with insufficient training, the overall quality of services would be adversely affected.

In a society characterized by rapid changes and alterations in labor force demands it is obviously necessary to develop ways of training persons to handle novel situations and to adapt whatever technical skills they may have to these changing demands. This also puts a much greater burden on those who are placed in a position of screening new applicants for positions which may alter considerably during the life-history of any given occupant. Tests and other criteria that are highly specific to narrowly defined tasks may prove much less useful predictors of future performance than overall criteria such as college or high-school grade-point averages. The latter averages are, after all, composites of performances in a variety of intellectual tasks: examinations in mathematics courses, oral work in language courses, term papers in political science, and laboratory work in chemistry. Presumably, they tap a combination of motivation, work habits, and abilities that vary in their proportions for each individual but that constitute a better overall predictor than any single criterion more narrowly defined.

Likewise, very general aptitude tests designed to tap overall quantitative and verbal reasoning ability (or training) may prove to be much better predictors than tests designed to evaluate specific knowledge of a technical subject. Such very general criteria seem especially important in the case of occupations that require qualifications and skills that are too poorly understood, at present, to be precisely evaluated.

In summary, then, I do not see how the tendency to blur standards of evaluation will have a positive long-run effect. Admittedly, it is an easy way out for many individuals, and it is also a short-run resolution of the problem of finding a speedy way of equalizing present inequalities between the races. But it may also be used as a device for discriminating against a particular minority or other subgroup. In government, a type of spoils system could readily replace the civil service system. Those persons who shouted the loudest or who could apply the most political or economic pressure could easily obtain a greater share of the pie for themselves at the expense of other individuals who, by objective standards, were more deserving. One might predict that, after a brief period of indifference to such a process, an intolerant white majority could very well use it to their own advantage. If so, many recent gains for minorities would have been lost.

For all of these reasons it thus appears as though the temporary expedient of the use of explicit double standards may provide a more satisfactory alternative. But this path, too, has some major disadvantages and poses a number of difficult dilemmas, one of which involves the degree to which the existence of such double standards should be explicitly recognized, brought into the open, and dealt with rationally. We shall deal with some of these dilemmas in the next section.

SOME DILEMMAS REGARDING QUOTAS

The ideal objective of strict universalism is easy to state, though as we have just seen it may not be easy to implement. As soon as we begin to recommend departures from such an ideal a host of nasty questions arise. If racial quotas are to be established, how large should they be? How can they be justified? How long should they be maintained? Who is to decide such questions? We open Pandora's box in terms of the possibility of prolonging racial conflict over such issues. Having argued that strictly universalistic criteria applied selectively at only a few points in the competitive system will produce only very slow rates of change, and also having rejected the solution of resorting to completely blurred standards as creating many serious additional problems in a competitive society, we must now face squarely some of the issues that would be raised in connection with quota systems based on competitive processes within each racial or ethnic group.

Let us assume that we are concerned with situations in which reasonably universalistic criteria are applicable, and are fairly applied, but where minority handicaps are sufficiently great that only a handful of its members are able to make the grade under these strictly competitive rules. Obviously if racial quotas are established in order to increase the minority representation, a double standard will result. Furthermore, the larger the quota of the minority, the greater will be the gap between the performance levels of average members of the two groups. Thus if under strictly competitive criteria only 1 percent of the student body at Harvard or Yale would be black, raising the quota of blacks to, say, 3 percent will result in a certain degree of inequality of black and white students. If this quota had been raised to 6 or 10 percent black, the average disparity would have been even greater. Therefore the relative sizes of the quotas and disparities are closely interrelated and one cannot adequately discuss the one without also dealing with the other.

What are the justifications for establishing racial quotas that favor a minority group? Three major reasons are obvious. First, quotas are a form of insurance against the discriminatory use of standards under the guise that they are strictly universalistic when in fact they are not. With quotas it cannot be argued that no qualified blacks have applied, and in fact the imposition of quotas forces the employer or educational institution actively to seek out the best minority candidates rather than merely sitting back and waiting for them to apply.

Secondly, favorable minority quotas constitute a kind of fair play by which persons who have been handicapped at one stage of the game see themselves advantaged at another. If one could accurately measure the previous handicaps it might become possible to decide on the degree to which a minority group member should be favored at a later stage. However, this would require much better data than are presently available, and in the absence of such data, minority members have a vested interest in exaggerating their relative disadvantage, whereas majority group members have an interest in underestimating this differential. A third important reason favoring the existence of quotas is that this will put blacks or other minorities in positions where they will be visible to other members of their group, thereby serving as role models and symbols of success, as well as in a position to influence policy and provide needed services to them.

What general guidelines, if any, can be given as to the establishment of minority quotas? Unless and until this question of quotas can be faced squarely we are likely to lack the kinds of data that will be necessary to guide intelligent policy. For example, approximately what percentage of blacks is necessary in specific occupations in order to make them visible to the general public and to other members of their race? Obviously this depends on the general visibility of the occupation as well as the degree to which blacks are put in public relations positions. If the number of black actuaries were to suddenly increase dramatically, I doubt if this would be noticed by anyone except employ-ees in the home offices of insurance companies. In contrast, black faculty would be very visible (and useful) to members of a student body though not to the public at large.

In the absence of such information and in the presence of heated debate, however, it is necessary to come up with some reasonable compromise working criteria for the sizes of quotas. The simplest resolution, it would seem, would be to set a uniform quota equal to the percentage of the minority in the overall population—approximately 11 to 12 percent in the case of blacks. But in many instances such high quotas would be grossly unfair to individual whites whose performance levels might be considerably higher, for some time to come, than most of their minority competitors. It would also raise the question of similar quotas on blacks in the few desirable occupations in which they are presently overrepresented. Should blacks be confined to 12 percent of the members of all professional football and basketball teams?

Let us consider an admittedly extreme case that is, however, not very much unlike the situation that presently prevails in many profes-sions. Suppose that by strictly universalistic standards only 1 percent of those admitted into the profession (or college) would be black. To raise the quota up to 12 percent immediately would require either a massive talent search for really qualified blacks or a very great lowering of standards that would undoubtedly create considerable resentment among whites. Obviously, if simultaneous attempts were being made to raise quotas of blacks in many similar occupations (or universities), the talent search would be unsuccessful.

A reasonable though very rough rule of thumb to follow in such circumstances would be to aim for goals or temporary quotas that are approximately half way between the existing percentage of blacks in the occupation (university, etc.) and the percentage of blacks in the relevant population. If one is in a region or metropolitan area containing, say, 20 percent blacks, and if the present percentage is only 2 percent, this would imply a goal of approximately 11 percent. Obviously, neither group would be completely satisfied by such a compromise, but perhaps both could live with it. If the quota were put at a very high level comparable to the actual percentage in the relevant population, then whites would very legitimately fear that blacks would demand this share on a permanent basis regardless of their performance levels, prior training, or seniority. But if it were set at a much lower level, gains for blacks would remain at a token level.

The obvious danger implied in the above discussion is that such goals become rigidified into fixed quotas and that they might be extended to almost any group that felt discriminated against—other minorities, women, the very young and the very old, ex-convicts, homosexuals, and so forth. Also, once quotas have been set and thereby made explicit there is likely to be a more or less continual conflict over numbers, with quality of performance becoming secondary. Clearly, quotas must be recognized as a very temporary expedient. But how temporary? This will of necessity depend on the time it takes to train blacks and other minorities to fill the positions concerned through a process of open competition with whites. In the case of occupations requiring a prolonged and expensive education, such as law and medicine, perhaps as much as two decades will be needed. In the case of skilled crafts, where a potential supply of black labor already exists, perhaps no more than five years would be needed. Again, one must anticipate major disagreements as to the length of time such quotas would need to be in effect and over the means by which they should be relaxed. For instance, if quotas are suddenly removed during a period of labor surplus, and if blacks lack seniority as compared with whites, this could result in sudden unemployment of blacks, rather than their gradual displacement into similar occupations.

Another dilemma that would have to be faced in any specific situation involves the extent to which the existence of a double standard in entrance or performance levels should be openly acknowledged and measured. On the one hand, if we pretend that it does not exist and if we discard all standards that tend to differentiate between the two groups (as well as among individuals, of course) there will perhaps be fewer hurt feelings and less condescension among whites. But then how can basic decisions be made concerning admissions to more advanced programs, job promotions, prizes or other awards, office-holding, and the like? In effect, there may be new informal quotas established by which it is agreed that the same percentages of blacks and whites will be moved up the ladder to the next level, but without ever admitting to the participants that the quotas really exist. Whenever a system is proceeding smoothly and performance levels are not visible to individual participants, this kind of informal way of handling the "unmentionable" is probably more satisfactory than any other resolution, provided that the working quotas are favorable to the minority and reasonably agreeable to the majority participants as well.

Such an implicit system is likely to be unstable for a number of reasons, however, particularly when there are outside demands to change the quotas or the bases of competition. If the system in question feeds personnel into another system, as in the case of all of our educational systems (since the ultimate levels feed individuals into the job market), then confusion is likely to result unless accurate information is being passed along. For example, if black and white students are being evaluated on different bases in high school, and if this is not known to those who select among college applicants or who give them jobs, then someone is likely to be in for a rude shock if the same standards are applied to both groups at a later time. Black students, for example, would suddenly find themselves at a marked disadvantage in college and would be unable to understand the reasons for their sudden drop in performance. Another obvious problem with attempting to hide the existence of a double standard is that performance levels are usually visible to all concerned, so that embarrassing questions are likely to be asked.

In this connection, the essential point is that if a double standard and quota system are being applied at any given stage, then knowledge of this fact must be passed along to those in decision-making positions at higher levels. But as more and more parties become aware of the existence of a double standard it will be increasingly difficult to hide it from view of the participants themselves. The existence of a double standard on many integrated college campuses is likely to be suspected by white students. It may not be openly discussed, but it seems likely to contribute to a degree of resentment, gossip, and condescension on the part of whites and may be a factor that encourages blacks to segregate themselves from extensive contacts with white students.

Of these difficulties, it seems far wiser to discuss the question openly than to attempt to hide the facts. An open consideration of the issues at least makes it possible to study rationally the nature of the criteria that are being used in the evaluation process, to find ways of improving performance levels of members of both groups, and to attempt to reach compromises that are reasonably well understood by both groups. This should be done with a view to working toward a conscious policy of systematically reducing the performance gap in as painless a manner as possible. In the case of individuals moving through time within a single system, such as a four-year college program, this could involve a set of standards by which a smaller and smaller gap is produced in each successive year, so that by the time of graduation approximately the same performance levels had been attained by each group. If we look at the process over perhaps two decades, we could also plan on reducing the average gap at any given level (say, junior class in college), so that a negligible gap existed by the end of that period.

Such a program of planned reductions in double standards will obviously depend on a lessening of most all forms of discrimination, so that black and white competitive resources can become approximately equalized. But it can also be helped along by auxiliary programs that help to provide compensatory training. In the case of education, for example, not only preschool but also precollege preparatory programs can be undertaken. Rather than encouraging poorly trained blacks to apply to the best of the predominantly white colleges and universities, it would seem preferable to rely heavily on community colleges as feeders and to set up special preparatory, post-high school programs for disadvantaged students. Decisions could then be made according to the best interests of the individual students, with some going to the most demanding institutions of higher learning after a flexible length of preparatory study. Some might be discouraged from continuing beyond this additional two years, while others may be advised to enter lesser four-year institutions as transfer students or to enter vocational schools.

This kind of remedial program requires sacrifices on both sides. From blacks it entails an admission that remedial work may be necessary, and that present criteria are not necessarily racist in nature. It also may involve a sacrifice of additional years of schooling. For whites the sacrifice must be one of bearing the largest share of the financial burden. Such additional schooling will obviously be costly. Families already near the poverty level cannot be expected to support an additional year or two of schooling, and therefore their children may not only need full financial support but also supplementary funds to compensate for income they might otherwise have earned during this period. If preparatory precollege programs were set up within the ghettos themselves, however, not only would living costs be reduced but additional job opportunities for blacks would be created. Compensatory programs of any kind will also have to be made available to disadvantaged whites, as well as minorities, if they are to receive popular support and result in an equitable distribution of resources.

HOW REALISTIC ARE QUOTAS?

It is always tempting to consider a range of possible solutions to a problem, rejecting all but one as being unrealistic, and then concluding that there is only one viable resolution that should be emphasized as the only way out. But realism in this instance does not seem to call for such a simplistic and perhaps optimistic conclusion. It may well turn out that there are no resolutions that prove even moderately satisfactory to all parties.

One of the favorite sayings of American whites is the following: "I'm very much in favor of _____ as an ultimate goal, *but* I am unalterably opposed to _____ as a means to achieve this goal." The blanks may then be filled in almost at will. In the 1950s one of the major issues was that of residential desegregation, and the means being opposed were various regulations prohibiting owners, landlords, and their agents from discriminating against blacks. In the early 1960s the goals were the abolition of various Jim Crow laws and the means being opposed were those of civil disobedience and mass protests. Now the goal is the desegregation of the public schools, and the means that are thought to threaten the very existence of the American system are those of mandatory busing. Busing, of course, is basically a means of achieving racial quotas in the schools without having first to break down patterns of residential segregation. If other forms of quota systems become a major political issue, we can undoubtedly expect the same "buts" to be applied to these means as well. It is no wonder that blacks denounce whites as being hypocrites! Are there any means that would be acceptable, other than those that are either extremely vague (such as relying on education or good will) or else appropriate only in the distant future?

In each instance where some specific means is proposed, important American values can be invoked in opposition, and there always is some important principle at stake. The use of quotas as a means is no exception since it sets up an opposing principle to that of restricted competition for positions. The fact that, in reality, the competition has never been a fair one is conveniently ignored by many whites and only grudgingly admitted by others. It seems clear that if quotas favorable to blacks and other minorities are to become an acceptable means to whites, there must be considerable compromise and flexibility on the part of the minorities. For one thing, it must be recognized that many whites are also handicapped and that perhaps similar quotas ought to be applied to them as well. When a sociology department in a southern state university began admitting disadvantaged black graduate students from within the region, the dean rightly pointed out that there were also many disadvantaged poor white students who should receive similar consideration. The problem, of course, is in properly identifying such students. Similarly, it has been noted that some of the black students who have received special scholarships have come from middle-class backgrounds and are in a few instances much wealthier than their white peers. Simplistic quota systems based on race alone run afoul of these kinds of considerations.

Quota systems favorable to blacks simply will not work unless the black participants recognize that the quotas, in themselves, represent a major concession on the part of their white competitors and that the matter cannot be pushed too far. If blacks have been admitted as high risk participants—though this phrase is no longer used, and rightly so, because of its obvious connotations—then they must accept the fact that failure rates are likely to be somewhat higher for their group. The temptation, of course, will be to find fault with whatever evaluative criteria have been developed and to label any criteria as racist if they differentiate between the two groups.

Another kind of minority reaction that is likely to have adverse effects is to demand quotas built upon quotas in such a manner that the whole thing becomes cumbersome and unwieldy, so that demands are seen as absurdly discriminatory against whites. In one southern community that actually created complete school desegregation by assigning almost exactly equal proportions of blacks and whites to all schools, black students began to demand various types of quotas in instances where it appeared to many outsiders that competitive criteria were being applied in a very fair-minded fashion. When black cheerleaders were underrepresented, demands were made that quotas be applied in spite of the fact that blacks were very much overrepresented on varsity teams, where of course no quotas had been applied. The whole thing reached absurd proportions when junior class marshalls were elected by a democratic vote of the student body. Two blacks were elected out of seven, which was slightly higher by a few percentage points than the overall black percentage in the school. Black students immediately demanded that half of the marshalls be black in spite of the fact that they constituted only a quarter of the school population and that there were no basic objections to the fairness of the election procedures. When it appeared as though school authorities were going to give in to these demands, white students and their parents strongly objected, and in order to resolve the dispute it was found necessary to eliminate the class marshalls altogether.

Another kind of danger of quota systems has already been discussed in connection with the problem of the blurring of standards. In any kind of a competitive system the losers must find some way of rationalizing or accounting for their poor showing. Up until very recently the whole American system, and the buttressing stereotyped beliefs about blacks and other disadvantaged groups, has operated so as to place the blame on the minorities themselves. Blacks have tended to see themselves as inferior, unable to compete with whites, and as more or less doomed to low-status positions. These beliefs and their encouragement within the white community have been gradually modified. But the process has been all too slow, and as a result we are now witnessing a dramatic effort to counteract these feelings of racial inferiority through an open challenge to the system. The danger, however, is that the new ideology may swing to the opposite extreme by always blaming minority failures on "the system." In the context of the present discussion, this could take the form of openly challenging every kind of criterion for evaluation that in any way differentiates between blacks and whites to the advantage of the latter.

The most tempting liberal reaction to this kind of tack is then likely to be the substitution of criteria that do not distinguish among any candidates, thereby blurring all such standards and relying heavily on subjective criteria that make it possible to apply informal quotas without ever having to admit that this is the case. If no one is permitted to fail at a given stage (say, high school), and if criteria that differentiate among candidates for the next stage (say, college) have been blurred, then either all persons will be simply passed along automatically regardless of performance, or else selection will have to be made on grounds that have little to do with this performance. Considerable dissatisfaction on the part of those who have performed well but have not made the grade is likely to result.

Thus certain persons will lose by a quota system and others will gain. There will be those who develop a vested interest in such a quota system and who oppose its being considered as merely a temporary expedient to speed up the process of integration or provide compensatory resources for the minority. Since it will generally be difficult, though not impossible, to specify either a precise timetable for removal of quotas or definite principles for fixing the sizes of these quotas, there will always be those who insist that quotas should be just a bit larger, or that they should be retained just a short while longer. Making the whole process explicit has the real disadvantage of increasing the amount of conflict that will occur. Nevertheless, such bargaining has become a regularized process in the case of labor-management relations, and there is no inherent reason why similar processes cannot be made to work in the case of minority relationships. In the latter instance, of course, there are many more factions or interested parties than in the case of the former type of bargaining situation, and the issues and criteria involved are much more vague and diffuse. The first step is therefore that of bringing the issues out into the open where they may be handled on a rational basis.

In some quarters there is the notion that any form of evaluation, per se, is discriminatory and unfair. The belief is that evaluation implies that some persons are rewarded more than others and that therefore the latter are being punished. The assignment of the letter grades A, B, C, D, and F for course work is seen as punitive and improper for motivating students, for example. Competition for scarce rewards is seen as somehow linked with a capitalistic economy geared to social inequality. Just what kinds of viable alternatives to a competitive system there are, however are not made clear.

Certain kinds of skills are obviously needed in any kind of complex society. Mathematical reasoning, for instance, is needed in an increasing variety of fields, including business and the social sciences. Not all persons have equal mathematical abilities, and certainly they do not perform equally well at mathematical tasks. It is extremely difficult to see how we can discover mathematical talents, design training programs pitched to different levels of skill and ability, and reward students for proficiency without some sort of a testing system. Likewise, many important positions require an ability to think abstractly, to generalize on the basis of diverse concrete instances, and to communicate ideas clearly and concisely. Testing procedures are also needed to evluate these skills and to pinpoint correctable weaknesses in performance.

Such skills and requirements are seemingly universalistic and are certainly not peculiar to white-controlled educational systems, capitalistic societies, or other social institutions. Demands for these skills undoubtedly vary with the complexity of the division of labor in a society, but unless one subscribes to extreme views that no such a division of labor should exist, it is difficult to imagine a social system that does not attempt to sort out individuals according to skill levels. This requires evaluative instruments, imperfect as they are, and some sort of timetable by which these are to be applied. It then becomes a practical matter to devise ways of improving these instruments and applying them so that they do not prematurely discriminate against those with high innate ability but disadvantaged backgrounds. The use of temporary quotas may be a necessary element in this process, but it should be clearly recognized that it is not by any means sufficient.

The celebrated *Bakke* decision of the U.S. Supreme Court appears to rule out the use of rigid, explicit racial quotas whenever there is no evidence of prior discrimination by the party responsible for instituting the quota. In instances where such a party really desires to favor the minority concerned, the impact of the *Bakke* decision may be to encourage the substitution of blurred standards and disguised quotas for explicit ones. In situations where the party has instituted a quota system primarily to satisfy external demand for affirmative action, however, the *Bakke* decision may have the effect of increasing the opposition to any procedure that works to the benefit of minorities (or women). Most certainly, the fundamental issues involved have not been resolved by the single decision, and we may expect them to remain with us for a long time to come.

In thinking about the pros and cons of quotas, Americans would do well to look closely at the major social experiment with "protective discrimination" currently being conducted in India. Embodied in its constitution as an effort to correct for previous endemic discrimination against the so-called Untouchables, the Indian government's policy created a number of reserved positions in its legislature, educational institutions, and government jobs for what are now called Scheduled Castes, Scheduled Tribes, and Other Backward Classes, with the last category being entitled only to positions in educational institutions and governmental jobs but not legislative seats. The sizes of these quotas are determined on the basis of the numbers of each group at the time of the 1931 census and vary on a regional basis.

As might be expected, objective poverty and other disadvantages do not coincide exactly with caste lines in India, just as in the United States not all members of "disadvantaged" minorities are in fact worse off than some members of white ethnic minorities or even the dominant white Anglo-Saxon protestant group. This has led to many types of conflicts in India. There have also been a confusing set of court cases, as for example those involving persons who had earlier overcome their Untouchable caste membership by converting to Christianity but who now wish to reclaim their status as a member of a "backward" caste so as to be eligible for its benefits! And of course there are numerous somewhat less improverished castes, including several of the Brahmin castes, that are not in this protected category. Evidence also suggests that some of the Scheduled Castes are benefitting at the expense of others, with the result that in some regions distinctions have had to be made between "Backward" and "More Backward" castes.

The situation in India is of course much more complex than that in our country, but there are a number of parallels. Basically, the fact that a single line has been drawn between those castes deemed eligible for special protection and those that were not has given the former a special vested interest in their "backward" status, a term that even seems to have positive connotations in present-day India. At some point, this deliberate policy of protection that has had very positive effects in reducing what was admittedly very open discrimination against a sizable segment of the Indian population will undoubtedly reach a point of diminishing returns, as several Indian social scientists have indicated to me orally.

It remains to be seen whether there will be any consensus as to when this point has been reached and, if so, whether the special protective quotas will be abolished all at once or progressively modified. Whenever there are several minorities or ethnic groups at different stages of advancement, this problem of arriving at a consensus will be all the more difficult. One wonders whether any of the major political parties could afford to take such a step. Possibly the system may become too complicated and controversial to enforce and thereby may result either in increased political conflict or a tacit agreement to ignore it. Clearly, if open conflict were to prevail and be aggravated by the existence of these fixed quotas it is difficult to imagine how they could be rationally removed in accord with some agreed-upon timetable.

The basic question to which we do not yet have an answer is: Once quotas have been established and made fully explicit, under what conditions can they be removed and with what consequences?

NOTE

1. Carnegie Council on Policy Studies in Higher Education, *Selective Admissions in Higher Education* (San Francisco: Jossey-Bass, 1977), pp. 11–12, 35.

5

Our Public Schools: Busing and Quality Education

IF THERE WERE NO RACIAL ISSUES or economic inequalities in America, there would obviously still be a large number of difficult policy issues relating to public education. Certainly, during the decade of the 1970s what has been called the "crisis of our schools" has come to the forefront and involves many problems, not the least of which are economic. Now that we are paying our teachers decent salaries and are providing students a wide range of course offerings, as well as the opportunity to attend community colleges and state universities at a reasonable cost, it is becoming readily apparent that education is a costly business. Taxpayers across the country are rebelling at the thought of ever increasing property taxes or special school levies, and they are also demanding accountability. At the same time, many citizens are becoming aware of the fact that what has been termed "quality education" may not be all that it is claimed to be. Performances on standardized tests have been slipping for at least a decade, but the reasons for these declines are not entirely obvious.

On top of these and other issues are those of racial integration and mandatory busing to achieve racial balance. Although newspaper and television accounts of racial disturbances in public schools appear to be declining in number, lurking behind the resistance to school desegregation is the fear on the part of many parents that their children would be in danger of physical harm in such settings. Even where this particular concern is not an especially predominant one, there is the closely related belief that a failure to maintain discipline in the classroom interferes sufficiently with the learning process so that much more strict controls need to be instituted. The liberal intellectual is blamed for much of what is seen to be a deteriorating situation, and there has been a rising demand to return to what are taken to be the "basics" of education, the "three R's" of reading, writing, and arithmetic. This demand is also sometimes coupled with efforts to cut out the frills and thereby save dollars. Just where the frills lie, however, is a matter of dispute, although there are many obvious candidates in most high school and junior high curricula.

What stance can and should the liberal take in view of what I honestly believe to be a genuine crisis in education? First, if we wish to hold onto the objective of achieving school desegregation within a reasonable period of time, given the existence of a high degree of residential segregation, there seems to be no viable alternative to assigning students to schools that are some distance from their homes. This undoubtedly requires busing in most instances.

If we are to insist on this objective, however, we mut be prepared to face up to the expressed concerns of the majority of white parents as well as many blacks. We cannot sidestep the issues of racial tension and the quality of the learning experience. I believe that this, in turn, will require a soul-searching look at just what quality education means and how we can counteract the trend toward a lowering of academic standards, grade inflation, and increasingly poor performance on standardized examinations. In short, we shall have to take seriously the demand for accountability and do whatever is necessary to raise our levels of expectations, assure discipline, and protect students against the threat of harm, and see to it that only the best teachers are retained in the system.

It is difficult to say just how much of the opposition to busing and mandatory assignments to achieve racial balance is due to resistance to contact, per se, with persons of another race. It may be that busing is merely another symbol for integration or racial mixture and that the white opposition to busing is primarily a resistance to any form of contact with blacks, regardless of their status, achievements, or behaviors.

Public opinion surveys have shown steadily decreasing levels of prejudice for at least two or three decades, however, and it is clearly the case that black professionals and other white-collar employees are becoming increasingly visible, even in the predominantly white suburbs. The kind of overt resistance to any middle-class black movement into many of these same suburbs that we witnessed during the 1950s has also diminished to a considerable extent, and the most overt acts of discrimination on the part of realtors and money-lending institutions have been virtually eliminated. It is therefore quite possible that the residents of white suburbs are prepared to see their children interact with blacks, provided that they can be assured that the learning atmosphere will not suffer as a result.

Perhaps it is naive to take the expressed concerns about the possibility of violence and quality education at face value when, in fact, they may only be convenient rationalizations for a strongly-held opposition to any form of contact between one's own children and those of another race. But in view of other liberalizing trends in connection with the acceptance of blacks who conform to middle-class behavioral norms, it seems sensible to accept provisionally these concerns as being the real ones that motivate the antibusing sentiments in most predominantly white communities.

It is difficult to believe that buses, per se, are the point of contention, although in some instances transportation costs may constitute a substantial portion of a school budget. Certainly, residents of suburbs and rural areas have been accustomed to busing for a number of years and, as has been cynically pointed out on a number of occasions, white children in the South were often bused long distances to avoid contacts with blacks. The time that students spend on these buses, as well as the attendant concern about possible violence or physical abuse, are factors of legitimate concern, however, and we shall return to this matter.

The emphasis in the remainder of the chapter will thus not be on busing, per se, or how best to achieve it. Instead, it will be directed toward the issues of how to improve the learning process so as to reduce the performance gap between white and black children, and on questions relating to discipline and the improvement of the general quality of interaction between black and white students. Our basic assumption will be that if these two kinds of issues can be successfully addressed, at least a major portion of the white resistance to school desegregation will be undermined. At the same time, however, we must be concerned with how the educational process can be used to compensate blacks and other minorities for handicaps they may have received prior to entry into school or in terms of the environments they may be facing throughout the period during which learning is supposedly taking place.

IMPROVING THE QUALITY OF OUR TEACHERS

It seems clear that we still know relatively little about the learning process and what it takes to motivate a child to perform well, to develop confidence and a positive self-image, and to make realistic appraisals of his or her interests and potential to do different kinds of work. Therefore, there is a tremendous need for ongoing research into all aspects of this learning process. Nevertheless, we also need certain very general guidelines for policy, as well as critiques of the present educational system. Thus the suggestions made in this chapter are made in the light of these reservations about the state of our knowledge, yet they are not made completely blindly.

One of the fundamental problems that must be dealt with on a sustained basis is the nature of the training that we provide our teachers and the processes through which persons become selected into the teaching profession, how they are later rewarded or negatively sanctioned for poor performance, and how their knowledge is updated and expanded. A basic fact of life with which we must deal is that the public educational system is to a large degree controlled by a combination of the educational establishment, concentrated in schools of education in colleges and universities, and very powerful labor organizations of teachers that bargain over teaching conditions, salaries, and seniority regulations. Issues such as the evaluation of teaching performance, the criteria to be used in hiring, just what kinds of credentials are necessary to teach at a given level, and policies relating to layoffs and teaching assignments often get settled at the bargaining table or in the halls of legislatures, rather than by local school boards, principals and superintendents, or independent groups of citizens or educational specialists.

One of the major sources of concern in colleges and universities ought to be what sort of training future teachers should have. For the most part, the professional educators have controlled this process and have insisted that teachers must have a very heavy dose of education courses, rather than intensive training in subject-matter fields. Insofar as is politically feasible, I believe this pattern needs to be modified, not only with respect to programs for training high school and community-college teachers, but also for junior high teachers as well. That is, someone who teaches high school physics ought to have much more training in physics, mathematics, and allied sciences than in pedagogic techniques. The same applies to other subject-matter fields. Furthermore, the selection process ought to be such that we pick as our future teachers persons who have a genuine enthusiasm for their subject-matter field and for the learning process. They should *like* to write poetry, read good books, work mathematics problems, or conduct experiments. They should be good to excellent students themselves and should not have selected an education degree because they could not make it in a stronger academic program.

It is of course not the case that all college students who elect a program in education are second-class citizens when it comes to academic standards, and it would be doing our present generation of teachers a disservice if we were to imply that this is the case. But we need to insist that these persons be the very best students and have genuine intellectual curiosity as well as a thirst for learning. I do not believe that public school teachers are presently being selected on this basis. Certainly, they are not required to have the strong endorsement of faculty in arts and sciences curricula, nor is their work in these substantive fields carefully scrutinized. Perhaps future teachers do need a few courses in educational instruction, and they most certainly require supervised student teaching, but there is far too great an emphasis on technique at the expense of substance in our educational training programs.

Post-college education for teachers has also become highly routinized, partly as a result of the necessity to work out standard formulas for rewarding work beyond the A.B. degree. Thus in most instances any credit hours beyond the A.B. in one's field count in equal increments, up to a certain point, toward pay increases. The work could have been done in advanced physics at Harvard or in a marginally graduate course specially set up to accommodate an influx of teachers at a nearby state college. The teacher's performance in this course could have been barely passing or superior. The course could have been designed to give participants valuable insights on the frontiers of knowledge, or it might be a catch up course that any normal physics major should have had as an undergraduate. Clearly, this sort of perfunctory attention to advanced training is ritualistic at best and totally hypocritical at worst. It says to the teacher that if he or she merely puts in some time earning extra credits, this will earn extra income.

There is now an oversupply of Ph.D.'s in many academic fields, as well as a number of others who hold the M.A. degree in some substantive fields. Not all of these persons ought to go into teaching, by any means, but many should be encouraged to do so and should not have to earn education credits on the side, again in a ritualistic fashion. Furthermore, these more highly trained persons should be permitted to displace those who are less qualified, using strictly competitive criteria that emphasize quality of teaching performance as well as expertise. Here is where the resistance of teaching unions will come into play and must be countered. If this cannot be done effectively, however, it becomes all the more essential to emphasize quality at the point of entry and to insist that work beyond the teaching degree be evaluated in terms of quality, rather than as a mere tabulation of classroom hours.

The reasons these quality of training issues need to be stressed are twofold. First is the fact that good teaching requires that one knows what one is talking about and that one be up-to-date on recent research. One simply cannot communicate problem solving in mathematics without a good grasp not only of the specific technique under discussion but also more general principles and alternative strategies for attacking a problem. Since the learning of mathematics, or any other subject, requires that these principles and strategies be communicated along with factual material, the persons providing the instruction must themselves have a basic understanding of these more difficult notions. It also helps, of course, if a genuine respect for learning and an enthusiasm for the subject matter are also communicated. Relatively advanced work in one's subject-matter field does not guarantee that the teacher will be able to impart these skills to one's students, but in many fields it is a necessary if not a sufficient ingredient that needs to be considered.

The second, and perhaps more important reason why the quality of training factor needs to be emphasized, is more subtle and more difficult to pin down. This is the ingredient of a generalized respect for learning and an understanding of what it takes to master a difficult subject matter. In the case of mathematics, some refer to this as "mathematical maturity." I am not sure that this fully encompasses the notion I have in mind, but it appears to be one element. Another is the experience of having to "fight through" a difficult intellectual challenge of the sort one encounters in an honors thesis, an advanced course in mathematics, a research experience in a course in one of the social sciences, or a substantial effort in creative writing. Such experiences convey the idea to the potential teacher that learning is a difficult and challenging process, the mastery of which is really worthwhile. They also provide one with a better grasp of the problems being faced by those who find it necessary to struggle in order to understand a new idea.

Often, the process of learning is taken to be so routine and simple that one never realizes the difficulties that are encountered closer to the frontiers of knowledge, where new ideas are difficult to generate and where common sense and folk wisdom lead one astray. If more of our teachers have, themselves, had to wrestle with ideas that are just a little bit beyond their grasp, I believe that they will prove much more effective in communicating with others. Perhaps it is unrealistic to suppose that a high proportion of our future teachers will be exposed to the kind of learning process I have in mind, but the greater the proportion who are, the higher the probability that some of this will rub off onto their own students.

A mastery of one's subject matter is not sufficient to assure teaching effectiveness, however. Teaching must be evaluated and the results of these evaluations used in some constructive way to benefit the instructor and, if necessary, to terminate his or her employment. But the evaluation of teaching is extremely difficult, especially when there are multiple views as to exactly what constitutes good teaching. Nor do those of us who teach really wish to be evaluated, since, needless to say, any form of evaluation is a threatening process. It is no wonder, then, that the teaching profession resists the notion that evaluation should be more than perfunctory after an initial year or two of probationary status. In particular, teachers' unions are dead set against the idea and would like to institute a rigid system of seniority in its place. More legitimately, there is also the genuine concern that negative evaluations could be used to get rid of controversial teachers in an infringement on academic freedom.

Given all of the difficulties and resistances to teacher evaluation, I am not at all optimistic that careful evaluations will ever take place on a systematic or widespread basis. If we add to the normal problems of evaluation the added complications of comparing white and minority teachers, whose training and teaching philosophies are likely to be quite different, it is perhaps naive to believe that the matter will ever be taken seriously. Yet, unless and until this is done it does not seem plausible to assume that our educational system can be markedly improved. Certainly, throwing money at the problem will not help the situation in these respects, though it may improve teacher morale and enable school systems to supplement present programs in ways that will be considered later. In spite of all these notes of caution, however, I do believe it sensible to suggest a few considerations relating to teacher evaluation.

First, the evaluations must be conducted carefully and systematically by those who are actually qualified to make informed judgments. Especially in the case of technical fields, and in virtually all high-school subjects, this means that at least some members of an evaluating team must be in the field of specialty itself or at least be well informed about the subject matter. If an assistant principal whose training is in history or physical education is asked to assess the performance of a biology instructor or teacher of nineteenth-century English literature, the most likely criterion invoked will be pedagogical technique, rather than the mastery of the material. This suggests that classroom visitations would need to be conducted by teams of persons, at least some of whom were specialists in the field.

Second, insofar as feasible, the evaluators need to be distant from the teachers being evaluated, so that personal friendships and animosities do not enter into the picture. Yet, they need to have reasonably close touch with the school, the nature of its student body, and any peculiar problems that the instructor is facing. They cannot be subject to retaliation, either by the teachers concerned, by a teachers' union, or by parents, the local school board, the school superintendent, or local principal. They must be free to make negative as well as positive judgments, as well as those that may be unpopular with various parties.

Third, ways must be found to tap student input without giving students control over the destinies of their teachers. On many, if not practically all college campuses, student evaluations of teachers are commonly used, in some instances as the only systematic evaluational tool. One suspects—though the data are unavailable to demonstrate it—that one of the reasons for the grade inflation is the tendency for instructors to try to please their students so as to improve these evaluations. In the case of high schools, and to an even greater extent in junior highs, we would not expect a degree of maturity from students to make the necessary distinctions needed to separate the merely popular teacher from those who are really successful in advancing students' knowledge, improving their skills, or having more than a temporary impact on their thinking processes. Yet, student reactions to teachers do tell us something and, at the very least, could be used to provide feedback to these teachers and, in some instances, to reassign them to courses more suitable to their particular skills.

Fourth, there is the very important issue of tenure, which is difficult to make compatible with the notion that teacher evaluations need to be taken seriously. Certainly, the probation period for new teachers could be extended to between four and six years, so that several evaluations could have taken place prior to his or her being awarded tenure. This might go a long way toward resolving the problem. But what about the teacher who gradually becomes dated or out of touch or sympathy with his or her students? What about the person who begins to slack off or becomes alienated from the teaching process? It is totally unrealistic to suppose that such persons will be let go in favor of younger ones. At the very least, however, periodic evaluations would be useful to help a principal or superintendent counsel such persons and perhaps reassign them to administrative duties.

The principle of tenure is extremely important for a number of reasons, particularly in situations in which there are ideological controversies or efforts by local community groups to control the educational process by getting rid of controversial teachers. Therefore the resistance to teacher evaluations is partly justified, at least to the degree that there is distrust between administrators and faculty. Since the former are appointed by school boards and may therefore intervene to protect their faculties only at the risk of their own positions, the principle of tenure becomes extremely important as a protective mechanism. In effect, it permits the principal or superintendent to say "Look, I cannot fire this teacher unless there is sufficient evidence of specific acts of incompetence or illegal acts." If teacher evaluations were ever used as a political weapon to get rid of controversial faculty in this fashion, it would totally undermine this evaluation process and justify opposition to it on the part of teachers and their unions.

Even this very brief list of considerations—and there are undoubtedly many more issues that could be raised—suggests that teacher evaluations would be both expensive and time-consuming, as well as opening the door for controversies of several types. As also implied, such evaluations would likely become the subject of dispute between blacks and whites, particularly if the evaluating teams were to impose academic standards that relatively few minority teachers were able to meet. For all of these reasons, I fully expect that the present situation will prevail for many years to come, even though a really marked improvement in quality would seem to depend upon careful evaluations. Therefore it seems more reasonable to suggest, as a compromise, that such careful screening occur at the time the teacher is hired and perhaps one or two years afterward.

SUPPLEMENTAL LEARNING PROGRAMS

The quality of a student's education also depends very heavily upon how much work one does, a simple fact that sometimes escapes notice. Not only must teachers be good, but they must also be able to induce their students to make the effort to learn, to provide them with adequate feedback that helps them understand their mistakes, improve the quality of their writing and reading comprehension, and—perhaps most important—to motivate them to want to extend the learning process beyond the classroom. Unfortunately, the teacher is not operating in a vacuum. Significantly, there are a number of competitors or detractors from the learning process that need to be removed. One such set, of course, is the student's peers who of necessity will have a major impact on the learning process. Another is the home environment and supporting institutions within the local community. If anything has been learned about the impact of school variables relative to those of home and peer groups, it is the negative finding that school variables, including such things as teacher salaries and teacher-pupil ratios, have very little impact when peer and parental variables are held constant. There may be one exception, however, if we can learn how to take advantage of it satisfactorily. This is the factor of time. The more time a student spends in the act of learning, the more he or she learns, other things being equal. This rather obvious conclusion may have some implications which we shall now briefly explore.

One common complaint of many parents is that their children do not receive sufficient homework. Some parents, however, complain that their children are overworked or that they can ill afford the time to do homework because of other commitments. We also fully expect that parents differ considerably with respect to the degree to which they reinforce teachers' expectations, insist that homework be done prior to TV watching, and encourage their children to select courses and a curriculum that is demanding with respect to homework expectations. Here, as a natural consequence of social class differences in parental education, there is probably a wide racial disparity that needs to be counteracted. Lengthening the school day would be one way of achieving this, especially if the added time were utilized to do homework and receive extra help as needed. But how could this be done without incurring additional costs, encountering opposition from the teachers and their unions, and (perhaps most crucial) still keeping the children motivated? Would not this extra time be wasted, or at the very least used unwisely by the very students who need it most?

There is nothing sacred about the school day that it should end at exactly 2:30 or 3 p.m. and contain exactly the same cast of characters during the entire period. It is quite possible, for example, to visualize a setup in which the regular teachers, exhausted by their continuous interactions with children and in need of time to grade papers and plan for the next day, depart promptly at 2:30 and be replaced by a number of part-time personnel, some of whom are volunteers. In a later chapter I shall stress the need to provide additional jobs to ghetto residents, at least some of which are part-time and do not require unusual skill levels. In particular, both mothers of small children and retired persons could be effectively utilized in these roles, as could teenagers and unemployed young adults. But what could be accomplished in these after-school sessions?

First, they could provide the children with a real change of pace and an opportunity to do tasks that seem to them relevant to their own interests. Here is the place where ingenuity can be used to create mathematics games, as for example in the format of relay races, or to develop mathematics skills by calculating batting averages of one's favorite ball players or making predictions as to outcomes of next week's football games. Writing projects might be geared to letter-writing, perhaps to local politicians about some problem that the students perceive to be important. Reading can be focused around the students' own interests—in science fiction, romance, biographies of their favorite sports figures or entertainers, and so forth. Black students may read about race heroes, girls about famous women. Educational films about Black Africa or problems faced by other minorities can be shown and discussed and might even serve as the basis for student essays. Feedback and encouragement can be given without recourse to a formal grading system and without the mechanism of the report card. In effect, the persons who are conducting these supplementary programs can operate almost totally independently of the school system, although it would of course be advisable if they were to maintain reasonably close contact with the appropriate teachers.

Second, such a supplementary program should be conducted for all age levels, ideally beginning at the preschool level. Perhaps the program would operate only two or three days per week in the case of younger children and four or five for older ones. For the very young, the most crucial aspect of the supplementary program would be to work on basic skills, particularly reading. As students reached the secondary school level, an increasing proportion of the time might be devoted, rather simply, to supervised study during which the children would be expected to complete their homework and receive tutorial guidance. At this stage, one of the most important things the student needs to recognize is that work is not always fun and that the mastery of any difficult task requires good work habits. At the same time, for these older students, a reasonable portion of the added school time could be devoted to projects that they have selected but that entail reading and writing exercises. For instance, a simple survey focused around some community need would provide the students with opportunities to read, use their mathematical tools, and also develop their writing skills.

These afternoon extensions would afford an excellent opportunity for minority students to receive extra help provided by members of their own race. For instance, in the case of children of Hispanic backgrounds whose command of English is inadequate, special multilanguage sessions could be set up to work on problems that uniquely concern these children. Similarly, black children experiencing difficulties arising from special dialects spoken in the home could receive extra help that might simultaneously enable them to understand their own racial and cultural heritage. Since the teachers or helpers associated with these special programs would be selected from within the minority community, there would be the further advantage of providing the children with additional role models to encourage them with other aspects of the learning process.

Supplementing our educational system in this fashion would of course cost money, which would probably have to be allocated on a need basis. Otherwise, the most prosperous communities would be those that also contained the largest percentage of qualified personnel and, perhaps, the parents most interested in developing such programs. This would hardly operate to reduce the racial differential in student performance unless programs of this nature were confined to the ghetto, a policy that would hardly be justifiable in any universalistic terms. It does seem feasible, however, to allocate funds in such a fashion that those school systems displaying the greatest need receive proportionally larger sums of money. Even so, the costs might seem staggering, especially in view of the fact that our public schools are presently suffering from economic cutbacks, to say nothing of expanding their offerings. Would the suggestion that part-time personnel and volunteers be used to encounter the opposition of the organized teacher lobby, which might sense that these kinds of supplementary programs would be used as a device to cut back on formal training and the number of teachers with the proper credentials?

These questions of cost and possible teacher opposition are real ones. One way to alleviate the problem of costs is to make maximum use of older students in the process. This would have the added advantage of motivating some of them to go on to college, as well as improving their own skills. If, for example, an eighth grader is attempting to help a sixth grader with a mathematics assignment or with a book that is somewhat too difficult for the younger child, this would afford both with an opportunity to learn. The mere act of explaining something to another person forces one to master it. Certainly, older children may be used effectively as assistants and as role models for the younger ones.

This kind of supplemental education function could also be performed by other community organizations, such as churches and lodges, although it is more difficult to visualize how such groups could compel a resistant parent to expose his or her child to the program. Nevertheless, there is considerable flexibility possible in the mechanisms through which these forms of supplementary education could be implemented. It could be done in the evenings or weekends, if more feasible. It could be done in individual homes on a rotational basis. Every added effort in this direction would help. The problem with such voluntary efforts, however, is that they are unlikely to be systematic or sustained with sufficient commitment over a long enough period of time to become really effective. It is by now obvious that many minority youth need real help, not just for a year or two, but for almost their entire childhood. I doubt that this can be accomplished without a national commitment and some way of creating an institutional structure for accomplishing this. Augmenting the programs of our public schools seems to be the most sensible way of doing so.

HOMOGENEOUS VERSUS HETEROGENEOUS GROUPINGS

We next turn to a very controversial subject about which there has been much more heat than light provided in the literature. From the standpoint of the learning process the question can be posed as follows: Do children learn best when they are asked to compete and when their relative performances are clearly apparent, or is it preferable to disguise their true performances or to use them only as bases for internal comparisons so as to evaluate rates of progress? Closely tied to these questions are those related to tracking and so-called social promotions. Should a child who cannot read and write be automatically passed along and eventually given a high-school degree?

In terms of questions having a more direct bearing on race relations, should black and white children be compared in terms of the same standards, namely objective test scores of some kind, or should such tests be eliminated or used only for intraracial comparisons? Does a minority that is initially handicapped by definition face discrimination whenever it is expected to perform at the same levels as those who have not suffered these handicaps? It seems as though these questions are interrelated and that the answers one gives to any one of them will predict one's answers to the others.

It should first be noted that, as of this time, we do not seem to have good empirically based answers to these questions, though there is no lack of opinions. Probably it will turn out to be the case that some children react positively to competitive stimuli, even where they begin near the bottom, and that they are thereby challenged to do better. Others, however, will respond in the opposite fashion, tending to give up prematurely or to develop compensatory responses. If we could predict, in advance, which children would respond in a given fashion then we could construct programs that would be tailored to their individual response patterns. If we cannot achieve this level of knowledge—and certainly considerable additional research is needed on the subject—then perhaps it will be possible to monitor each individual child and find the kind of setting that is optimal for him or her. Even this second alternative, however, will be difficult to achieve and will certainly be costly in terms of time and effort. Therefore, perhaps the optimal solution is to strike a compromise of some sort. But precisely where and how?

My own experience teaching applied statistics to undergraduates and graduate students convinces me, as it has many other teachers, that an extremely heterogeneous class poses almost insurmountable communication problems. If the mathematics backgrounds of students in statistics range all the way from several years of college calculus to virtually no high-school algebra, it becomes almost impossible to satisfy both extremes. A teacher can attempt to pitch the class close to the median level, in which case those at both extremes will suffer. Or one can try to teach three classes at once, something that may be feasible with extremely small classes but which becomes virtually impossible when the numbers reach even 25 or 30 students. So-called individualized instruction is often suggested as a way out, and perhaps this works satisfactorily under certain circumstances. But it places a very great burden on both student and instructor.

If a group of students is not relatively homogeneous with respect to backgrounds and performance levels how does one then proceed to evaluate their work? One resolution is to grade performance in terms of the level of improvement achieved. Of course if students catch on to this device, they may easily beat the game by deliberately doing poorly at first and then improving at whatever rate they choose so as to obtain the desired grade. Leaving aside this problem, however, we encounter the basic difficulty of how to prevent the increasing heterogeneity that is likely to develop under such a system. Some children will perform at one or two grade levels above their assigned level, whereas others will fall several years behind. Are they all to be assigned to the same class next year? If so, then after several years of this process the heterogeneity will become so obvious to everyone, including the children themselves, that marked invidious distinctions will be impossible to avoid.

Another kind of resolution is basically that of holding back the fast learners by giving them meaningless repetitive tasks (such as working hundreds of similar addition problems), while concentrating primarily on the slow learners. This is precisely the kind of educational philosophy that has created the concern about quality education, as well as the white resistance to busing and school desegregation. The fear of these white parents, whether realistic or not, is that their children will be held back by slow learners who usurp most of the teachers' time. This fear may be based on colossal egotism on the part of parents concerning their own children's abilities, but this does not mean that the fear or concern does not exist; it needs to be counteracted. But this cannot be done if blacks and other minorities resort primarily to the argument that their own children are handicapped or that nationally-based examinations are discriminatory. This tack merely reinforces the basic fears of the white parents, who nowadays accept the cultural heritage theory of inequality but who are basically concerned about the present performance levels of their children.

A third resolution is that of tracking, by which children are placed in what are believed to be relatively homogeneous groupings according to ability level. The problem with this approach is twofold, as its critics have forcefully stressed. First, a child tends to become stigmatized and relegated almost permanently into the level at which he or she begins. This works very much to the disadvantage of the minority child, who learns to think of himself or herself as inferior and basically incapable of competing on equal terms with whites. The second difficulty with tracking, quite apart from that of stigmatization, is that of measurement error. How can we be sure that a given child really belongs in the slow learner group? How does one evaluate something so vague and general as "intellectual potential" at such an early stage of development? Because of the initial handicaps faced by minorities and possible cultural biases in the screening tests, almost any measuring devices we develop are likely to be biased and may therefore be used by a dominant white group determined to hold a minority in its place.

Is there any way out of this impasse? Clearly, a segregated system of education itself constitutes a form of tracking, though only insofar as minority performance levels are in fact distinctly different from those of whites. As a student reaches the level of high school and is afforded a high degree of flexibility of choice with respect to course selections, another voluntary form of tracking takes place through which students select themselves into courses that are more or less demanding. We may assume that students who have come to perceive themselves as less capable than others will tend to select the easier of two paths, particularly if they find themselves in classes with other students more like themselves. Thus even though tracking may have been avoided at the earlier levels, it may reappear at a later point in time, thus preparing these older students for very different types of occupational careers.

It seems to me that if middle-class white parents are ever to accept the notion of school desegregation without retreating to suburbs or sending their children to private schools, some degree of ability segregation will become necessary. At the same time, this separation of children cannot be permitted to become rigidified. That is, each child must be encouraged to move from one group to another at reasonably frequent intervals during the year, or at the very least every academic year. This implies a great deal more flexibility in terms of teaching assignments and the use of classroom space than our present system may currently afford. Such flexibility alone would not be enough, however. It would have to be accompanied by intensive efforts to supplement the training of those who have been temporarily placed in the slow learner category. This poses additional problems.

One problem is that of finding ways of avoiding stigmatizing these children, say by making them stay after school (assuming the longer school-day suggestion has not been implemented). For very young children, who may as yet be only dimly aware of their dubious status, perhaps this can be accomplished by having them meet in special play-oriented groups either after school or on weekends. Specially trained experts could be assigned to these groups, rather than having them supervised by volunteers or part-time helpers. Basically, then, they would be exposed to a remedial program that appeared to be something else but that was closely coordinated with their school work. Presumably, successful efforts directed toward very young children would do much to reduce the heterogeneity in later years.

As the children age, I see no simple way of avoiding the risk of stigmatization altogether, except that the children would not be assigned to any one group for more than a short period of time before being reevaluated. The process would undoubtedly require a great deal more sensitivity on the part of teachers than seems warranted on the basis of present experience. The temptation would be, of course, to attempt to reduce the inequalities by assigning the best teachers to the slowest classes, by holding back the others, or by other devices that would have the net effect of creating blurred standards situations in which it was merely pretended that all students are basically alike with respect to both actual and potential performance. As argued in the previous chapter, I do not believe that such a blurring of standards is compatible with what is basically a highly competitive economic system. The plain fact is that there *is* competition for the best jobs. At some point, students need to learn this fact of life and to evaluate their own performance in relation to that of others.

The above recommendations are in effect double-barrelled and therefore are subject to the risk that was noted in the introductory chapter. Basically, I am arguing that performance differences need to be noted and that students need to be placed in reasonably homogeneous groupings. I am also arguing that those who are placed in the slower-learning categories must receive extra help by well-trained specialists. The first of these suggestions would involve minimal extra costs, whereas the second would be expensive and much less appealing to those who control purse strings, namely upper-middle-class whites. Therefore we may anticipate pressures to slack off on the extra help, and whenever budget cuts become necessary, to cut corners if possible. If so, the proposed loose-knit tracking system would degenerate into a dual educational system and would be far less satisfactory, in my opinion, than one in which all students were thrown together and performance levels blurred.

Perhaps a second reasonable compromise would be that of assuring that tracking would not result in racial segregation by assigning students to schools primarily on the basis of socio-economic class level. To an important degree, this is occurring anyway. The aim would be to pair black and white schools on approximately the same class level, so that it would then be highly unlikely that black students would be disproportionately represented in the slower sections and whites in the faster ones. But given the marked class and educational differences between the races, this would leave many black and white schools totally unmatched and would be vulnerable to the charge made by lower- and lower-middle-class whites that the upper-middle classes favor integration only because their own children can avoid it.

Clearly, no final solutions to the basic problems are in sight, nor does it appear that anything other than a compromise solution can be found. Such a compromise will be far less likely to be achieved during periods of racial unrest or tension. Unless both sides to the controversy are willing to admit to the basic problems involved, there may be no short-term solution at all. If so, the quality of our educational system will certainly suffer and our children will continue to be the objects over which the racial battle will be fought and our schools will remain the battlegrounds.

THE NEED FOR BETTER COUNSELLING

If the quality of public education has not improved over the past decade or so, certainly the variety of offerings and range of choices open to students have increased. Furthermore, most of our colleges have either lowered their entrance standards or drastically reduced the number of college-preparatory courses required for entrance. This has been especially the case with respect to language requirements, mathematics training, and work in the sciences. The result of all this is that high school students have been opting to avoid many of the more rigorous or esoteric courses in favor of those that seem more applied or that are considered more relevant to them. Instead of courses on Shakespeare, which are still available, they are likely to take courses on American movies or science fiction. Instead of geometry or trigonometry they are likely to opt for business math or a course in jewelry making. Foreign languages have perhaps suffered the most of all in terms of enrollment.

The decision-making process is not an entirely random one, however. Those students who have parents or older siblings who have previously been to college are much more likely to get informed advice than are those coming from lower-class backgrounds. Paradoxically, the increase in choice that was instituted in response to student demand

and a broadening trend in the public school curriculum may have served to handicap most those whom it was intended to benefit. Obviously, intelligent choices can only be made when a person is well informed about the consequences of these choices and, in particular, when the long-term implications are taken into account. A student who freely elects not to go beyond two years of high school mathematics may not realize just how many career lines are being cut off by this decision. Even if the implications are dimly recognized, the short-term benefits of taking easier courses may outweigh, in the student's mind, the longer-range costs. Minority students, in particular, may be especially vulnerable in this free-choice process unless they are adequately counselled and encouraged to take the more difficult path whenever they appear to have the necessary capabilities.

There are basically two kinds of counselling that need not be performed by the same persons. The first is supportive personal counselling that involves a friendly, big brother or big sister relationship with the student. The second is academic counselling that usually requires a greater amount of expertise and technical knowledge about the kinds of training needed in each of a number of different fields in which the student might be interested. The former type of counselling needs to take place frequently and at all stages of the learning process. It can of course be supplied by interested teachers, parents, neighbors, or older peers. The latter type needs to occur at critical decision points in a student's career and to be reinforced by periodic assessments of the realities that confront him or her. Unfortunately, neither type of counselling seems to occur very frequently for many students and particularly for those who need it most. Sometimes the persons who are best informed about a student's situation will not be in a position to have their advice accepted or actually acted upon by these same students.

It seems as though this counselling function can be taken on as a kind of supplementary activity by persons who are hired part time or who volunteer for this service. Young mothers, college students, and retired persons certainly come to mind. The problem is to institutionalize the counselling process so that it does not occur on a hit-or-miss basis and so that it really benefits those who need it. Ideally, someone who has really followed a student's career over its entirety would be admirably suited for the first type of counselling role. Usually, when a student is promoted from elementary school to junior high or a middle school, he or she entirely loses contact with former teachers. A person who could serve as a link, and who could work closely with academic counsellors, would be especially useful to those students whose own parents are unable or unwilling to fulfill such a function. Here is an opportunity for minority service clubs, lodges, and churches to play an important part in the educational process. I am assuming that in most communities taxpayers will be unwilling to support what they perceive to be a frill but which is especially needed by most minority youngsters as well as their majority counterparts.

THE PROBLEM OF DISCIPLINE

Whether based on realistic fears or not, it is certainly true that one of the major reasons why both black and white parents say that they are opposed to busing and school desegregation is that they are concerned about violence and problems of discipline that would interfere with the learning process. Such fears are undoubtedly also linked with concerns about high crime rates in general and such acts as assaults, muggings, and rapes in particular. Although the mass media never seem to lose the opportunity to play up themes of violence whenever they occur, and although reports of such acts in school settings seem to be getting much less attention than five or six years ago, there still seem to be a sufficient number of racial disturbances, as well as nonracial assaults on students and teachers alike, that these concerns cannot be passed off as being unreasonable or based on prejudice. Were these acts brought under control, we suspect that one of the important causes of resistance to desegregation would be eliminated.

Just as there has been a recent awakening of the need to show a concern for the victims of criminal and delinquent acts, there must also be a corresponding interest in the rights of those students and teachers who fall victims to assaults by other students or who are constantly being intimidated and restricted in their movements by these students. It is often pointed out that our legal system is full of safeguards for those who are accused of criminal acts, and the corresponding seems to hold true for students who constantly create disturbances or who in other ways detract from the learning process of their peers. The use of corporal punishment of students is usually prevented by law, and any teacher choosing to use this means would, in any event, be subjected to severe sanctions.

Yet, those students who continually threaten or even attack their teachers may not be subject to similar constraints. Indeed, since they have much less to lose by engaging in physical violence, this gives them considerable power over teachers, school authorities, and the other students. If a student can be expelled only under exceptional circumstances, if discussions with parents do little good, and if the sanction of lowered grades is also irrelevant because no student can ever be permitted to fail, then how can these behaviors be controlled?

This problem, too, is a sticky one because of our reluctance to give up on any individual and our tendency to believe that he or she is the victim of something. To the degree that a disproportionate percentage of the troublemakers are black or members of other minority groups, the charge of racial discrimination is also likely to be leveled against any administrators who take a tough stand. Here, incidentally, it seems essential that minority members interested in quality education and integration must learn to give up the notion that any inequalities are, ipso facto, signs of discrimination. If, in fact, it is black students who are terrorizing whites, then this must be stopped, just as in the reverse case. A no nonsense approach seems absolutely essential to protect the rights of those students who are interested in learning. The same holds, of course, for lesser forms of deviance such as classroom disruptions.

Achieving a greater degree of control is perhaps easier said than done, however. If it can be applied consistently and nonpunitively in the grade schools and then maintained during the difficult junior high ages, presumably there will be many fewer problems in high school, where the students are physically much more capable of inflicting damage. Presumably if schools have been integrated beginning with kindergarten and first grade there will be many fewer racial disturbances than in situations where blacks and whites are confronting each other for the first time as high school students. What specific steps can be taken, then?

If corporal punishment is ruled out, it still seems possible to utilize a form of punishment that extracts from the student considerable immediate costs. I have in mind such things as making the student do five or ten laps around the track, do hard physical labor, or perhaps distasteful work such as removing garbage, picking up papers on school grounds, or even such old fashioned, but effective, things as having to write one's name 500 times or staying after school to help janitors, do homework, or sit with one's head on the desk. Funds permitting, in many schools it would seem to make sense to hire one or more persons, who might be part time, to serve as a combination of nightclub bouncer, army drill sergeant, and older sibling. Such persons should have imposing physical appearances and be able to break up fights in a forceful fashion, while during periods of calm act as friendly observers and big brothers (or sisters) of the students. They should also be capable of gaining respect, of making troublesome students do strenuous exercises, and of exacting strict discipline on those occasions in which it is needed. The existence of a few such persons in each school would also free most of the teachers of the necessity of, themselves, having to serve as disciplinarians. The aim would be to announce to would-be troublemakers that their acts will immediately be met with punishment that, although not physically harmful to them, will most assuredly be distasteful.

Many students are also in fear of what may happen to them off campus, especially if they were to rat on those of their class who are causing them difficulties. While it would of course be impossible to police the behaviors of all children while not in school, the presence of several part-time protectors on and around the school campus immediately after school closing might also be helpful. Funds permitting, such persons might also be hired part time to ride the school buses. Not only would this help to keep order, but these persons—if sufficiently skillful—could be useful in heading off disputes before they became too intense, in helping members of both races see each other as individuals, and in trying to get to know some of the problem children on more personal terms, not as a policeman but as a big brother or sister.

The above suggestions may sound punitive and, if not even-handedly applied, might lend themselves to charges of racism or discrimination. They would work only if supplemented by more positive efforts to help this small minority of troublesome students gain genuine self respect by finding alternative outlets for their aggression or tension. Minority students and their parents would likely be prone to expect that this kind of "punitive" approach would be differentially applied and would not, in fact, be complemented by these more positive ones, which are often more difficult and costly. If this fear turned out to be realized, then the approach would undoubtedly backfire. Without it, however, I fear that it is very difficult to find short-run solutions to the problems that these students create for their teachers and peers. Somehow, they must be controlled if genuine education is to take place and if white and black students are to gain mutual appreciation for each other.

6

Occupational Inequalities and Discrimination

JOB OPPORTUNITIES ARE OBVIOUSLY OF CRUCIAL IMPORTANCE to minorities, as well as all other persons desirous of entering or remaining in the labor force. Not only are they a source of economic livelihood, and therefore a necessity for many other valued objects, but at least in the United States and other industrialized nations one's occupation is intimately linked to one's self-respect and socio-economic status and thus to one's sense of psychological and economic security. Furthermore, the perceptions of job opportunities that exist among the younger generation are obviously important in motivating them to achieve the necessary education and technical training that will later enable them to compete successfully for these jobs. Therefore to the degree that job opportunities are actually unequal, or even perceived as being unequal, there will be important ramifications throughout many different social institutions and activities.

There is no question but that racial discrimination in the job sphere has been blatant, widespread, and persistent throughout virtually all sectors of the American economy. In a few instances, where it has been explicitly incorporated into written policies, such discrimination has been easy to document. But for the most part, given that discrimination is either illegal or at least contrary to the American Creed, practices have been much more covert than overt and thus difficult to pin down and measure in any precise terms. Virtually no employer or professional group, for example, will ever admit to discrimination. Others may do so, perhaps, but not us! There will always be disclaimers or alternative reasons given for the existence of inequalities, and as a matter of fact these alternative explanations can practically always be found to contain a grain of truth.

We shall postpone a consideration of this difficulty of distinguishing between actual discrimination and other reasons for racial and ethnic inequalities until the next section. Here we merely note the fact that the extreme difficulties one has in pinning down responsibilities in this area mean that there will be complications for policy, as well as major differences of opinion concerning responsibilities for correcting the situation.

Although there have been substantial recent gains for minorities in the occupational sphere, it is perhaps well to begin this chapter with a major note of caution having some pessimistic implications. Many of these minority gains have occurred during a period of economic growth and overall rise in the American standard of living since the end of World War II. Now that the effects of our prodigious population growth and industrialization on the world supply of food and energy are becoming apparent, and in particular as the costs of extracting fossil fuels are rising at an accelerating rate, we are beginning to see some of the very important restrictions on economic development that appear almost inevitable unless there is some major technological breakthrough in energy production. With this, we are experiencing the strains of an inflationary spiral that has major implications for the job opportunities of many Americans, particularly those whose lack of education or skills place them in marginal positions in the economy.

Along with these basic trends are another set of social phenomena that bode ill for those who are least able to compete in the American economy. We are witnessing a growing number of strikes and symptoms of labor unrest indicating a tendency for each occupation to look out for its own self interest, often at the expense of others. There is a realization that many occupations and services are in competition for slices of a pie that must be cut in ever smaller pieces. This is especially apparent in the public sector as taxpayers become increasingly restive about their taxes, and as federal and state legislatures cast about for ways to reduce services and cut agency budgets. Whether these cuts come primarily from welfare services, educational institutions, public employment programs, mental health centers, correctional programs, or elsewhere, the losses for those who are in the weakest competitive positions are likely to be greater than for those near the top. Racial and ethnic minorities, in particular, are likely to be among the principal losers.

On the attitudinal level, we may also anticipate that most citizens will not fully appreciate the importance of impersonal demographic, economic, and technological factors and will, instead, search for villains on whom the blame can be placed. If so, it may be increasingly difficult to hold onto political office long enough to develop long-range programs, as there may be a growing tendency to throw each set of rascals out if, say, inflation and employment cannot be simultaneously brought under control. We may also anticipate a rising distrust of other occupational groups, including most of the professions and businesses.

Minorities have their own special fears, if we may learn any lessons from history, because under these conditions they often make ideal scapegoats. Liberals, as a category, may also be vulnerable in this respect. Although it is difficult to predict with any degree of accuracy just what groups or categories will be hurt most in this situation of contracting opportunities and possible decline in living standards, it seems safe to predict that there will be increasing suspicion and distrust as well as overt conflict. At least this will be the case unless the economic situation can be stabilized or unless the American public can learn to adjust itself to a decreasing rate of growth and continued social and economic problems brought about by a combination of forces that are only partly under our control.

This issue of occupational opportunities and unemployment is thus a very serious one indeed, and it would be absurd in the extreme to assume that everything will work out for the best without our taking a careful look at what is occurring. This is of special concern for liberals and for those population elements that seem most vulnerable if economic changes force us into increasing competition for scarcer and scarcer goods and services, while at the same time there is a conservative movement among taxpayers and political leaders. Under such circumstances, we may anticipate growing strains among the rather loose-knit coalition of persons who have tended to favor a redistribution of these goods and services so as to protect those who are least able to compete. In particular, I am thinking of the various and ethnic minorities, the aged, women, physically and mentally handicapped persons, and various deviant subgroups in American society.

Cooperation and mutual sympathy among these groups have been weak or latent, at best, and one can well imagine a scramble of all-against-all in which each type of disadvantaged group becomes increasingly eager to disassociate itself from the others, with one or two becoming scapegoats to the advantage of the others. Were this to occur, it would signify the downfall of liberalism, at least in the sense of a coherent political philosophy or reasonably integrated program of action. It would not be the first time, however, in which a supposedly progressive social movement turned into a paradoxical combination in which idealism and extreme bigotry were combined. One need only remind oneself of the populism of a Tom Watson or certain signs of antisemitism among blacks to visualize the kinds of processes that remain a distinct possibility, though we hope only a remote one at this time.

INEQUALITIES VERSUS DISCRIMINATION

Occupational inequalities are very easy to document, but it is another matter to link these inequalities in a simple one-to-one fashion with job discrimination. For example, blacks are very much overrepresented in one of the highest-paying professions, that of professional basketball. This does not imply that white players are being discriminated against, although this might be the case. It could even be that black players are being discriminated against and that if there were no discrimination whatsoever the proportion of blacks would be even greater. Similarly, the relative shortage of black doctors and dentists does not necessarily imply discrimination within the medical profession, although in this particular case at least a degree of discrimination is suspected. Clearly some clarification is needed.

Minority activists—as well as some members of the Women's Liberation Movement—are often quick to jump to the conclusion that inequalities, per se, must have resulted directly or indirectly from discrimination. The amount of inequality may even be taken as a measure of degree of discrimination with no questions asked. If there are relatively fewer women full professors than assistant professors, this is assumed to imply discrimination. It might, of course, simply mean that relatively more women have dropped out of the labor force after having children, and/or that older women in the lower ranks had only recently returned to the labor force.

A very low percentage of blacks in a particular occupation could be due to any number of factors in addition to discrimination. The favorite explanation of employers, of course, is that very few qualified blacks have applied. The issue then turns to what one means by qualified. If it can be shown that only five percent of black college graduates have been hired, whereas 20 percent of white graduates have been employed, does this constitute good evidence in favor of discrimination? Not necessarily, unless one is willing to assume equality of preparation on the part of both groups. But what are the relevant characteristics upon which the judgments are based—grades in college? If so, are the colleges equal with respect to quality? Are they based on aptitude test scores of some kind? If so, perhaps these are deliberately discriminatory against blacks. If based on personality characteristics, how are they being assessed? Are there any objective ways of measuring these traits, or is the appraisal merely based on the superficial judgment of the interviewer? How is the applicant's overall potential assessed? If this is based on past performance in a similar position doesn't this handicap those who have never had previous experience?

It might seem as though questions like these can never be satisfactorily answered since, in fact, there are extremely few occupations or jobs for which a person's qualifications can be adequately judged prior to being hired. Likewise in the case of promotions the best that often can be done is to reward conscientious service and to extrapolate from the person's past performance to potential performance in some other presumably more demanding position. To the degree that it is possible to develop ways of accurately forecasting a person's future performance on the basis of past performance, test scores, or any other method of assessment, we may say that practices are completely nondiscriminatory if these characteristics alone are used to make the decisions. Race, religion, sex, and other supposedly irrelevant characteristics are completely ignored. Ideally, the individual's race or religion is not even known to the person making the decision. The interviewing process obviously makes the race of the applicant known in most instances, though not his or her religion. Sex will practically always be known unless only initials or a code number is used on the application.

We have noted that it is currently being argued that this kind of completely universalistic criterion may also be discriminatory, and admittedly it is often difficult to tell in any particular instance whether or not the stated criteria are, in fact, the real ones. Certain of these criteria will be correlated with race (or sex, age, or ethnicity). We have already encountered this problem in connection with our discussion of aptitude testing and the double standard. Suppose blacks are found to do poorly on whatever screening test is being used. Then it may be argued that, ipso facto, the process is discriminatory. Pushed to the extreme this argument would of course mean that any screening device that distinguished among persons in such a way as to give any category of persons an advantage might be labeled discriminatory. Thus performance tests give the advantage to college over high school graduates. The criteria by which professional football players are selected obviously discriminate against women, the aged, small persons, and those who lack speed, strength, endurance, and (of course) the ability to play football.

In the case of a profession like that of football or basketball the criteria used in selecting new recruits are rather easily defined. Basically, they involve the past performance of players in much the same kind of setting as they will later experience. College athletes will have been previously selected by an elaborate process of scouting the high-school talent. They will have been trained for professional careers during four years of college, with most potential recruits having dropped out along the way. Some may have taken their studies sufficiently seriously so as to have found more attractive alternatives. The wider range of occupational choices for white players, outside of athletics, undoubtedly provides one mechanism for the selective recruitment of relatively more blacks into the profession. We also noted that there are numerous well-standardized measures of athletic performance, particularly for the offensive players—scoring records, yards gained, passes completed, and so forth. In few occupations known to man—including that of the Presidency of the United States—is there such a systematic, elaborate, and expensive search for talent. And in very few occupations is there less discrimination against blacks, though of course sex discrimination is blatant.

Most white-collar occupations are by no means this selective, nor are the criteria for evaluating performance as clearcut. As one might expect, therefore, the standards for hiring and promotion are much more blurred. Many white-collar occupations require combinations of personality traits such as perseverance, ability to make contacts easily, pleasantness of personality, and soundness of judgment, all of which are exceedingly difficult to measure or to appraise during a brief job interview or by reading a few letters of recommendation. Nor have the applicants been previously evaluated in terms of earlier performance that is anywhere near comparable to that expected on the job. How does one evaluate an A in English literature, a B in psychology, and a C in calculus in sizing up a candidate for a position in an insurance company or bank? How does one throw extracurricular activities and a membership on the track team into the equation? How about personal appearance? Are all of these irrelevant or are they reasonable indicators of abilities and personality characteristics that will make for a successful career? Suppose a black and a white candidate have roughly equivalent academic records but the black appears to be openly hostile toward a white interviewer. Will this affect his or her performance on the job and relationships with one's peers? If the black candidate is rated down on personality does this constitute racial discrimination? What if several whites have also been bypassed because of rather nebulously defined personality traits?

Obviously, one needs a working theory to interpret whatever data are at one's disposal. Sociologists have at least until recently tended to believe that whenever employers said that virtually no qualified blacks applied for jobs, this was a mere rationalization. Or we assumed that blacks, hearing about these discriminatory practices, simply did not apply because they knew they would be rejected. Perhaps the employers were telling the truth, however. The reason white sociologists are now not so sure of themselves on this point is that they, themselves, have recently been accused by blacks of being racists. The evidence—there were very few black professors, even a smaller proportion in the name universities, and also very few in the committee structure of the American Sociological Association. We have been trapped by our own very loose criteria!

It may well be true that occupational and income inequalities are due to discrimination somewhere in the system, but it does not follow that they imply discrimination at the last stage of the process, or in any other particular stage. One obvious reason for the shortage of black sociologists, doctors, and bank presidents is that there are very few blacks who have obtained the necessary educational credentials. In the case of sociologists who had earned the Ph.D. degree, the relatively small proportions who held offices in the professional organization may have been due to weaker publication records or the fact that blacks tended to be concentrated in the black colleges of the South. Does this mean that the profession was discriminating against blacks by relegating them to schools that required heavier teaching loads and that were out of the mainstream of the profession? Again, not necessarily. These black professionals may have received their degrees from easy programs and have been less qualified than their white counterparts. Is this mere rationalization? It is of course difficult to say without much better data and sharper evaluation criteria than we presently have. We may try to duck the issue by arguing that the truth is probably somewhere in between. But where in between? Policy decisions, if rationally based, ought to depend upon the answers given to such questions.

We noted in our discussion of quotas the tendency to develop fuzzy criteria through the process of eliminating those that discriminate. Discrimination is used, here, in a double sense—discrimination against minorities and discrimination among the candidates. We also argued that this blurring of standards, although providing an apparent escape from the dilemma, is less satisfactory than the explicit use of a double but unblurred standard. An employer is likely to wish to use at least a certain number of quantifiable criteria, such as grade point averages and various test scores that his or her company has found predictive of later success.

If these criteria are eliminated as racist, the employer must then rely on subjective impressions and on difficult-to-interpret letters of recommendation. The best predictors of success on the job may have been ruled out, and future employees may be selected on the basis of guesswork or the impression they have made during a half-hour interview. Their four-year college record and their performance on tests that may have been specifically designed to predict to job performance may be ignored. To the employer this may seem completely unreasonable.

This does not mean, however, that legitimate criticism of employers' criteria cannot and should not be made. We strongly suspect that in most cases there will have been no systematic investigation of the predictive value of these criteria. Certain of the tests may be treated in a perfunctory manner but deliberately used to screen out undesirable personnel whenever the employer is pressed for a justification of his or her practices. In many other instances the criteria (e.g., a high school degree or certain minimum test scores) may not have any bearing whatsoever on the job skills at stake. They may be treated as indicators of abilities or motivation for tasks that are almost completely unrelated to the job itself. To the extent that the high school or college degree becomes a necessary union card for positions at a particular level, the school drop-out is handicapped for life regardless of his or her other qualifications.

Thus it seems very reasonable for minorities and their allies to ask a number of specific questions concerning the adequacy of criteria for hiring and promotion and to demand that these be justified. At the same time, it is not reasonable to claim that every criterion that is being used to discriminate among applicants is also discriminatory against the minority merely because the minority, on the average, does not perform well according to these criteria. If, for example, specialists can construct testing instruments that predict just as well to later job performance, but do not penalize blacks or other minorities, then there will be a very legitimate reason for asking that these be substituted for the present criteria. If they cannot, then the present criteria should be retained, though always recognized as fallible and replaceable. As in the case of educational testing, I would prefer to see a temporary double standard utilized so that, for example, blacks would not have to pass a particular set of tests at the same level as whites. This would permit the same distinctions to be made among black applicants as are made among whites, rather than forcing the employer to develop fuzzy criteria that, in effect, make it extremely difficult to reward past performance in school or previous jobs or to utilize test scores of any kind.

The essential point is that inequalities cannot be directly used to locate or identify discrimination unless one uses an extremely simplified working theory or a definition of discrimination that makes the two concepts virtually identical. The notion of discrimination, as it is used popularly as well as in the sociological literature, involves the idea that certain persons are being unfairly or differentially treated because of their membership in some social category. It does not imply that all persons are equally qualified or eligible for a given position or even that all categories of persons, on the average, are equally qualified. Thus if one finds inequalities among these categories this does not necessarily imply that discrimination has occurred, though this may very well have been the primary source of the inequality in question. Unfortunately, there will seldom be agreement on this point among parties that have divergent interests and perspectives!

PROFESSIONAL AND MANAGERIAL OCCUPATIONS

There are obvious inequalities between blacks and whites with respect to the relative percentages of each group in the various professional occupations, in managerial positions, and in most all white-collar occupations. Have blacks been gaining ground relative to whites? This all depends on how one measures the changes. The proportion of white-collar workers has been increasing for both groups over the past three or four decades. If one constructs rates of change by comparing the ratios of later to earlier occupants, then blacks appear to be gaining ground.

The reason is obvious; if you start with a very low figure the rate of change may be made to look phenomenal. If the total number of black actuaries increases from 2 to 12, there is a sixfold increase! Suppose this is compared with a white increase of, say, 3,000 to 4,000, a one-third increase. The blacks are obviously gaining ground through this increase of ten black actuaries as compared with a thousand whites! These hypothetical figures are of course extreme, but they should make the point. In general, the absolute differences between the numbers of white and black professionals have been widening, as have the differences in black and white incomes at most all occupational levels. But the percentage changes often look much better for blacks.

First-year class	Total first-year enrollment	Disadvantaged minority enrollment	Disadvantaged minority percentage
1968–69	9,863	292	3.0
1969–70	10,422	501	4.8
1970–71	11,348	808	7.1
1971–72	12,361	1,063	8.6
1972–73	13,677	1,172	8.6
1973–74	14,159	1,301	9.2
1974–75	14,763	1,473	10.0
1975–76	15,295	1,391	9.1
1976–77	15,616	1,400	9.0

The point is well illustrated by the above figures taken from a very recent study by the Carnegie Council on Policy Studies on Higher Education.[1] The data refer to medical students enrolled in their first year of medical school between 1968 and 1977.

We see that, during this brief period, the minority percentage actually tripled. There were approximately 1,100 more minority students in 1976–77 than in 1968–69. Even so, there were approximately 4,600 more nonminority medical students in the final cohort than the first, representing almost a 50 percent gain.

Figures such as these imply different things to different people. On the one hand, they do mean that minorities have been making considerable headway in breaking into an occupation that, until recently, has been virtually closed to them. On the other hand, we infer that much of this progress has been due to the general expansion of medical schools, and more generally in the white-collar and professional labor force. Certainly, whites have also made gains and numerically speaking have often profited more than blacks. It is also true that the great masses of blacks and other disadvantaged minorities have not been markedly affected by these particular changes. But are they meaningless? Do they merely reflect tokenism? Or do they indicate that, once the opening wedge has been formed, racial discrimination in white-collar occupations will virtually disappear?

Once more the interpretation one gives to these facts depends on one's working theory of the causes of the original inequalities. To many conservatives the extent of genuine occupational discrimination has never been great and inequalities have been due to the small number of qualified blacks. To many liberals these gains are real but would not have come about except through a constant barrage of education efforts, black protest, court rulings, and governmental policies. To the radical or militant extremist these are not real gains at all but merely the result of a deliberate policy of trying to win over a few of the more highly educated blacks while refusing to deal with the basic problems of the urban ghetto and rural poor.

The liberal position has, I think, been consistent over time in one very important respect. It has accepted the notion that the job market must be truly competitive and that the only ultimate solution to job inequality will be to build up the competitive resources of blacks and other minorities, while at the same time eliminating discriminatory policies that have placed roadblocks in their way. The removal of these roadblocks requires pressure, but once removed, a minority must then rely on its own resources if it is to compete successfully in the system.

Conservatives have often denied the existence of these roadblocks, or if they have not denied them they have disclaimed any personal responsibility for them. The fault is assumed to be the poor education blacks have received within the South (if a Northerner is speaking), or broken families, or the welfare system, or with meddling by Washington bureaucrats. These conservatives are essentially correct in one respect: the fault does partly lie elsewhere. But it also lies close to home too, and this is the difficulty.

Whatever the reasons for the small number of black doctors, sociologists, and statisticians, the fact is that now—after considerable pressure from blacks, white liberals, and those who control the purse strings in Washington—there is a scramble to attract black professionals, to apply double or blurred standards for admission to training programs and job openings, and to promote and otherwise reward black professionals at least as rapidly as their white counterparts.

Any special privileges that may be given to minorities as compensatory rewards are, like quotas, resented to varying degrees by members of the majority group. There are therefore practical limits beyond which demands for such compensations will be met with stiffening resistance, quite apart from the question of the extent to which they are actually justified. There are some blacks who have not been especially handicapped and perhaps a few who have been helped along at numerous points under the assumption that they were more deserving than their white competitors. Usually, however, these particular blacks are not distinguishable from the remainder of their group, just as the handicapped whites are not easily identified. A truly universalistic program of compensatory rewards would therefore require a much more complex system than one based merely on race (or sex). The mechanisms for working out handicap points would then become so complex and subject to debate that a return to strict universalism would seem to be the only solution. Likewise, if every minority group were to demand special privileges and quotas, the system would also become unworkable. If carried to the extreme, therefore, a compensatory program begins to look ridiculous and also begins to alienate nearly all of the participants, each of whom believes that he or she is not getting a fair break.

The opposition to compensatory programs would also seem to be dependent on questions of supply and demand. In times of a shortage of labor, such as existed in many academic professions in the 1960s, good jobs are sufficiently plentiful that white males are not especially resistant to granting relatively better opportunities to blacks, or even white females. As the market becomes tighter however, there will undoubtedly be much greater resistance and resentment. The fact that a decade or two ago the white and black candidates might have been in opposite positions is, to the present victim, no satisfactory explanation for what is perceived to be reverse discrimination. From the standpoint of one's individual rights one would have to agree, though from the standpoint of motivating blacks, as a group, a certain amount of compensatory rewarding also makes sense. Once more, the dilemma is real since it involves several conflicting principles, each based on important American values.

Another factor that undoubtedly affects the tolerance level for what is perceived to be reverse discrimination is the relative numbers involved. After all, there are still very few blacks who receive advanced degrees beyond the A.B. Compare this with the large numbers who could rather easily qualify to become carpenters, masons, electricians, or plumbers. Blacks have encountered much greater resistance among white members of the building trades, both with respect to racial quotas and to plans that would enable black apprentices to attain journeyman status more rapidly than whites. Since there is no real threat that blacks will easily enter the professions en masse, the small number of exceptions can be more gracefully accepted.

Also, many professions are extremely sensitive concerning their public image and the need to appear liberal, reasonable, and unconcerned with protecting a vested interest. In an economically secure profession, the members are almost as concerned with their public relations as with their incomes. In the case of the university community, those academic fields that are most eager to capture the minds of today's socially-concerned students are especially eager that they not be labeled racist or sexist. Threats by blacks to boycott the national professional organization, or to create scenes that will produce unfavorable publicity, are therefore much more likely to affect, say, sociologists and political scientists than statisticians and chemists.

As an overall assessment, it appears as though some of the most difficult hurdles in actual job discrimination on the professional and managerial levels are now being overcome.[2] At least for every such occupation in which there is presently discrimination against blacks there seems to be another in which blacks and other minorities have a competitive advantage. But given the fact that there is a substantial scarcity of qualified blacks at this level, we cannot be fully assured that the present situation is not one of mere tokenism. This can only be evaluated once blacks obtain these qualifications in sufficient numbers that token blacks are no longer needed. I have argued in another work that pressure tactics and governmental policies, alone, cannot give blacks and other minorities the necessary competitive resources, though they may force this kind of token representation on most employers.[3] Many black militants and white radicals claim that tokenism is all that blacks will be able to get voluntarily from whites. It is premature to tell whether or not they are correct in the case of these kinds of white-collar occupations.

It must be recognized, however, that recent gains by blacks in these fields have not been obtained without a considerable amount of militancy and—one might add—without an effective alliance with white liberals. Were it not for directives from Washington and the fear of losing government contracts, many businesses would not be scrambling to locate qualified blacks. Most certainly, major efforts to recruit disadvantaged students and to hire black faculty were a direct result of student disorders on campuses, combined with government threats to cancel research contracts and fellowship programs.

In addition, the younger generation of business executives and administrators have been more exposed via college courses, literary works, and a favorable press to rather consistent efforts by liberals to get across the message that they, too, are responsible for the plight of blacks and other minorities. Presumably, their resistance to change is now considerably less than that of their elders. Some, in fact, have taken the initiative to search for blacks and other minorities long before the pressure was actually applied and to convince their colleagues to do likewise. It would therefore be a mistake to state baldly that it has only been through pressure that gains have been won. Certainly, however, the pressure has been of fundamental importance.

BLACKS AND AMERICAN LABOR UNIONS

Between the ranks of professional and managerial personnel, on the one hand, and the unskilled laborer, the unemployed, and the welfare recipient, on the other, are the vast majority of Americans. These are the small farmers, the semiskilled operatives, the craftsmen and foremen, and the lower levels of the white-collar labor force. Obviously, if blacks are to move from the unskilled level to the highest ranks of the white-collar labor force, the overwhelming majority are going to have to pass through these intermediate ranks in the job hierarchy. With small-time farmers becoming less and less important to the overall economy, and with increasing urbanization of the labor force, it is clear that occupations presently associated with organized labor hold an important key to the problem of racial inequality.

We can expect white members of labor unions to have ambivalent attitudes toward their black brothers and sisters. On the one hand, they are fellow members of the working class. To the degree that they can be exploited as a cheap labor supply or as strikebreakers, the labor movement as a whole is weakened. On the other hand, they are competitors of white labor. When jobs are scarce an obvious way for white labor to protect its interests is to exclude blacks and to immobilize the black resistance by any means possible, including the ultimate threat of violence.

The relationship between the American labor movement and blacks has been a mixed one that has remained basically static over the past thirty years. The facts have been well documented and can be summarized reasonably adequately by drawing the familiar distinction between craft or trade unions, which for the most part were identified with the A. F. of L., and the industrial unions, generally associated with the old C.I.O. and epitomized by the United Auto Workers under the leadership of Walter Reuther. The latter type of union must of course depend on its numbers for bargaining power, whereas the former depend upon their ability to monopolize particular skilled trades by a process of restricting their size and regulating the training of apprentices.

Particularly since World War II, industrial unions found it advantageous to include blacks on a more-or-less equal basis with whites in order to control a labor force that could otherwise readily be used as strikebreakers. Strengthened politically during the Roosevelt era of the 1930s and early 1940s, these industrial unions played an important role in enabling blacks to retain a reasonable share of the jobs that became available to them during the labor shortage of World War II. Thus, in contrast with the situation following the first World War, blacks maintained a foothold in semiskilled jobs associated with automobile manufacturing, steel, and other heavy industries.

With the possible exception of a few highly industrialized cities, however, blacks made many fewer gains in the southern economy owing to the overall weakness of labor and the difficulty in reconciling black-white rivalries. Today, there are sincere efforts being made by both black and white union organizers to unite black and white unskilled and semiskilled labor, but these unions are finding it extremely difficult to develop the strength and unity needed to overcome substantial handicaps. For one thing, they are attempting to organize relatively unskilled workers in the textile industry, hospitals, or municipal employees such as sanitation workers or janitors. Given the large surplus of black labor and the relatively inefficient use of poorly paid employees who are easily replaced by other workers or by automated processes, the bargaining power of these unions is very weak. In addition, they do not receive the necessary degree of support from the national chapters or from predominantly white labor unions in the local area.

Attempts to organize black hospital workers in the South during the 1960s illustrate another basic dilemma. The dramatic and prolonged strike of hospital workers in Charleston, South Carolina, which was supported by Reverend Ralph Abernathy and the Southern Christian Leadership Conference, seemed to imply a new hope for black-dominated union movements in the South. The power element in this case was a real factor. Although the black labor force was not especially skilled, a sudden strike in a hospital setting posed an immediate threat to the health and lives of the patients. Similarly, strikes among sanitation workers create health hazards as well as considerable inconvenience to white members of the community. But by the same token, strikes by hospital or sanitation workers in such sensitive occupations are likely to produce a strong reaction among whites, not only locally but across the country as well. Thus black unionists are in the unenviable position of lacking the economic leverage to make their strikes or threats successful, while at the same time not being able to take advantage of noneconomic bases of power. We would anticipate, however, that if blacks become sufficiently desperate these noneconomic weapons may become increasingly important.

The policy recommendation in this instance seems clear enough. Since one can hardly expect government economic support of union activities, this is one place where the national union organizations must make every effort to collect additional funds to support both predominantly black and predominantly white union locals in the South. Protracted strikes are particularly costly to workers whose wages are close to the poverty level, and there is little in terms of a union tradition that can be used to induce these workers to take the high risks involved. But can we realistically expect American labor unions, that have now become quite conservative in nature, to make such an overall effort in the South? Certainly in most other respects northern liberals have been unwilling to make comparable economic sacrifices. Nor can government pressure be applied to force the unions to allocate their funds in this manner. I am not at all optimistic, therefore, that steps of a sufficient magnitude will be taken.

Basically, the black labor problem in the South, as well as in the many urban ghettos, stems from the large oversupply of available unskilled and cheap labor. The relatively large number of black women in the South who even now must find work as domestic servants is another indicator of this general oversupply of black labor. Fundamentally, then, the problem must be corrected by means of a combination of population-migration policies and by a national program designed to provide meaningful jobs at this skill level. The first of these possibilities will be discussed briefly in the next section, and the second will be our focus of attention in the next chapter.

The story is somewhat different in the case of skilled labor. It has been well documented that many of the craft unions, particularly those associated with the building industry and railroads, have been highly exclusionist for a long period of time. This was pointed out and documented by Herbert Northrup, in a book published in 1944, and the practice has continued with only negligible change.[4] Black carpenters, electricians, plumbers, masons, and painters have until very recently simply been excluded from apprenticeship training and therefore, of course, journeyman status. In the South, in particular, one finds them in numerous helper roles in which they may actually be doing basically the same work. But they are not paid anywhere near the same wages, do not have as much economic security, and do not enjoy the union privileges of the journeymen members. And where there tends to be an oversupply of journeymen relative to actual jobs, they find themselves out of work. The strength of these trade unions clearly depends upon their ability to control the supply of "qualified" workers, and this control has meant that only a token number of blacks have been accepted.

Does this indicate that tokenism in these unions is basically the same as tokenism within the white-collar professions? There are many differences, as we have already implied. The most important of these seems to be the relative numbers of potential black workers who could fairly easily qualify to enter the respective occupations. What other leverage do these labor organizations have, other than to exclude most of those who wish to enter? They cannot rely on the educational union card of the A.B., M.D., or Ph.D. to screen out most potential competitors. Political power in general, and a strong influence within the Democratic Party in particular, is thought to be an absolute necessity in maintaining their competitive status. It is no wonder, then, that politicians (particularly Democrats) have been reluctant to challenge the racial policies of these unions.

Yet this is precisely what must happen if blacks are to break through the craft-union barriers in reasonable numbers. Perhaps only the Republican Party will be in a strong political position to enforce strict nondiscrimination or even racial quotas on, say, the building trades. But if this was pushed too far, they might be merely alienating the union vote in exchange for the black vote, and the latter would in most locales be less important. Of course, at present, both sets of votes happen to be in the Democratic camp so that the best political strategy for both parties seems to be that of attempting to obscure the conflict and to make vague and undeliverable promises to blacks. Once more it does not seem that blacks have the necessary political leverage to make substantial gains unless they attempt the kinds of dramatic means that are also most likely to produce a backlash reaction.

Steady progress in breaking down these union barriers would seem to require expanding the demand for these types of labor to such an extent that white members will feel sufficiently secure that they will be willing to admit a substantial number of black apprentices. It seems unrealistic and unfair to individual whites to demand that black apprentices be upgraded much more rapidly than whites, but it does seem reasonable to insist on policies that set definite quotas or goals for new black apprentices each year for perhaps one or two decades.

The railroad industry is obviously too sick to call for such an expansion. But the housing industry is not, particularly given the large potential demand for low-rental public housing in the black ghettos. A major effort to expand the number of public housing units—even in segregated areas—would thus kill two birds with one stone provided that the building trade unions were made to take in and train larger quotas of blacks. If public housing could not be constructed with the cooperation of these unions, then ways should be found to bypass them altogether by creating a separate labor force of black construction workers for these projects. If a public housing program were planned on a long-term basis, so that the number of jobs involved could be accurately estimated, one expects that the unions involved would begin to cooperate.

Public housing, itself, is a controversial subject. Would either political party care to give high priority to such a doubly controversial program? Probably not, unless there were substantial pressure from both the black voter and a sizable number of whites as well. Given the very high costs of purchasing new homes, perhaps such a pressure will materialize if the current biases against public housing that exist within this country can somehow be overcome.

POPULATION AND MIGRATION POLICIES

There is a commonly held belief that is substantially supported by research findings to the effect that the size and distribution of a minority affect both prejudice and discrimination, thereby influencing the rate of progress toward integration and full equality. The argument applies most forcefully to minorities that retain their visibility, either because of racial characteristics or cultural traits that are distinctive and not easily changed. In the case of blacks in America, research findings show very clearly a positive correlation between the percent black in an area and many types of economic inequality, particularly educational inequality and income differentials. This holds true not only in the case of comparisons between the North and South, but within the South as well—even within the individual states. Certain forms of inequality and residential segregation are only weakly related to the percentage of the black population, however, and the exact mechanisms responsible for the correlations are not entirely clear.

We have noted that inequalities are of course not perfect indicators of actual discrimination, and one possible explanation is that the most poorly trained blacks tend to cluster together through a process of selective migration. (There is no evidence to suggest, however, that the most recent black migrants to our urban centers have poorer educations or lower earning potentials than black nonmigrants of comparable ages.) More plausible, perhaps, is the argument that the association is spurious. In the case of the South we know that blacks are still concentrated in the areas where cotton was most profitable and therefore where slavery had its strongest roots. It could therefore be argued that it is the lingering tradition of slavery, together with practices originating shortly after Reconstruction, rather than the size of the minority, per se, that have been responsible for greater discrimination.

In view of the facts that there has been considerable migration since the Civil War and that the correlation between minority size and inequality holds up (to a lesser degree) within the border states and in northern cities as well, it seems more reasonable to suppose a more direct causal connection. One line of argument runs that it is the fear of economic competition that increases the motivation of whites to discriminate, and this fear is increased as a minority becomes more visible and numerous. Another possible explanation that seems especially plausible in the light of recent developments is that as a minority increases in size it poses a greater threat to the majority, both in terms of voting power and (ultimately) actual dominance.[5]

If there is in fact a direct causal connection between a minority's size and discrimination then this would have important policy implications. In particular, it would argue for programs to limit the minority's size and to encourage geographic dispersion. Both kinds of policies, however, would inevitably be extremely controversial, and we must therefore examine them carefully. Any attempts to limit the minority's size are likely to be appealing to the dominant group but not the minority; those aimed at dispersion will meet not only minority resistance but also that of members of the dominant group into whose area the minority is migrating. Therefore although I believe that the ultimate goal of complete integration almost by definition requires minority dispersal and will be facilitated by stabilizing the relative sizes of the two groups, I do not see much immediate hope for the acceptance of genuine programs in this area.

Prior to the Civil War and during the period of active slave trading, the percentage of blacks in America reached the level of approximately 20 percent. As the slave trade was cut off, and during the period when white immigration in large numbers was encouraged, the black percentage dropped to slightly under 10 percent by 1920. Since that time the percentage has risen very slightly to about 11 or 12 percent. Assuming approximately the same trends as have occurred in recent decades, it would not be unreasonable to estimate a figure of about 13 percent by the end of the century.

The black population has also been migrating both urbanward and northward, with huge concentrations developing within the largest metropolitan centers. There has been a marked westward movement since World War II, and we may anticipate that this will also continue for at least several more decades. Without any major changes in these trends we may therefore expect a resettlement pattern resulting in growing numbers of racial islands concentrated in the largest cities of the nation. What was once a rural and southern minority will thus become urbanized and located primarily in urban pockets of larger sizes. It is not unreasonable to expect that America's 50 largest cities will contain black percentages ranging from 30 to 80 percent by the year 2000. Many of these blacks will spill over into what are today white suburbs, and it is possible that quantitative measures of residential segregation will show slight decreases over time. But without basic changes in the present picture, something like the above pattern can be anticipated.

The desirability of formulating policies aimed at stabilizing the percentage of blacks at somewhere near the present level depends not only on whether one is black or white, but also on one's working theory of the causes of discrimination. Anyone suggesting that controls be placed on population growth would of course immediately be labeled a racist or a fascist as well. But what about those who stress the need for planned parenthood, governmentally financed abortions, or other fertility programs aimed at limiting the number of unwanted black (and white) children? If one sees this as a middle-class plot to do away with the race problem by eliminating blacks, then much the same reaction can be expected. Therefore about the best white liberals can hope for in this respect is a program that makes available and virtually free of charge birth control techniques and clinic facilities. If the issue is pushed too strongly it is almost bound to fail.

There have apparently not been any serious claims that the black cause will be significantly aided by deliberate attempts to increase the black birth rate so as to achieve a greater relative size. There have, however, been arguments to the effect that black power requires the geographic concentration of blacks so that power can be consolidated, black representatives more easily elected, and a basis for genuine self-respect created. We have already discussed the segregation aspect of this question and will have some additional remarks concerning a possible migration policy. Let us therefore briefly consider the problem of differential racial birth rates.

High birth rates imply rather long periods during which there is a high dependency ratio produced by the large number of nonproductive children who must be clothed, fed, housed, and educated. Without massive day-care centers or other arrangements it also implies the immobilization of a large proportion of the potential female labor force. Traditionally, of course, the existence of discrimination and high unemployment rates among black males has forced a very high proportion of black mothers either into the labor force or onto relief payrolls. Patterns that have simultaneously sapped the self-respect of the black male, or have encouraged him to leave home in order to make his family eligible for relief funds, may have also encouraged a higher degree of promiscuity and financial irresponsibility resulting in higher birth rates.

The conservative white reaction that has threatened to reduce unemployment benefits, aid to families with dependent children, financial support for abortions, and other forms of relief has only aggravated the situation, since it has not been accompanied by genuine efforts to remedy the basic economic discrimination. We may thus find ourselves locked into a type of vicious circle that cannot be broken by frontal attacks on the black family or on population control, attacks that also have obvious moralistic overtones that are offensive to blacks.

Yet the advantages of lowered birth rates, with an emphasis on quality child rearing and education, must somehow be made to seem real. If black families that restrict the number of children cannot reap the rewards as readily as their white counterparts, then exhortation, free birth control facilities, and other white-dominated efforts cannot possibly hope to succeed. Fundamentally, then, there must be basic economic changes within the black community. As a supplement, the institution of black-run and black-staffed birth control clinics might then make it increasingly the norm within the black community to exercise more effective family planning.

High current birth rates in lower-class black ghettos mean that there are already alive a large number of lower-class black children who, as they reach late adolescence, will attempt to enter the labor force. If these persons are as poorly trained as their elders, and if government labor policies remain basically unchanged, then we can anticipate very high levels of black unemployment for several decades. Even if the birth rate were drastically lowered overnight, it would take a long time for this unemployment to work itself out if no specific remedial action were taken. Obviously this is all the more reason why we need a flexible employment program capable of absorbing varying amounts of available black labor in many different communities across the nation.

A well planned migration policy might serve to alleviate some of these problems, but even the mildest suggestion that blacks be encouraged to migrate (usually from the South to other regions) has been met with icy silence on the part of liberals from the potential receiving areas. "Why should *we* take over *your* problems and attempt to fit poorly trained blacks into our more highly skilled labor force?" There is of course considerable hypocrisy in this typically northern position in view of the fact that the development of the southern economy has been discouraged, in part, through northern efforts. Now the problem is clearly a national one, however, and the kind of migration program that is needed is one that will encourage resettlement within each region of those blacks who are presently concentrated in the very largest cities.

Gunnar Myrdal also noted this tendency of blacks to pile up in our largest cities and even recommended an explicit migration policy with dispersion as the objective.[6] Population planning has never appealed to the American public, however, and there are inevitably many kinds of objections that can be raised. The notion of planning poses a threat to many; it appears to violate the basic freedom of movement postulated in the American Creed. (Such complete freedom of movement has never been possible for blacks, a fact that is often forgotten, however.) Planning does not necessarily imply coercion. It can merely involve a national policy of collecting information concerning employment and housing opportunities in various areas, together with efforts to assist potential migrants to make wise decisions, to enable them to make initial contacts, and to obtain needed employment in new locations.

The migration process is not as well understood as might be hoped—in part because research funds in the field of population have been much more available for the study of fertility then migration. We do know, however, that much migration results from rather inaccurate information concerning job opportunities at the destination, combined with glamorous images of the big city and informal contacts with friends and relatives who have recently moved. All of these features favor the movement to the larger metropolitan areas, particularly when long-distance migration is involved. Why should a Mississippi black want to move to Waterloo, Iowa when all he or she has heard about is Chicago or Detroit, and when a sister's family has just moved to Chicago? Having settled in Chicago and learned the true facts of life, and not being able to find employment there, how would one ever find his or her way to a smaller northern community? If one learned more about such a community, who would help out when he or she arrived?

If there were agencies within the black community capable of giving really adequate advice, assisting with loans, and making contacts with distant employers and real-estate agents, the probability of moving to smaller communities would undoubtedly be increased. To a degree, organizations such as the National Urban League handle this function, but they lack the necessary resources to do a really adequate job. There are other major obstacles, however, many of which reside in the potential host communities. For the plain fact is that these predominantly white communities do not want additional blacks. Even if they did, they recognize that a sincere effort to create new jobs and to put out the welcome mat could very well result in a flood of newcomers, since other communities in the area would not likely follow suit.

In order for the effort to succeed, there would need to be a simultaneous effort made in numerous small cities and local communities. For this reason one cannot be very hopeful that a carefully planned migration policy would ever be supported by either political party. But this does not mean that data should not be collected on economic opportunities in various localities, with this information being disseminated into the black community. Such information could undoubtedly be obtained as a by-product of research being conducted to obtain standardized social indicators.

As a long-range objective a greater dispersal of the black population seems absolutely necessary. Obviously, the present pattern represents an extremely high degree of segregation that is incompatible with the objective of complete integration. At the very least, as a means of achieving the objective of integration, I believe we must work toward the migration of blacks into the relatively smaller nonsouthern communities. But I do not see how this can be achieved dramatically or in the immediate future without the benefit of economic policies consistent with this objective.

NOTES

1. Carnegie Council on Policy Studies in Higher Education, *Selective Admissions in Higher Education* (San Francisco: Jossey-Bass, 1977), p. 109.

2. William J. Wilson, in *The Declining Significance of Race* (Chicago: University of Chicago Press, 1968), makes much the same point while also emphasizing the desperate plight of lower-class blacks.

3. H. M. Blalock, *Toward a Theory of Minority Group Relations* (New York: Wiley, 1967).

4. Herbert R. Northrup, *Organized Labor and the Negro* (New York: Harper, 1944).

5. Blalock, op. cit., Chap. 4.

6. Gunnar Myrdal, *An American Dilemma* (New York: Harper, 1944), Chap. 17.

7

Programs to Reduce Unemployment and Provide Minority Jobs

WE CAN IDENTIFY THREE GENERAL MAJOR OBJECTIVES relating to work and the allocation of economic resources, two of which are probably in theory noncontroversial, and a third on which there is undoubtedly at least a reasonable degree of consensus. Our problem, however, consists in reconciling the apparently incompatible requirements that each imposes, given a real world of limited or scarce resources and less than ideal human beings. These difficulties do not seem so great as long as the discussion is confined to a very general and abstract level, but they appear much more fundamental when it comes to finding specific ways of implementing them and assigning priorities.

The first is the obvious need, on both a nationwide and worldwide basis, to increase and maintain high levels of production efficiency and distribution of goods and services, so that overall average levels of living and consumption may be improved. If this cannot be achieved we will be involved in what game theorists call a "zero sum" game in which the total sum of winnings remains fixed (or may decrease). In such a game every dollar that I win is lost by someone else in the system, and all of the players are involved in a cutthroat type of competition that makes for interesting games, perhaps, but a very vicious and conflictful situation in the larger society.

In such a world there is no incentive for the "haves" to cooperate with the "have nots" except on the basis of very temporary and expedient coalitions designed to wipe out or handicap some of the remaining participants. Clearly, a "positive sum" game is more advantageous in absolute terms for the participants and is also one that has been shown to be much more productive of cooperative arrangements. Over the past several centuries the Western world has, of course, experienced such positive sum games in which absolute living levels have been steadily rising. The total pie itself has been getting larger even though one's relative share in the pie may have been determined by outcomes of more strictly competitive processes.

The second very general objective is that of providing meaningful work for a steadily increasing proportion of those persons who are willing and able to perform such work. This work should afford a wide range of alternatives for each individual, provide avenues and incentives for mobility, and be meaningful in the sense of helping the individual gain self-respect, ideally enabling him or her to perceive the contribution to some worthwhile objective. Furthermore, the avenues to each position should be multiple, so that if one means is blocked others will still be open. Status should ideally be awarded the individual according to how well he or she performs the duties of the role, taking into consideration his or her potential.

Obviously we have not been able to find ways of making this second objective totally compatible with the first, and we have in fact evolved an elaborate ideology in order to explain these failures. The general flavor of this ideology is of course familiar to all adult Americans—the necessity to reward the most able and conscientious persons with power, prestige, and higher incomes in order to provide the incentives for a capitalistic system. Hence those whom we find at the top are assumed to be the most deserving, and any effort to tamper with this system would only interfere with the goal of achieving greater efficiency of production. The fact that this ideology is both familiar and widely accepted in America does not make it either empirically true or false. It does mean, however, that the overwhelming majority of Americans can be expected to act as though it were true, and in so acting will make it much more difficult to introduce major social experiments creating new incentive systems, methods of assigning individuals to jobs, or new job categories of the type that do not evolve naturally from the free-enterprise system.

The third and more controversial general objective is to affect the allocation of rewards, quite apart from the occupational division of labor itself. Traditionally, of course, a rate of pay or salary is derived for each occupation by a combination of supply and demand dynamics together with political bargaining. For example, a coalition may in effect exchange votes for specific government policies or perhaps obtain jobs in exchange for a promise not to boycott or to disturb the peace and tranquility of the community. But there is very general consensus that certain kinds of persons—the aged, the handicapped, small children, and a few others—must either be maintained in some way outside of this competitive system or must be given some sort of bonus arrangement.

This consensus breaks down with respect to the details, however. Just who should be eligible for these bonuses and for how long and under what conditions? How large should the bonuses be in order not to destroy the nature of the competitive system for everyone else? Who is entitled to make these decisions? Should the handicapped themselves be entitled to bargain in their own behalf (say, through political organization), or do they forfeit this right by their inability to play the game according to the rules by which all of the other players must abide? And what happens to the morale of the regular players when they see their own winnings doled out to nonparticipants, or awarded to those who have been playing only half-heartedly (as they perceive it)? If demoralization results, what happens to the game itself?

There is of course no necessary one-to-one correspondence between the quantity and quality of one's work performance and the distribution of economic rewards. Other forms of incentives such as community recognition, medals and prizes for meritorious service, or added power and influence may be used as alternative or supplementary rewards. In fact, in the American tradition there are many volunteer positions—including numerous political offices—that are so rewarded. The work involved is by no means considered meaningless. Nevertheless the greatest noneconomic rewards of this type have typically gone to those who needed them the least: upper-middle class, middle-aged males, and, less frequently, their wives.

There is no necessary reason why such volunteer labor could not be used in, say, lower-class black neighborhoods, with the volunteers being supported by regular cash incomes automatically coming from the federal or municipal governments and not being dependent upon the nature or amount of work accomplished. Such a pattern would be the obvious counterpart of the wealthy lawyer who takes out perhaps as much as a decade from his or her career in order to run for political office. In terms of present-day American values, the difference seems to be primarily one of social definition. The lawyer is esteemed because of "sacrifices" made on behalf of the community or government, whereas the lower-class counterpart would more likely be considered a "welfare" case who should be advised to get a "real" job. In truth, both might be contributing an important service to the community while not receiving a direct economic payment for such services. The point is that there are many more possible ways of motivating persons to do useful and psychologically meaningful work than are presently being utilized. But are we sufficiently flexible to give them a try?

SPECIFIC PROBLEMS FACING BLACKS

The above general objectives involve many issues over and above those of racial discrimination and the problem of upgrading the job market for blacks. But the sticky practical issues encountered whenever one or the other objective is given priority over the others are especially obvious in the case of present-day black-white relations in the United States. Nowhere do we confront the issues more squarely than in the problem of the extremely high unemployment and welfare rates among urban blacks. Nowhere is the American Creed put as directly to the test, and nowhere are its apparent inconsistencies more obvious. The unemployment rate among blacks has, for several decades, been consistently double that of whites. These official rates actually underestimate the true ratio, since the census definition of unemployment requires that a person be actively in search of work. Those who have given up the struggle to find decent work are therefore not counted among the unemployed. Today, estimates of the true unemployment rates among young, urban, black males and females range from 30 to 50 percent! It is no wonder that embitterment and cynicism regarding the American value system have been acted out on the streets of the urban ghetto.

The desperate problems of urban black ghetto dwellers have been described for more than a half century. There were clear warnings in Myrdal's classic study, *An American Dilemma*, published in 1944.[1] But one of the most recent pessimistic interpretations of black unemployment appears in Sidney Willhelm's *Who Needs the Negro?*[2] It is Willhelm's general thesis that, thanks to automation, economic exploitation is no longer the major problem for blacks. Blacks were forced into the New World to provide the slave labor for the plantation economies of the American South, the Caribbean, Brazil, and several other colonies. After slavery, their hands were still needed in southern agriculture and to provide unskilled labor in urban areas. The need for such unskilled labor is now minimal, however, and is being reduced each year. Automation has meant that no more than perhaps 5 percent of our labor force is really needed to produce an actual surplus of agricultural goods—though of course the distribution of this surplus is another matter. Willhelm provides an impressive set of data illustrations to argue that before long no more than 5 to 10 percent of our labor force will be able to produce enough to satisfy most of our industrial needs as well.

What future exists for blacks? They are simply becoming redundant and unncessary, in much the same way that American Indians became redundant and were merely pushed off their land to make room for whites. Similarly, blacks are being confined to the urban ghettos with the possibility that they will remain there almost as wards of the government. Perhaps they will not make too much trouble, but Willhelm's prognosis is that if they rebel they may very well suffer the same fate as the Indian, mass annihilation. What about the American ideology that stresses equality and universalism? Is this primarily a clever trick to make blacks believe that there is, after all, some hope? Willhelm argues that most blacks are systematically denied the means with which to compete—quality education and true equality of opportunity. When they then fail to compete on equal terms, say by doing poorly on standardized tests, they are asked to believe that they have only themselves to blame, and the resulting lowered self-esteem only further inhibits the ability to compete. White liberal ideology, even if advanced by naive but sincere individuals, merely tends to support the system, he claims. The egalitarian and universalistic ideology is therefore nothing but a coverup in a capitalistic system in which a growing percentage of individuals can be taken as expendable. If automation can do the job more quickly and cheaply than persons, then the latter will be replaced. Those least able to compete will be pushed downward and ultimately will, in effect, drop out of the productive economy.

Willhelm's thesis is somewhat more complex than this, and many of his points are overstated. Some of the characteristic biases of the New Left social science are also in evidence, particularly the conspiracy theory that tends to see the white establishment and liberal intellectuals as a close-knit, homogeneous, and terribly unscrupulous group. But is the general thesis entirely unreasonable? There is much that has occurred since Willhelm's book was written that tends to support the basic thesis and little to deny it.

If blacks remain concentrated in urban ghettos, whereas industry continues to decentralize by moving increasingly to the suburbs, these blacks and other similarly situated minorities will experience yet another handicap. In particular, the suburbanization of businesses and industry can be expected to have a special appeal to middle-class women and older persons who wish to take part-time jobs, who do not wish to commute to the central city, or who may fear to enter certain high-crime neighborhoods. The latter types of employees may, in fact, serve as an incentive to industry to accelerate the suburban movement, at the expense of ghettoized minorities. Government incentives to industries to remain in central cities, combined with efforts to reduce crime and make these areas attractive to those who commute into the central cities, are obviously needed to counteract these forces favoring a peripheral movement. Once more, the timing and magnitude of such efforts seem crucial if an accelerating trend is to be avoided.

Still in the pessimistic vein, we may add one more ingredient to the potentially explosive mixture. Women, another minority group, are entering the labor force in increasing numbers, a trend that has continued for several decades. Currently the women's liberation movement is emphasizing that there must be sexual as well as racial equality with respect to employment opportunities and promotions. Their appeal, although theoretically not class-linked, has been aimed primarily at the upper-middle classes, women college students, and at the very lowest classes of welfare mothers.

If this movement succeeds in opening up to women many more occupational opportunities in the professional and business worlds, and if increasing proportions of college-educated women become oriented to full-time occupational careers, then the impact on lower-class blacks is predictable. Many middle-class men will be displaced downward in the occupational pyramid. These persons, in turn, will displace downward other white men and women who, in turn, will displace those at the very bottom. Assuming that most husbands and wives will have approximately equal levels of training and abilities, this will in effect mean nearly double incomes (before taxes) for the upper-middle class families and much greater unemployment rates for both husbands and wives in the most disadvantaged groups. Thus without compensating policies of some kind, the superior competitive resources of white women as compared with black men will result in still greater family income differentials between the races.

In addition to competition from the increasing percentage of women in the labor force, blacks face two other possible types of rivals for jobs. The first is the growing number of illegal immigrants coming largely across the Mexican border and settling primarily in the Western states but also moving into some of the same metropolitan areas, elsewhere in the nation, that are supersaturated with low-income blacks. If population and economic pressures within Mexico continue to produce a very large differential between living standards in the two countries, it is difficult to see how this immigration pattern can be brought under control without incurring substantial economic and social costs. At least in the urban areas, these immigrants will be in direct competition with the most disadvantaged among the black population and will not only undercut them in the unskilled labor market but will also add to the total welfare budget in these cities.

The other group of potential competitors may be the increasing numbers of older workers who, as a result of congressional action, will now be able to remain in the labor force beyond the age of 65. It is too early to tell how many of these persons will choose to remain in the labor force, and this will undoubtedly depend upon such factors as inflation rates and the adequacy of social security benefits. Such elderly workers will have certain obvious advantages over younger persons, including whatever power and status they have achieved within their professions or labor organizations, their ability to gain sympathy as a result of friendships and prior service to the employer, and their increasing proportion of the electorate. With a fixed number of jobs, we may obviously expect that whatever number of these older persons are retained in the labor force beyond their previous levels of employment there will be a displacement of others, presumably those who are just entering or those who can be most easily squeezed out. A disproportionate number of the latter will undoubtedly be blacks or other minorities.

The answer, of course, is not to suppress white women and the elderly or to play off the one minority group against the other, but to attempt to find new kinds of employment opportunities that are less directly tied to economic market mechanisms. The thrust of the black-white liberal coalition's movement has in the past been in the direction of attempting to improve the relative competitive resources of blacks through education and to break down the barriers to white-collar occupations. The results have been satisfying in some respects, though it has become fashionable in militant circles to assert baldly that they have been meaningless. But it is certainly true that only a tiny fraction of the black minority has directly benefited from these efforts.

It is important to emphasize that the improvement of training and educational opportunities does not resolve the overall employment situation unless there is, in fact, a poor fit between job demands and the capabilities of the occupants of these positions. If we merely increase the educational levels of the populace, we are thus apt to find an inflation of job entrance criteria, so that for example a high school degree is required in many occupations for which a much lower degree of training is really needed. Such an inflation of requirements for entry or promotion then obviously works to the disadvantage of any category of persons who are unable or unwilling to obtain this higher level of education, whether it be a high school degree, a college diploma, graduate or professional training, or experience in an apprenticeship program.

Basically, then, employment opportunities and training are only loosely interconnected. Individuals who obtain the requisite training may have a decided advantage, but unless the overall employment levels are increased, a collective effort to improve educational levels may merely result in an oversupply of eligible persons. This may improve the overall quality of the labor force, and may have added social benefits, but it cannot compensate for a total increase in the number and diversity of positions in the labor force. Thus a dual emphasis on training opportunities and on increasing the overall number of jobs becomes crucial. An emphasis on one without the other makes no sense, and thus the basically conservative concentration on education as a solution to economic problems faced by minorities and other disadvantaged groups is only a very partial solution at best.

One potential resolution to the problem of developing a larger number of job opportunities that is periodically mentioned but rarely systematically explored is that of making meaningful part-time employment a really viable alternative for more persons. I have in mind, here, not merely a set of basically marginal occupations, such as those of part-time helpers during peak periods, but genuine career opportunities that involve part-time employment. Obviously, this would entail certain sacrifices in terms of complications in work schedules and a division of labor among persons with different work schedules, but the problems do not seem insurmountable.

It would be necessary to modify certain American values, as for example the importance attached to the male partner being the head of household and primary breadwinner in the family. It would also require that industries, businesses, and public agencies offer prorated fringe benefits to part-time workers so that they did not become second-class citizens or a cheap alternative source of labor used to undercut the full-time labor force. More serious, perhaps, might be the problem created by persons who elect to moonlight by taking *both* a full-time and a part-time position, thereby aggravating still further the unemployment problem. In particular, an opening of part-time positions to middle-class housewives who entered the labor force to supplement the incomes of husbands, who continued to work full time, would only result in a displacement of those at the bottom of the skill hierarchy.

Thus a splitting of full-time positions into part-time ones might not have any overall impact on the minority employment situation unless, at the same time, a reasonably high percentage of white families decided to reduce the total number of aggregate hours in the labor force, say by arranging for both the husband and wife to work only part time. In fact, it might very well turn out that an increase in the flexibility of work hours would only aggravate the situation for those least able to compete.

In considering any policies to reduce the overall unemployment rates among blacks or any other population segment it is necessary to recognize that there are still some powerful vested interests that basically favor high unemployment, though of course these sentiments cannot be publicly expressed in this form. Obviously, there are employers that rely on the existence of a cheap and docile labor force, particularly one that can be called upon whenever seasonal needs demand it. Agricultural industrial farming that depends heavily on migrant labor is an obvious case in point. There is also a demand for domestic service, particularly within the South, that capitalizes on a large supply of unemployed or underemployed black female labor. Many small businesses that periodically employ handymen have a similar interest in this type of labor market, even though there may be frequent complaints about its inefficiency.

Fortunately, the demands for these kinds of services are gradually diminishing, as implied by Willhelm's thesis. For example, as housewives increasingly rely on household gadgets to reduce their domestic chores, the demand for black maids steadily declines. But this has merely helped to swell the ranks of the unemployed in many instances, particularly since many of these black women have found it desirable—though sometimes impossible—to enter the labor force so as to supplement the very meager incomes of their husbands.

Given the reduction in the demand for this cheap labor, we may anticipate that the employer opposition to providing "full employment" will also diminish, but it seems likely that it will be replaced by a growing concern about the costs of such programs in terms of the tax bite involved. In other words, the nature of the economic opposition to achieving full employment can be expected to shift from those who have direct interests, as potential employers, to those who stand to lose the most from the standpoint of tax payments. In many instances these will be the same sets of individuals, but perhaps the opposition will become more diffusely spread and also less highly organized and focused.

PRIVATE VERSUS PUBLIC EMPLOYMENT

In considering alternative programs to reduce unemployment it is necessary to examine two prevailing myths, namely that the public sector of the economy involves a disproportionate number of make-work or needless jobs that are basically nonproductive, and that the growth of the public sector inevitably involves creeping socialism. Both of these myths are perpetuated by conservative ideologies and are a source of vulnerability for those liberals who wish to improve this public sector and who do not see any viable alternative for reducing unemployment.

We need to ask about any kind of work: Does it contribute to the welfare of some segment of the population, either by actually producing something that is worthwhile to consume or by providing valuable services to some class of individuals or to the society at large? In effect, then, we need to ask what things need to be done and which of these are most appropriately accomplished through the private sector, which for the most part is oriented to making a profit, and which through the public sector, which must be financed out of common funds.

Clearly, many objects that are produced by the private sector are of questionable value even to the individuals who eagerly purchase them. To be sure, we may be producing cigarettes, pornographic magazines, cosmetics, candy, movies, and many other goods through the private enterprise system, but precisely in what sense is this productive or more useful than, say, the services provided by public employees in areas of education, health, parks and recreation, and so forth? Is the production of something tangible—no matter what it is—the overriding criterion of worth? If we are willing to endorse the production of luxury goods, then why not luxury services that are paid for at public expense? A clearcut dichotomy between productive and nonproductive work, if it could be justified, would undoubtedly not be coterminous between the private versus public dichotomy. Things are much more complex than this.

Aside from the obvious difference in type of ownership between private and public enterprises there is another basic difference that bears directly on the welfare of minorities. When a good is produced privately and sold in the market place, there is a direct exchange between two parties both of which supposedly gain from it. The producer makes a financial profit, which may be shared with employees and stockholders, and the buyer gains some kind of psychic or economic benefit because he or she has purchased something of value. In the case of publicly produced products, which are usually services of some kind, there is more often an indirect exchange in which those who pay for the service, namely the taxpayers, are not necessarily the direct beneficiaries. Some taxpayers gain directly in the process, but others do not.

In particular, since many public services are competitors of private ones, which usually carry a higher price tag and may even have snob appeal (e.g., an elite private college or expensive medical clinic), the public services are much more likely to be used by relatively poorer clients. Indeed many public services are intended exclusively for the poor. Overall, this indirect exchange involving the taxpayer, the public agencies, and their clients involves a redistribution of the wealth of a society in a direction favoring the nonelites. No wonder, then, that this type of exchange is looked upon with disfavor by wealthier members of a society who could very readily get along without them or, at least, could survive adequately with much reduced services. Such groups obviously have a vested interest in poking fun at the inefficiency, costliness, and supposed uselessness of the public services, while neglecting to notice the same defects within the private sector.

This resistance to expanding the public sector is nonetheless real, as we all recognize. To the degree that there are defects in public delivery systems as well as meaningless jobs created merely to use up public funds, the opposition will have effective ammunition to support its arguments. Therefore those who wish to expand the public sector as a complement and competitor to private enterprise must be extremely careful to develop programs that are really cost efficient, that offer genuine rather than token benefits, and that are most capable of fulfilling needs that are not being met in the private sector. In many instances the two kinds of systems can exist side by side, as in the case of public and private colleges and universities or hospitals. Incidentally, in the case of institutions that are primarily oriented to providing services, such as colleges and hospitals, it often turns out that the public institutions are much cheaper to operate as well as being less costly for their clients. Sometimes it is claimed that this is primarily because they enjoy public funding, but it may also be due to efficiencies of scale and the necessity of cutting out frills that are rather more status-giving than functional.

Turning specifically to the question of jobs and unemployment, and assuming that the private sector will continue to absorb a major portion of the total labor force but will be motivated more by the goal of maximizing profits, we must ask: What specific kinds of jobs and services are really needed and would really prove beneficial to the public at large or some important segments of it? A thorough answer to such a question would involve imaginative efforts to identify many kinds of services that are not being offered at all. In order to provide job opportunities for persons who are relatively uneducated, who may only find it possible to engage in part-time work, and who may wish to use the job as a stepping stone to more permanent employment elsewhere, it will also be necessary to think beyond the kinds of technical services that are ordinarily provided by professionals, though not necessarily by paraprofessional assistants of one kind or another.

In developing a set of priorities with respect to needed services it seems sensible to rely, initially, on national and local surveys that ask samples of citizens what needs they define as most important and how they believe the quality of their lives could be improved by rather specific kinds of facilities or services. Armed with such a set of priorities, specialists could then begin the task of assessing the relative costs of providing such facilities or services and suggesting ways in which as many of these as possible could be provided locally by relatively unskilled personnel. Ideally, a set of job specifications could be developed such that these persons could learn useful skills in the process and be graduated from one type of task to another. Such a process of rational planning of tasks in the public sector would not be unlike those that take place in private industry, except that the priorities would be set by the responses of citizens who, presumably, would benefit from these services.

We can imagine such a process resulting in a number of conservation and beautification projects, additional services to the elderly, modifications in transportation services, improved recreational facilities, efforts to renovate older homes and apartment buildings, various supplementary programs oriented to child care and educational programs, auxiliary services to police and fire stations, improvements in building inspection and sanitation programs, and various supplemental programs in the creative arts and entertainment fields.

Some of the suggestions made in the next section obviously presuppose what these prioritized projects will turn out to be, but they are made primarily in order to illustrate the kinds of public sector jobs that are possible, rather than to serve as any kind of definitive list. The problem, of course, would be to sell such a program to taxpayers who are increasingly looking for ways to reduce, rather than increase, their overall tax burden. Two obvious selling points are that such a program will contribute directly to the public good, in the sense of providing needed services, and that it will subtract substantially from the very burdensome public welfare budget by providing all those who can do so with meaningful work.

A PROGRAM OF SERVICE WITHIN THE BLACK COMMUNITY

Broadly defined, the service sector contains occupations at all status levels, ranging from those of the surgeon, lawyer, and teacher to those of the custodian, domestic servant, and garbage collector. Although a number of persons whose occupations fall within this wide range are employees of municipal, state, or federal governments, many others are privately employed. Our major concern, however, will be with the employment of the most unskilled portion of the labor force, and our recommendations will assume that the vast majority of these persons will have to be supported by public funds. Thus we will be dealing with only one subset of the entire range of possibilities, though it is of course this particular subset that has been the subject of intensive debate and the target of many unsuccessful experimental projects within the past decade.

The word "service" has very different implications to low-status

142 / BLACK-WHITE RELATIONS IN THE 1980s

persons, and blacks in particular, depending on who is being served, by whom, and under what circumstances. The medical doctor enjoys high status and is well rewarded because he or she is highly skilled, performs crucial services in emergency situations, and is perceived to be his or her own boss, so to speak. The black domestic servant or garbage collector, however, is performing menial services to whites under circumstances in which it is clear that the one who is providing the service can find no satisfactory alternative means of support. In other words, the service is voluntary only in a very literal sense of the term, and the provider of the service is clearly a person of lower status than is the one who receives the service.

It has recently become common to point to the rising expectations of the black population, with the clear implication that these expectations are utterly unrealistic in terms of the educational and skill levels of perhaps two thirds of this group. Black leaders often point out that blacks need to have meaningful jobs and that they will no longer be satisfied with artificially created, temporary, make-work jobs that are rightly seen as dead ends. Yet most of the blacks with whom we are concerned in this discussion are unskilled, and for many it is too late to return for additional schooling or training. Furthermore, the experience of the Job Corps and other programs designed to reach the so-called hard core unemployed indicates that it is probably unrealistic to attempt to train such persons directly for positions in industry. It has also been repeatedly emphasized that a high percentage of the welfare recipients in the black ghetto—as well as elsewhere—are not in a position to hold down full-time jobs. They are predominantly mothers with small children, elderly people, or the handicapped. How can such persons find meaningful work under the circumstances?

The key to the problem, if there indeed is one, may lie in the notion of service to the black community. A menial, unskilled position is almost by definition a psychologically unrewarding one unless it involves an obvious service to persons who are deemed deserving and who would find it difficult to perform this task by themselves. For example, helping elderly persons carry groceries to their apartment, escorting them to a nearby clinic, or helping to make minor kitchen repairs can be rewarding to a totally unskilled black youth. Working part-time in a day-care center, helping to collect and repair old clothing and blankets, or helping an elderly couple with rodent-control may likewise be satisfying work for a young mother. Handyman carpentry work, combined with part-time apprenticeship, may offer the beginnings of a reasonable career line for, say, a presently unemployed male in his late thirties.

Many of these services are, in fact, badly needed within the ghetto, but we are not presently organized to provide these types of work on a viable and flexible basis. They are the very kinds of work projects that used to be designed by groups like the American Friends Service Committee to stimulate self help and to enable middle-class participants to better understand the nature of poverty. They are also the kinds of projects sponsored by the Domestic Peace Corps (VISTA). For the most part, the participants in these volunteer projects have been outsiders who have been attracted to service work for various reasons, some commendable and others not. These participants have not been local community members who needed the income, who have grown up in the area, and who could receive the basic satisfaction of making a long-term contribution through service to their own particular neighborhoods.

The program I have in mind must have a number of characteristics. First, it must be locally organized and supported. This means sufficient control over financial policies so that funds can be allocated according to local needs. Second, it must be conceived as a long-range program, not just a temporary stop-gap measure. Implied here is the notion that each participant must perceive that there are a number of distinct career lines possible, with outlets into the outside world for most, but with visible opportunities for advancement within the local system itself.

Third, there must be a wide variety of types of work and considerable flexibility with respect to work schedules and movement into and out of the program according to the nature of outside opportunities. Finally, the program must be financed on a very large scale and cannot be merely another token gesture on the part of white politicians. At the same time, there must be some method of appraising its success and holding each community accountable for its own policies and practices. Implied, then, is the necessity of some degree of budget control that must be kept as free as possible from partisan political pressures.

Elliot Liebow, a white anthropologist who studied a lower-class black neighborhood in Washington, D.C., argues in his book, *Tally's Corner*, that one of the major facts of life in the world of the lower-class black male is the necessity of living in the present.[3] The young male, seeing about him a group of older men whose life style is no different from his own, comes to realize that his own future is likely to be exactly the same as the present—basically, hopeless. Therefore long-range planning makes no sense even if the individual were rationally thinking about his future. Why work an eight-hour day and try to save when you are likely to be laid off next month, or even next week? Why develop the kinds of work habits and attitudes toward a career that white Americans so feverishly attempt to instill in their children?

Edward Banfield, in *The Unheavenly City*, makes this thesis an important ingredient in his basically conservative orientation to the urban lower class.[4] If the bulk of the lower-class population has this orientation to the present, then Banfield argues that perhaps our labor policies should take this more explicitly into account. He therefore urges that many opportunities be made available for part-time hourly work, where for example an individual may work for two or three hours at a time in order to earn sufficient pocket money to avoid the temptation to earn a quick $5 by mugging the most convenient victim. Clearly, this view of the lower class is extreme, as Billingsley has pointed out in his study of lower-class black families.[5] Only a relatively small proportion of this population is so present-oriented as to require this kind of odd-job approach. Many persons who might begin by working on a very irregular schedule can be induced gradually to take a more long-range outlook, particularly if they are able to perceive definite career lines that are not being continually disrupted.

The major lesson we may draw from this dispute concerning the perspectives of (black) lower-class persons is that a diversity of opportunities must be made available. There must be part-time work for those who care to drop in periodically to earn enough for a couple of meals. There must also be regular part-time opportunities, say, for the young mother who wishes to leave her children three mornings per week at a child-care center. And there must also be full-time opportunities that vary in their number according to the state of the economy. Also, those blacks whose regular jobs do not pay well enough to take care of medical bills or to save for the education of their children must be given opportunities for weekend or evening work to supplement these incomes.

Flexibility and variety of opportunities are the main essentials, and this of course means that specific details must be worked out according to local conditions and the needs of the community, as defined by the residents themselves. So must the methods by which work is allocated, the relative pay scales, and the ways of providing noneconomic rewards for conscientious service as well as sanctions against those who exploit the system unfairly for their own benefit.

Some Specific Examples

While detailed plans would have to evolve over a period of time and on the basis of considerable experimentation, and although such plans should originate within the community itself and be guided by priorities determined by blacks themselves, it is necessary to give a somewhat more specific indication of the kinds of programs I have in mind. Obviously, most of these suggested projects have been tried before, though often without the benefit of adequate publicity and careful evaluation of successes and failures. The principal feature of the proposal is the suggestion that such programs be tied together into a reasonably well-planned package and that they are conceived in terms of decades and billions of dollars rather than in years and small sums for experimental projects.

First, as implied earlier, there would need to be arrangements for drop-in hourly types of work for those individuals who initially resist more rigidly defined work schedules. The pay for such work should be at a lower rate than for the other kinds of projects, and undoubtedly the work would have to be more closely supervised and such that extremely minimal skills would be required. Also, the work could not entail any fixed time schedule for completion. Possibilities would include trash cleanup programs, toy repairs, and various kinds of assistantship jobs in connection with some of the projects mentioned below. Presumably, efforts would be made to induce participants to begin work on a more regularized basis, perhaps several half-days per week.

Depending on the nature of the other demands placed on the participants—for example, young children or relatives to care for—some sort of flexible schedule might be worked out so as to provide as varied opportunities as possible, within whatever economic limits were imposed by budgetary considerations. One possibility would be to attempt to get part-time participants to devote three or four half-days per week to perhaps two different kinds of projects. Persons who are free to take on full-time work, but who for other reasons have been defined as hard core unemployed, might be initially put on a three-day schedule but given the opportunity to work a fourth day with, say, a 10 percent increment in pay and perhaps a fifth day with a 15 percent bonus. Perhaps those who wanted to work the extra days would be given the incentive of greater choice of type of work.

An important feature of reasonably large-scale programs as compared with much more delimited ones would be the larger variety of types of work that could be made available. Especially in the case of persons who are entering the labor force for the first time, or who have been removed from it for a long period of time, it would seem advantageous to offer these participants several types of work simultaneously. For example, a person working on a three-day schedule might work one day in a day-care center, one day helping elderly persons, and a third on a cleanup or beautification project. As an incentive for working additional days, such persons might be given a choice of projects for their fourth and fifth days, thus affording an opportunity for specialized skills to develop, while at the same time providing the individual with a sufficient variety of experiences that he or she could begin to assess the relevant skills needed as well as his or her own interests and abilities. A varied work experience of this sort would also have the presumed advantage of making participants aware of the scope of community projects, the needs of different types of individuals, and giving them some broader perspective on and ego-involvement with the total project. It might also make the participants aware of diverse avenues of mobility as they come into contact with supervisors who have previously moved through the same channels.

Projects would of course have to tap the skills and interests of a variety of persons: youth, normal adults, and the elderly; males and females; the physically active, mothers tied to the household, and the handicapped. They would also have to serve genuine needs within the community and not just be make-work projects designed to keep people busy and off the streets. Presumably, once viable programs were underway, numerous practical suggestions would flow in from local residents. We can mention briefly a few of the more obvious kinds of possibilities.

• Work with children under five years old. Day-care centers, reading readiness, art and music, and recreation. Mothers of such young children might be encouraged to leave their own children at such centers two or three days per week, while performing other kinds of service work. They might be charged a fee of perhaps a quarter of their own wages.

• Work with school-age children. Sports and recreational skills, tutoring, trips to parks and museums, ghetto work projects, rap sessions about community needs and service, periodic trips outside the city.

• Auxiliary personnel in schools. Helping teachers, tutoring, playground and cafeteria supervision, sports and hobbies after school, directing traffic, making school and playground equipment.

• Work with aged and handicapped. Shopping, running errands, writing letters, minor repairs to apartments, taking them for outings and protecting them from muggings, teaching skills, general recreation, providing information about and transportation to health facilities.

• Health-related work. Auxiliary personnel in hospitals, clinics, and nursing homes. Informing residents about alternative health facilities.

• Part-time work in local businesses, such as delivery services to elderly. (Since this would be publicly supported, it would in effect constitute a form of subsidy to local businesses, enabling them to provide additional services and compete more effectively with chain stores.) This could be a type of apprenticeship program leading to full-time, regular employment.

- Crime and drug control. Policing the streets to report crime or dope pushing and to reduce muggings and burglaries. Work as auxiliary personnel in prisons, corrections programs.
- Building inspections, search for fire and health hazards. Auxiliary personnel for legal aid services e.g., reporting of landlords who do not comply with fire or health regulations).
- Organized recreational programs. These would take over some of the functions of the old settlement houses, with the advantage that programs would not be planned and run by outsiders.
- Projects involving handicrafts for persons confined to their homes for prolonged periods—the elderly, handicapped, and mothers of young children. Products could be sold locally for nominal prices.
- Cleanup projects and beautification. Here there are opportunities to develop building-trade skills of painters, carpenters, electricians, plumbers, or masons. Clearing of vacant lots for playgrounds, planting shrubbery, painting, rodent control. Work on these projects could lead to work in the construction industry.
- Conservation and beautification projects outside the ghetto, as for example state parks or scenic highways.
- Development of job placement centers and counselling services, staffed by local blacks who have served for several years in the program and who may therefore serve as role models. Such a placement center may screen candidates for positions outside the ghetto and may also serve as an information center, providing realistic assessments of the nature of these outside opportunities.

There is no reason why many such projects cannot be dovetailed with work-study programs within the schools and with remedial educational programs for adults. For example, health-related work may be linked to high school biology and health programs; various community projects with social studies courses; and tutorial services for younger children with the learning of mathematics and reading. A rather vague demand for relevance of all school work is, I believe, often a foolish one and is sometimes an excuse for intellectual laziness. Certain things, such as high school algebra are not going to seem relevant until a student has gone much further with his or her studies. Likewise, reading and writing skills depend on a considerable amount of drilling and concentrated hard work that often cannot be justified in terms of immediate connections to the experiences of the students. In short, much learning requires disciplined work habits and a degree of faith that applications may (or may not) be found in the future. Certainly if these abstract subjects are mixed with experiences that tie more directly to the student's environment, then school work will seem more meaningful to a larger proportion of black youths.

It should not be too difficult to include students in many of these types of projects, initially as observers and incidental helpers and later as part-time employees. The advantages of local control over ghetto schools and the above kind of job program is that—at least ideally—the two can be coordinated. One can imagine, for example, students becoming interested in health problems by initially visiting with elderly people and escorting them to clinics. The nature of these health services, their diverse functions, and their shortcomings could be studied in social studies courses. Biology courses could be deliberately designed to focus on the study of health, while at the same time giving the student the necessary tools to study human biology and, later, medicine or nursing. Other students might engage in woodworking projects, say repairing furniture or toys, and later serving as apprentices on real neighborhood construction projects or helping with the improvement of parks and other recreational facilities. Still others might begin by tutoring younger children, becoming teachers' assistants during their last year or two in high school, and then become motivated to follow a teaching career after graduation from college. Others could begin to learn about crime and drug control, first as observers, later as helpers, and finally as regular employees of ghetto agencies or the municipal police.

All of this sounds very simple and idealistic, and it would be foolish to propose projects of this nature with the notion that within a few years nearly all motivational problems would have been resolved and that participants would be well on their way to respectable middle-class careers. Many would fail, but even more are doing so under the present system, or (more accurately) lack of system. One of the major hurdles is likely to be a high initial level of confusion, rivalry, and dissension among diverse ghetto groups that might serve as sponsors and coordinators. Daniel Moynihan's *Maximum Feasible Misunderstanding* provides a clear warning concerning the kinds of difficulties that may be expected if a massive program were launched without adequate planning, experience with pilot projects, and mutual trust between city hall and the various ghetto organizations that would become the active participants.[6] We therefore need to consider seriously the problems that can be expected in connection with the implementation of large-scale programs of this nature.

Implementation

In considering the difficult problem of implementing a very large-scale program such as the above proposal we encounter the fundamental issue of financing and control. On the one hand, we have the notion that blacks should be able to choose their own leadership accountable to the black community, rather than to the white power structure. On the other hand, the sheer scale of such projects requires that they have the strong endorsement of a sizable portion of the white electorate and certainly that of the president and Congress. In a sense, then, it is impossible for black leadership to be appointed by fellow blacks, unless the president and a majority of both Houses were black—an exceedingly unlikely possibility. Obviously, the best that blacks can hope for in this respect is that such programs be planned, administered, and evaluated by a responsible group of black leaders who, in turn, must be accountable to the predominantly white leadership in Washington and in various state capitols.

The War on Poverty fiasco, described by Moynihan, suffered not only from less funding than seemed to be promised but also from a combination of too much haste plus poorly conceived, though well-intentioned efforts, to permit maximum feasible participation of the poor. The result was a series of scandals, battles over the process of decision-making itself, and black-white confrontations that—almost inevitably, according to Moynihan—led to a rapid drying up of funds. Not only were white politicans put on the hot seat, but far too large a proportion of the funds went into staff salaries and half-baked experimental projects that were never properly evaluated. Obviously, if a large-scale program is to receive steady funding over several decades it must have bipartisan support, and it must begin to show tangible results after perhaps a period of three to five years. The major outlines of such a program, as well as budgetary control, must be developed from the top, with allowances being made for a reasonable degree of flexibility of options at the local level. A commission of highly respected blacks (and other minorities) of varying political and economic persuasions would seem to be the obvious body to develop the details of such a program.

Given such a planning commission of minority leaders who would be responsible for a frank evaluation of successes and failures perhaps five years after the program had been initiated, it might not be too difficult to obtain the necessary funding from Congress. Of course blacks may rightly ask why they should be held accountable to Congress when the Pentagon, the C.I.A., and the F.B.I. are only minimally so, but clearly this will be necessary for continued support. The difficulty, of course, will be that of persuading the Congress and the public to think in terms of a major reallocation of funds and a shifting of national priorities. It will certainly not be adequate to have a mere repackaging of programs, taking funds away from other urban projects in order to shift them to such new programs. An obvious temptation will be to cut back too drastically and too quickly on welfare expenditures under the assumption that these will no longer be needed.

Such a minor shifting of funds would indeed be shortsighted. At the very least, a period of from three to five years would seem necessary in order to provide a period of transition from welfare status to job support and to assess with any degree of accuracy the extent of welfare aid that would be needed for those who were unable to take part in the program. Also, rapid shifts in the funding of programs leave the impression that all are likely to be short-lived, and the result will inevitably be to heighten rivalries among organizations and between cities as each attempts to grab as large a share as possible before the funds are exhausted. Also, it takes time to locate and train the proper local officials and supervisory personnel, to say nothing of providing incentives through the example of persons who have advanced through the system.

For all of these reasons, plus the fact that this and other needed programs will initially be exceedingly expensive by present standards, the number of major sources of funding appear very limited. One obvious possibility is that of diverting funds from the huge allocations that go each year to the Pentagon. In fact, it would not seem at all unreasonable, in view of the prolonged period of favoritism to the Pentagon, to simply announce that the military budget would be cut by five billion dollars the first year, ten the second, and fifteen in succeeding years. This would leave it to the military establishment to do as every other bureaucracy must do—force itself to evaluate efficiency and drop out low priority programs. If, say, twelve to fifteen billion dollars per year were added to existing programs involving blacks and other minorities as well as disadvantaged whites, we would be taking a very tangible step in the direction of giving these groups the economic resources with which to begin to help themselves.

As is true with most other segregated projects, programs that stress self-help within the black ghetto will seem very appealing to many whites who just want to be left alone. Appealing, that is, until it comes time to pay the bill, then the stalling and temporizing will occur. The result is likely to be a major launching with much political fanfare, a modest funding for initial projects, and a gradual disenchantment and withdrawal of economic support in favor of whatever other priorities have developed. This, in turn, is likely to signal to blacks the necessity of dramatizing the issues and keeping their plight in front of the TV cameras and in the newspaper headlines, as occurred during the 1960s.

There is also a fundamental dilemma from the standpoint of the black beneficiaries of such a massive economic program. Through bitter experience blacks have learned that money is not enough. For example, what can be done about the landlord who refuses to make needed repairs or the local business that charges usurious interest rates—report them to governmental officials? The resulting delays, litigation, and expenses may be prohibitive. Instead, direct action appeals for rent strikes and boycotts may be much more effective. But these types of militant approaches, particularly if they are associated with violence of any kind, are not likely to be supported by the very government officials who may be brought into the fray and attacked as racists. This point has been emphasized by Charles Silberman, in his *Crisis in Black and White*, who supports Saul Alinsky's thesis that genuine community action projects must be self supporting.[7] Both Silberman and Moynihan, who differ markedly in other respects, agree that the Mobilization for Youth program in Manhattan failed because of the inevitable conflict of interest between government and foundation support agencies, on the one hand, and the community action agents, on the other.

Therefore a well-financed program requiring the annual approval of Congress for its budget is likely to become establishment-oriented and relatively timid about setting up controversial projects that might create bad publicity—bad, that is, in the eyes of the whites who are paying the major portion of the bill. Obviously, then, whatever projects are funded by such a program will have to be supplemented by others sponsored by financially autonomous groups. A certain amount of tension within the black community becomes almost inevitable—and of course is already present. This is a difficulty that must be handled within the black community itself, however, since very little white influence can be brought to bear. The role of the mass media seems crucial in reporting results to both white and black audiences. If only the most dramatic acts and results are thought to be newsworthy the program will have two strikes against it.

Another problem to resolve will be that of precisely how funds should be allocated. Should they be awarded to state governments, municipal governments, a single agency within each ghetto, or to much smaller units on the basis of specific applications? The overall policy would seem best served if flexibility becomes the general guideline. Some states may develop very sensible plans of action, delegating detailed responsibilities to black organizations with supra-city member-ships. Other states may be totally unwilling to act or to delegate sufficient control to local residents. In some instances a city govern-ment may have a sufficiently close working relationship with grass-roots leaders that awards may be granted to an entire city, with certain stipulations as to approximately how the funds must be allocated to particular districts or for specific projects. In many instances, however, cities will be so torn with internal cleavages or so subject to political corruption or patronage that it will be most wise to allocate funds to agencies that have been specially set up for the purpose, or to existing organizations or groups of organizations.

The essential point, here, is that decisions of this sort should be made by blacks themselves, and not by a group of white politicians or by the predominantly white membership of one of the presently constituted executive branches, such as HEW. This will in itself be a novelty— a totally black or minority Board of Commissioners having sufficient control over substantial funds for which state and local governments, as well as nongovernmental agencies, must all bid on more or less equal terms. Would either major political party buy such a program on more than a token basis? Conceivably they would, if they became sufficiently desperate and could not find an alternative resolution. But it would also require a considerable amount of pressure from the black voter, as well as a reasonable amount of support from a substantial portion of the white electorate.

The proposed Board of Commissioners would also be put on the spot. There would be a considerable need to avoid any hint of political patronage or financial scandals. Mechanisms would have to be developed to prevent politicians from using the funds to buy votes or radical elements from terrorizing other blacks into following a militant line. For example, there is always the possibility that a local group that has taken over policing functions within the ghetto may use this power to extort money for their own ends or to engage in open warfare with the regular police.

Here, as elsewhere, it is essential to evaluate each program as objectively as possible. White social scientists may not be trusted to do so, but there is a growing number of minority social scientists who are in a position to perform this vital task. It might be argued that other (white) minorities have had their political machines, their scandals and graft, so why should any more be expected of blacks? In principle, this may be correct. But such patterns did leave their marks on these minorities, which did not have the handicap of being racially visible, and which always seemed to be followed by other minorities that adopted the same patterns. Most important, they did not have to be financed on such a large scale and on a national level. Blacks, in short, will not be able to afford this luxury. The program—and any others like it—will simply be pronounced a failure and quietly buried.

Being a basically segregated program for most participants, there is always the possibility that success could lead to a relaxation of efforts to achieve integration in the schools, in the job world, and, equally important, in housing. There is no reason, in principle, why the education portions could not be carried out in integrated schools since the same types of programs would also be of benefit to many white youth. Also, the job training aspect of the program could be linked directly with efforts to place many more blacks in predominantly white occupations. But vested interests in segregation are almost certain to develop, and these would need to be evaluated carefully and counteracted wherever possible. In addition it should be emphasized that the proposed program would be designed for only that portion of the black population that is the most severely handicapped. Presumably, even though the program itself might become a long-term one, the major purpose would be to enable the vast majority of the participants to obtain better positions after a period of no more than three or four years. It would also be a mechanism for providing part-time supplementary work for many others.

On the white side of the fence there is also the likelihood that such a program may be seen as a trade-off of economic support against an informal understanding that the effort toward integration will be reduced. If the program were working smoothly, and if tension within the black ghetto were to subside as a result, then there is also the danger that white interest and support would subside. The whole venture, like that of public welfare, could be defined as a gift to the indolent, rather than as a mechanism to support a large-scale self-help effort. Even today, some leading politicians have defined full employment as involving an unemployment rate of 4 or 5 percent. This means an actual black unemployment rate of perhaps 9 to 15 percent, with the rates for black youth probably running between 20 and 30 percent. This would obviously not be full employment in the minds of the black population. The existence of a relatively modest program that would reduce these figures somewhat might then be used by whites as an excuse for doing nothing more.

Finally, a major move to support a substantial portion of the unskilled labor force that is not being employed by private enterprise is likely to reinforce those whose primary fears are those of creeping socialism. Certainly such plans do not constitute socialism in the sense of public ownership of the means of production, since it is the steady improvement in the efficiency of production that has been displacing much of the labor force, particularly the most unskilled members. It would indeed seem foolish to argue that private businesses should hire additional personnel merely to keep them out of the ranks of the unemployed. If a file girl is displaced from an office job in an insurance company, why not consider that she has been freed to do some other kind of work, perhaps in a day-care center or nursing home? If a worker is no longer needed in an assembly line, why can't he or she be hired as an auxiliary member of a school staff? This is certainly not socialism but just good sense. It does mean, however, that an increasing percentage of the labor force becomes employed by governmental agencies, either municipal, state, or federal.

The fear of socialism that is shared by most citizens of whatever political persuasion seems to be primarily that of a concentration of power in Washington and therefore in the hands of the political elite. Here, the only realistic resolution is that of attempting to develop as many functions as possible at the state and local levels. Blacks and other minorities have had good reason to distrust the political processes at these levels. The States Rights movement has, of course, been associated with southern conservatism. But also in the North there have been very few state-level officials, to say nothing of rural- and suburbia-dominated legislatures, who have strongly endorsed the causes of blacks and other minorities.

Furthermore, if all funds were to be turned over to state governments, policies would be extremely uneven. Those states that pressed forward with positive programs would likely attract blacks from the remaining states, giving the latter states little incentive to improve their own services. Much the same difficulty would also occur on the municipal level, though blacks would undoubtedly find generally more sympathetic politicians at this latter level. Thus another major dilemma: how to assure uniformity of practice while at the same time dispersing the decision-making process. Once more, insofar as programs are developed to aid blacks, we need to give blacks a much greater voice in making such decisions concerning the allocation of resources and controls over basic policies. The same of course applies to other minorities and disadvantaged whites.

NOTES

1. Gunnar Myrdal, *An American Dilemma* (New York: Harper, 1944).

2. Sidney Willhelm, *Who Needs the Negro?* (New York: Anchor, 1971).

3. Elliot Liebow, *Tally's Corner* (Boston: Little, Brown, 1967).

4. Edward Banfield, *The Unheavenly City* (Boston: Little, Brown, 1970).

5. Andrew Billingsley, *Black Families in White America* (Englewood Cliffs, N.J.: Prentice-Hall, 1968).

6. Daniel Moynihan, *Maximum Feasible Misunderstanding* (New York: The Free Press, 1969).

7. Charles Silberman, *Crisis in Black and White* (New York: Vintage Books, 1964).

8

The Issue of Power

TO MANY AMERICANS WORDS SUCH AS "POWER" AND "EXPLOITATION" are ugly terms that are used by Marxists and militants but that are shunned in polite company. So are references to violence, unless the violence applies to our relationships with outside enemies or appears to us in the escapist form of murder mysteries, TV police stories, westerns, and war stories. Whenever a social system is running smoothly, inequalities in power are not openly challenged and they are accepted as legitimate by most of the parties concerned. Those deviants who defy legitimate power, or what we call authority, are punished in such a way as to set an example for those who might be tempted to follow in their footsteps. Differences in power form the backdrop for differences in income or prestige, but it is the latter that become the focal point of our attention.

American sociologists have likewise tended to neglect the study of power until relatively recently, though the topic has long been a subject of interest in European academic circles. In part this was because the sister discipline of political science had been formed to study the political processes in which discussions of power were a bit more open. But even so, there was a surprising neglect of the subject by American social scientists, and this no doubt stems from biases and tendencies in the larger American scene. We had become accustomed to prolonged periods of internal political stability, with the War Between the States being considered a peculiar aberration. There had, of course, been a few sociologists who had stressed power relationships prior to the 1960s, the most notable of whom were Robert Lynd and C. Wright Mills, who became heroes of the New Left movement, and Floyd Hunter, whose study *Community Power Structure* published in 1953 stimulated considerable controversy over the question of the degree of concentration of power in American communities.[1]

In the area of race relations a number of scholars had pointed out that power considerations lay beneath all minority relationships, but the predominant interests of American scholars were on class and economic differences, the study of prejudice, and on minority adaptations to inferior status. Studies of black leadership dealt with power relationships, of course, but always in a circumscribed way. It was pointed out that black leaders seldom had the leverage to achieve their objectives, that for the most part they were dependent upon the support of liberal and moderate whites, and that they lacked an organizational base within their own group. But there was no really detailed analysis of how power entered into the picture.

Conflict has also been neglected by American social scientists for much the same reasons. The study of war has been left to the historians and political scientists, while lesser forms of conflict have been relegated to so-called social problems. It is almost as though conflict has been considered as a very rare form of human interaction that periodically breaks out into the open but that is rather easily brought under control. Within sociology, for example, the study of social control placed an overwhelming focus on relationships between the larger society (and its agents) and more or less isolated deviants. Thus the conflict was taken to be very one-sided, and the problem was seen as that of finding ways of bringing the deviant into line and in rehabilitation making the deviant a conventional citizen.

Power and conflict are now very much more openly discussed and in fact they have become the slogans of those who are most actively challenging the system. Perhaps because we have tended to sweep them under the rug until now, these challenges have become all the more frightening to many white Americans. In fact, of course, there has always been "white power" that has succeeded for so many years in keeping blacks in their place. But because this power had been so secure and unchallenged it had become possible to ignore it or to use it only in those few instances in which an overt rebellion seemed likely. White violence had been extensively used against individual blacks in the case of lynchings or against larger numbers of blacks in the form of race riots. Rarely had the roles of the two groups been reversed until the 1960s, however. The liberal tradition of scholarship and journalism had seen these acts of violence primarily as deviant acts of lawless elements, even where they had been with the collaboration, if not active participation, of the police and other legal authorities.

When "black power" became a slogan and black violence a frightening thought to many white Ameicans during the late 1960s and early 1970s it was necessary to give explicit attention to the power aspects of race relations, in particular, and to questions concerning the distribution of power much more generally. Because the word "power" has ugly connotations, however, it is not an easy matter to discuss the subject in reasonably objective terms. Nevertheless we must do so if we are to reach any genuine understanding of the kinds of racial relationships that are likely to confront us over the next several decades.

Power means different things to different people, as evidenced by the considerable confusion that exists, among blacks as well as whites, as to the meaning of "black power" as a strategy of action. To some, power connotes dominance, control, and physical force. To others it merely means the potential for achieving one's goals or improving his or her life chances. In some cases power is conceived as a potential for action, whereas in others it is action itself. Let us therefore turn briefly to a consideration of the various meanings that can be given to the term and to the kinds of factors that affect the amount of power one wields or the ways in which it is exercised.

RESOURCES AND THEIR MOBILIZATION

Possible ambiguities between power as a potential and power as exercised do not arise in the physical world because the appropriate laws and properties of materials are well understood. Thus, in physics, power is defined as work accomplished per unit of time, implying that the measurement of power would be in terms of work actually accomplished under standardized conditions. Yet one speaks of 200 horsepower engines as though the horsepower were a *property* of the engine. What is meant, of course, is that the engine has been designed according to well-known principles of physics in such a way that even though this particular engine may not have actually been put to the test, it is *capable* of doing the work of 200 horses under standardized conditions. We know that it has the potential because it has been constructed in a certain way and, perhaps, tested once or twice. It is assumed that its properties will remain constant over some reasonable period of time. Thus power as potential and power as work per unit of time are easily linked through our knowledge of the workings of machines and the assumption of constant properties.

In the social realm we obviously lack both the well-defined theories and the constancy of properties. Suppose an individual is extremely wealthy or holds an important political office. Does this automatically give one power? To do what? Can a governor have his or her political rivals legally executed? Assassinated? Bribed? Discredited through control of the press? Defeated in an election by buying up most of the TV time? Can a major conglomerate buy a political party by helping to pay for its conventions? Can blacks exercise power through the ballot or through economic self-help? Through threats of violence? And what if the tactics of one party tend to arouse the opposition of previously neutral third parties? Is their power thereby diminished? Suppose a politician takes a very unpopular stance on some issue, thereby losing some of his or her political support? How can one assess the degree to which some of this power has been used up?

All of these questions point up the obvious fact that the measurement of social power is exceedingly difficult, partly because constancy between one application of power and the next cannot be assumed, but primarily because there is no simple hookup between power as potential and power as exercised. An extremely wealthy individual may merely choose not to engage in political activity or to offer support to any of the parties involved. Does this mean that he or she lacks power or influence? The potential is obviously there, but unlike a machine we cannot simply push a button and make a person work to full capacity.

Because of this difficulty of linking power as potential to power in action, social scientists often consider them as distinct though possibly correlated entities. We usually refer to the potential aspects of power as power *resources*. The most obvious kinds of resources in the case of race relations are economic and political ones, but resources would also include the potential to commit violence, knowledge or expertise, and any other possessions one may have (including sexual attractiveness) that may be used to influence the behavior of other persons or to achieve one's objectives.

Since resources are expendable in most instances, and since they may be saved or stored to be used for many different objectives, it is also necessary to ascertain the extent to which these may be *mobilized* in any given instance. Obviously in American society the white majority possess the political and economic resources to do almost anything they please to blacks. But many courses of action would be extremely costly and repugnant according to present values. Some would involve slight gains for most whites but major losses to a few others. Furthermore there is no general consensus among whites, and there are many diverse economic and political interests involved. Therefore although the distribution of resources between the races is very uneven, it does not follow that they will be mobilized in any given manner by either group. Knowing that these resources are unevenly distributed of course affects the way blacks may utilize their own limited resources. They face the fundamental dilemma of finding ways to mobilize their resources in such a manner as not to produce a large-scale countermobilization (the so-called "white backlash") in the opposing group. Theories of power in the social sciences must take these mobilization factors into consideration, as must anyone who is attempting to make policy recommendations.

In a very fundamental way, the resources of party A depend upon the needs and motivation of other parties involved, both the opposition party B and other third parties C to the interaction. Thus if I have money I may use this money to buy the services of someone, or to induce someone not to act in a certain way, only because money is valued by these parties. On a desert island this resource would be worthless. If I have the power to take away someone's life, this is an important resource only if that person desires to continue living. An executive can control the behavior of subordinates only to the extent to which they desire promotions, prestige, or higher income more than other values that may be sacrificed in the process.

Obviously, then, much of the struggle for power depends on influencing values and hierarchies of goals. To the degree that these can be modified, relative resources can also be affected. Many values are based on important biological needs, particularly survival needs. This is why military and police powers generally tend to undergird all other forms of power, even economic. Military power depends upon control over the physical means of violence and those who have been trained to use them. Economic resources are often sufficient to pay for and supply an army, but recent events in Vietnam and throughout the Third World indicate very clearly that much more than this is involved.

The mobilization of resources by party A against party B depends on the needs and values of party A, as well as its assessment of B's (and C's) resources and willingness to mobilize. Each party will have multiple goals, and if resources are allocated to one objective they may have to be directed away from another. In a world in which decision making is a completely national process, each party would assess its probability of success in every venture and weigh this against the expected loss. But knowledge will always to some extent be imperfect, and this of course includes knowledge of the resources and intentions of the opposing parties. Therefore bluffing becomes a major component of the process, the aim being to keep the other party from employing its resources by making it believe that the outcome will be disadvantageous.

Unlike the situation that often holds in experiments in the physical sciences, relative powers cannot be accurately measured because of the impossibility of replicating encounters more than once or twice at most. If one party has won the previous encounter, it is often difficult to assess the degree to which its resources have been depleted or its priorities shifted. It is no wonder, then, that considerations of power in the social realm lead to major ambiguities and that theories of power are in a very rudimentary state.

Power also depends on the nature of the objectives under consideration. Each of us obviously has the power to do certain things but not others. Resources that may be used in the service of power to achieve one particular kind of goal may not be of any value in the case of another objective. In American society, however, there are two important kinds of resources that have a high degree of generalizability across different objectives. These are control over economic resources and the ability to control votes. It is of course well known that money can influence political decisions and that votes may affect the distribution of economic resources through taxation, regulations, and labor policies. But there is considerable debate over the relative power of such major parties as business and labor, government and business, government and labor, and so forth.

Our discussion of power must be made much more specific to the context of race relations if it is to be at all useful. We have noted that the resource advantages are very much in favor of whites. Only a small fraction of these potential resources are actually being utilized to keep blacks in their place, however, and therefore the mobilization factor becomes the really crucial one. At the same time, blacks possess certain resources in the form of veto power over the ability of the dominant whites to maintain peace and tranquility if they choose to employ extreme forms of discrimination. This veto power has from time to time been threatened by black militants under the assumption that whites may value this peace and tranquility over other important values, including their vested interests in status superiority.

Power is often distinguished from influence, which generally has the connotation of involving a more voluntary kind of persuasion that entails changing a person's values, goals, and priorities through a process of advancing intellectual or emotional arguments, rather than applying sanctions. In practice, however, this distinction between power and influence is often difficult to draw. If a large corporation donates considerable sums of money to a political party, and at the same time attempts to persuade it by intellectual arguments to change certain policies, does this represent influence or power? One's assessment depends on a knowledge of the motivational structure of the recipients, and since this knowledge is seldom attainable each observer is free to develop his or her own interpretations.

Nevertheless, it is useful to make certain analytic distinctions in order to clarify one's thinking on the subject. One set of distinctions that has been made by French and Raven is between "reward power," "punishment power," and "referent power."[2] Actually, all of these terms basically refer to what we have termed resources. Reward and punishment power obviously refer to resources that may be used to either reward or punish another party. Referent power refers to one's ability to influence another through a process of identification, by which the influenced party takes on the values of the other party, so that he or she will act in accord with the wishes of the first party without the necessity of surveillance. The application of both reward and punishment power, in contrast, generally requires such surveillance. According to French and Raven, one major difference between reward and punishment power is that the former often leads to referent power because the rewarding agent comes to be viewed favorably by the recipient, who is much more likely to take on the same set of values and priorities as the donor. In contrast, a resort to punishment or negative sanctions is much more likely to lead to rebellion, a rejection of the aims of the first party, and a constant need for surveillance.

In the context of race relations in the United States, whites have in the past relied on a combination of reward and punishment power. Paternalism is an obvious form of reward power through which the dominant party does not relinquish any real power, while at the same time attempting to reward those forms of minority behavior that it deems desirable. Given an assumption on the part of the minority members that the prevailing distribution of power and status is justifiable or at least unchangeable, these reinforcements of loyal behavior are seen as rewards. The recipient often develops a loyalty that may take the form of gratitude, internalization, or acceptance of the paternalistic arrangement, and a willingness to "do the master's bidding."

What are rewards to one person may not be so to another. Parents, for example, are familiar with the fact that what may begin as a reward to a child may soon become expected in due course, so that the withholding of this reward becomes, in effect, a punishment. Candy given every day may be a reward until it becomes routinely expected. Then if it is withheld, the child claims that a right has been withdrawn. Obviously, then, any particular resource may change in its reward or punishment value according to the expectations and goals of the recipient.

This presents the wielder of power with a fundamental dilemma and tends to prevent a system from stabilizing for too long a period without the benefit of strong ideological forces designed to reinforce the existing system. In the case of paternalistic relationships between blacks and whites, what were at one time considered as rewards deserving of loyalty to the patron now tend to be seen as rights, the withholding of which is cause for rebellion. No longer are blacks willing to accept such token gestures as though whites have a God-given right to dispense them as they see fit. Demands have replaced hat-in-hand requests, and as a result one of the important forms of reward power has all but disappeared.

Along with such reward power, however, has gone punishment power as well. The essence of a paternalistic system is the simultaneous rewarding of subservient behavior and the harsh punishment of those who dare to step out of line. But unless punishments are to be meted out on a group basis, with innocent victims being punished for the deeds of those who cannot be caught, the exercise of punishment power depends on one's ability to witness the deviant act and to catch the perpetrator. As blacks have moved into large urban centers where they have become increasingly anonymous and invisible as individuals, it has become more and more difficult to apply many kinds of punishment power.

In the roughly 50-year period prior to 1930, lynchings represented the ultimate form of punishment power. In many instances, even here, it was impossible to locate the actual perpetrator—if in fact there was any perpetrator at all—but the lynch mob could at least be assured that the lesson had been gotten across to the lynch victim's neighbors and relatives. Today such extreme forms of punishment have been basically ruled out of the white arsenal of control mechanisms, though we should not be too certain that they will not be revived in the form of more or less random acts of violence.

The weakening of these two important kinds of control mechanisms has considerably reduced white power over blacks. The surprisingly rapid rate at which this change has occurred has also meant a major change in the face that blacks have presented to their white audiences. Whereas whites were reasonably assured as recently as the early 1950s that most blacks were basically happy and accepting of the status quo, and that they could be easily appeased by token rewards, there can be no doubt in the 1970s that this is not the case. There have been many references to the so-called rising expectations of blacks. What does not seem to have been noted, however, is that these changing expectations have implied that what were previously accepted as rewards for good behavior are now no longer taken as such by blacks. The withholding of "rewards" that are considered to be basic rights guaranteed under the Constitution is now defined by most blacks as a form of punishment. And this, in turn, means that their reactions to basically the same behavior on the part of whites have shifted dramatically.

Today there are relatively fewer ways in which whites can reward blacks. This is having fundamental consequences in terms of black acceptance of the system, black reactions to various forms of control, and the degree to which open rebellion is replacing conformist behavior. An orientation toward conflict, rather than cooperation and accommodation, is becoming more prevalent. Genuine attempts to reward may be cynically interpreted as signs of weakness that have only been extracted as a result of threats of violence or disruption.

There is one important kind of reward power that still remains in white hands, namely that of rewarding blacks as individuals in just the same way that white individuals are motivated. This would imply, of course, treating them as equals—offering exactly the same educational opportunities as whites, the same job and income opportunities, and so forth. If this is done in an integrated setting, where blacks are afforded reality checks in comparing themselves with white competitors, these rewards may be seen as such. One of the dangers inherent in the separatist movement, however, is that if blacks remain segregated they may more easily misperceive the gestures of the white majority. They may not realize, for example, that difficulties they are experiencing are also faced by whites. Improvements in ghetto schools may seem to be minor as compared with those that whites are thought to be receiving. Demands may become unrealistic in the sense that they involve expectations that are out of line with those of the white majority.

If hostilities between the two groups develop to the point where those members of either group who attempt to reward the other group are always rebuffed as being either hypocritical, as in the case of white liberals, or Uncle Toms in the case of black moderates, then reward and referent powers will be confined to relationships within either racial grouping. Whites and blacks alike will find it increasingly necessary to depend on punishment power, and this is likely to mean an increasing escalation of hostilities.

Different minorities have available different kinds of reward and punishment resources. The anthropologists Charles Wagley and Marvin Harris have emphasized that one of the important factors that influences the outcome of contact situations between dominant and minority groups is what they refer to as the minority's "adaptive capacity," or ability to compete on reasonably equal terms and to offer tangible goods or services that may be exchanged for other benefits.[3] In previous chapters I have referred to much the same thing under the label of competitive resources, by which I mean resources that are sufficient to provide employers or other persons with positive rewards in exchange for employment or other benefits. One of the major goals of the liberal movement has been to improve blacks' competitive resources so that they may move more rapidly, as individuals, out of the lower class. Such competitive resources are obviously not rewarding to all white persons, but primarily the employing elites. At the same time that they may be of benefit to employers they also serve as a threat to potential white competitors in the labor market.

Blacks and other minorities also possess what we have referred to as pressure resources that generally involve a form of punishment power. Generally such pressure resources require a high degree of organization on the part of a minority or its allies (e.g. the federal government) and must be either continually applied or threatened. Being a form of punishment power, they also require continued surveillance to make sure that there is no reversion to previous discriminatory policies. Because of this, they have often been useful primarily in opening the door to blacks in the case of positions that have been previously closed, whereas competitive resources seem necessary in order to achieve more than token representation. In the case of professional sports the admission of Jackie Robinson to the ranks of major league baseball in 1947 produced very rapid and lasting effects because black athletes possessed the necessary skills to compete effectively with whites. These competitive skills were easy to evaluate, helped to produce winning records, and had noticeable effects in terms of ticket sales. But pressure to open predominantly white social clubs to blacks has produced only token representation at best.

Pressure resources have, however, provided blacks with a kind of veto power over the policies and planning of various kinds of white-controlled institutions. Basically this is a veto power over their ability to return to peace and quiet and to proceed in a routine fashion toward other objectives. In effect, these blacks have learned to say: "All right! If you won't listen to us, we'll never leave you alone." In blocking others from attaining their objectives, it is often possible to bargain to achieve certain of one's own goals, though at the expense of possibly arousing retaliatory responses.

The case of campus unrest is an excellent illustration. Many college administrators are basically moderates rather than liberals. Their objectives are often those of operating a smooth-running organization, holding down overt conflict through expedient compromise, and attempting to persuade state legislatures and influential alumni that their institutions are performing a useful function, while not rocking the boat too severely. The student uprising of the 1960s by both white and black militants radically changed the rules of the game. Administrators who were used to being addressed with respect and merely requested to make certain rather minor alterations in policy were suddenly confronted with demands, were called all sorts of names, and in some instances even subjected to physical violence. Educational institutions that relied heavily on paternalism were no longer able to depend on this device and in the resulting confusion found themselves in disfavor with nearly all groups in the larger society. From the standpoint of blacks there were considerable tangible gains in the form of special minority programs and a lifting of entrance barriers, an increase in the number of black faculty and administrators, scholarship aid, and increased representation on important university committees.

It is doubtful, however, whether this kind of veto-power over the peace and tranquility of selected whites can be used on a sustained and large-scale basis without stirring up a major counterreaction. In the case of colleges and universities the attack was made on relatively liberal institutions that were vulnerable from the political right as well as being in basic sympathy with the cause of minority groups. Also, in spite of the fact that black students for the most part tended to reject the support of white students and faculty, they had numerous white sympathizers who tended to support their major demands. If similar attacks were made on General Motors, the U.S. Senate, or a state legislature, it is much less likely that they would succeed.

One very important fact must be recognized, however. It is sometimes the case that a very small minority can exercise effective veto power if it is sufficiently desperate to be willing to give up other goals in the process. In particular, the goal of peaceful integration can be jeopardized rather easily by perhaps 5 percent of either the black or the white population if these individuals have become persuaded that all nonviolent approaches are hopeless. The extreme possibility of guerrilla warfare cannot be ruled out, particularly if contacts between the police and black ghetto dwellers are again permitted to deteriorate, as they did in the late 1960s and early 1970s. We shall have some recommendations to make on the subject of violence in the following chapter. Suffice it to say that the kind of open warfare that now exists in Northern Ireland could set us back fully a half century. Once underway, it would be exceedingly difficult to bring under control. In this very real sense, extremists on both sides have a kind of veto power over the rest of us, though they would find it necessary to pay a terrible price of their own for such actions.

As a general rule, white liberals, white moderates, and black integrationists have all stressed the desirability of blacks attaining competitive resources. But there has been less than complete agreement over the means and the rate of change that is considered satisfactory. White moderates have tended to give lip-service to the goal, while decrying practically all means that have been tried other than education and the gradual change of attitudes. The use of pressure resources to attain these ends has been disclaimed by most moderates, who have generally argued that such tactics are self-defeating in the long run and that competitive resources can only be developed very gradually. Associated with this argument has been a reluctance to attack head-on *white* resistance to the development of these resources. The old Booker T. Washington philosophy that blacks must pull themselves up by their own bootstraps has been the backbone of the conservative and moderate positions, with perhaps a grudging recognition that there are also whites who must be educated.

An abhorrence of overt conflict and a personalistic rather than institutionalistic approach to prejudice and discrimination have also been major ingredients of the moderate ideology and working theory. The role of power has tended to be neglected altogether, so that any emphasis on black power and Marxist tactics and rhetoric become very frightening to these moderates. To the degree that they are emphasized at the expense of less threatening kinds of approaches, we may anticipate that these moderates will be driven further and further into the conservative camp. With them will go considerable economic and political resources.

White liberals and black integrationists, in comparison, have been much more ambivalent about the use of pressure resources. Having been in the forefront of efforts to utilize less extreme approaches, and having encountered stubborn resistance on the part of those who have served as gatekeepers of discrimination, many of these persons have come to learn the realities of power and to appreciate their own lack of resources. In my own case, for example, I recall that it took fully three years to get one college administration to remove pictures of applicants for rooms in women's dormitories. Numerous unsuccessful efforts to persuade another college administration that black janitors and maids were being badly exploited by lower administrative personnel likewise convinced us that unionization and active protest by blacks presented the only alternative. Nonviolent protest tactics and the use of pressure through legislation and executive order have generally been approved by liberals as legitimate means, whereas moderates have tended to resist even these means until they have become accomplished facts.

Violence and overt conflict, however, have generally been repugnant to liberals as well as moderates. The result has sometimes been a tendency to overstate the case against the use of violence—as when, for example, it is dogmatically asserted that violence *never* results in positive outcomes, while at the same time supporting an overseas war and a military budget in the billions of dollars. The truth is, of course, that we simply do not have good ways of accurately assessing the gains and losses that result from any particular means, including the use or threat of violence. Instead, we rely primarily on whatever working theories seem most appealing and compatible with our own interests and values.

The use of pressure tactics and the ultimate threat of violence is one way a minority may attempt to improve its competitive resources, but it is not the only route. Many minorities have been numerically so small that they could not hope to achieve success by this method. Perhaps the most obvious possibility, and the one that has been tried most often, is simply to attempt to disappear as a distinctive group through the process of comformity and intermarriage. Racially distinct groups, however, cannot lose their visibility so simply, in which case they may try to compensate for this handicap by overconforming to important societal norms and capitalizing on whatever cultural traits may give them a competitive advantage. We have already noted that Japanese-Americans have successfully employed these means. There is a decided risk in this strategy, however. Overconforming groups are sometimes damned for this very reason. Jews are thought to be overly zealous and hard working. Japanese-Americans were similarly accused of using unfair labor practices by employing their children on their very successful truck farms.

In a highly industrialized society it hardly seems likely that blacks or other disadvantaged minorities can ever hope to develop specialized skills that give them distinct advantages over whites. We have noted that to a very limited extent this appears to be happening in the case of professional sports, but the number of openings in this occupation are of course extremely limited. Nor can blacks capitalize on a cultural heritage that gives them some sort of competitive advantage, as was possible in the case of, say, the agricultural skills of Italian or Japanese immigrants or the trade backgrounds of Jewish, Armenian, and Greek immigrants from Eastern Europe. Blacks are going to have to rely on the same means as used by practically all white citizens, namely the formal educational system. This point is perhaps so obvious that we may forget, however, that different minorities (including racial ones) have relied on other devices in addition to that of success through formal education.

A racially distinct minority is faced with a major dilemma. Since it is visible, too great a success may mark it for scapegoating in times of crisis, as for example when there is high unemployment or political instability. But unless it can develop strong competitive resources it is extremely vulnerable to strictly economic shifts that may have nothing to do whatsoever with prejudice and discrimination. We have already noted that in the case of blacks this could very well mean relatively permanent high rates of unemployment and a very marginal and dependent position in the economy. It appears as though blacks have really no choice except to place heavy reliance on achieving competitive resources through the educational system. The next question to which we shall turn is that of whether or not they can develop sufficient consensus and resources to achieve this on their own or whether they must rely on coalitions of various forms with particular sectors of the white population.

POWER AND COALITIONS

Even a casual observer of the race relations scene in the 1970s must be impressed by the confusion that exists over policies and priorities. In effect, there are so many plans and proposals and so many parties with differing viewpoints that we seem to be stagnating and badly confused. Each major grouping has a kind of veto power over any important program that may be proposed, so that little by way of consistent policy ever gets implemented. This is not simply a case of white hypocrisy. Nor would the situation be resolved if all cleavages within the black community were suddenly removed. It is an example of a very low level of mobilization in both groups that stems from an inability to form working coalitions with sufficient resources to implement any consistent program.

We have noted that one of the major arguments advanced by black separatists is that blacks must learn to free themselves from coalitions with whites unless these be on their own terms. The thesis is plausible enough as far as it goes. Stokely Carmichael and Charles Hamilton, in their book titled *Black Power*, developed the argument as follows.[4] For too long, blacks have had to rely on coalitions with white liberals and moderates who practically always usurped leadership positions and virtually dictated policies. Blacks were operating from a position of weakness and were therefore always junior partners in the process. Token leadership roles might be thrust upon certain of their members, but these persons were never able to develop autonomous policies of their own. Furthermore, in their view white liberals proved to be unreliable and unwilling to go the whole way toward genuine equality. When the chips were down, they would desert the cause, leaving blacks to do the dirty work. Coalitions are always based on the self-interest of the respective partners. In order for them to work, each party must be bargaining from a position of strength and must have something tangible to offer the other. Blacks must first develop the cohesion and unity of purpose to provide such a power base, then they may form coalitions with whatever groups are willing to join them on their own terms.

There is much valid reasoning in this position, but it tends to neglect two important facts that dominate the present race-relations scene. The first is that the two major kinds of needed resources, economic and political, are in the hands of whites who constitute the overwhelming majority. The second is that insofar as pressure resources have been effective in the past, the application of pressure tactics requires a low degree of mobilization and consensus on the part of whites. For instance it is very true that a black bloc vote may prove pivotal in important elections, thereby giving blacks an important leverage, but this presupposes a divided white vote. The argument in favor of black power neglects or minimizes the possibility that a countermobilization on the part of whites could actually result in *reduced* power for blacks. For instance if there were a high degree of consensus among whites against public welfare, coupled with inaction in providing additional job opportunities commensurate with the skills and needs of persons currently on the welfare list, black power alone would be of little use in finding jobs for these persons.

A small number of black extremists have gone so far as to say, in effect, that they don't care how whites react. Some may really mean this, but it seems more reasonable to conclude that most of these extremists are making the working assumption that whites are already about as highly unified in practice—lipservice to the contrary—as they will ever be. Therefore an increase in black mobilization is thought not likely to increase the mobilization of whites, nor to shift their central tendency to the political right. I wish I could believe this to be the case. It is certainly possible, but in view of the potential consequences it becomes a very dangerous working assumption. If there is one thing that white liberals know for a fact, and that blacks are not in as favorable a position to understand, it is that there is not a high degree of consensus within the white community and that there is considerable potential for a major counterreaction.

In this connection, the word "power" has different connotations according to the audience involved, and the slogan "black power" can have the unfortunate effect of changing white behavior as much as it does black. Of course if another term were substituted it could very well come to have the same connotations. Carmichael and Hamilton, as well as many others who have used the phrase, have tried very hard to indicate that they do not imply violent means, race hatred, or the goal of taking over American society. They are using the term power in a very general and scientific sense, namely power to achieve objectives such as full freedom and equality. But such intellectual discussions of the notion of black power seem much less persuasive than when these are used as ideological slogans. It seems much more likely that the phrase "black power" connotes naked power and violence to those who perceive of race relations in these terms and something quite different to those who do not. The essential point is that it may become a potent negative symbol in the conservative white ideological arsenal, and if this is the case the barriers to full equality will have been increased rather than decreased.

Thus a no coalition strategy, or more correctly a coalition based on strength policy, makes very good sense under some conditions but not others. If the strategy cannot be implemented without increasing the cohesiveness of opposing forces, then it may backfire. There is little that white liberals can do directly to affect the nature of the internal processes within the black community, other than to emphasize that the problem is not so simple as is sometimes implied. White liberals can, however, try to reduce the probability of such a white counterreaction taking place. One direction these efforts can take is to explain the reasoning behind the need for black power and to encourage its more constructive aspects, while at the same time taking steps to reduce the number of contact situations that are most provocative of violence and extremism. In the next chapter we shall turn to this question of conflict and violence, as well as conflict resolution mechanisms.

NOTES

1. See especially Robert S. Lynd and Helen M. Lynd, *Middletown in Transition* (New York: Harcourt, Brace & World, 1937); C. Wright Mills, *The Power Elite* (New York: Oxford University Press, 1957); and Floyd Hunter, *Community Power Structure* (Chapel Hill: University of North Carolina Press, 1953).

2. John R. P. French and Bertram Raven, "The Bases of Social Powers" in *Studies in Social Power*, ed. Dorwin Cartwright (Ann Arbor: University of Michigan Press, 1959), Chap. 9.

3. Charles Wagley and Marvin Harris, *Minorities in the New World* (New York: Columbia University Press, 1958).

4. Stokely Carmichael and Charles V. Hamilton, *Black Power* (New York: Vintage Books, 1967).

9

Violence and Crises: Are They Inevitable?

BOOK TITLES ARE DESIGNED TO STIMULATE THE IMAGINATION AND, of course, to sell the book. References to crisis, violence, and revolution in titles of books written by black militants, white radicals, or even white humanists are more or less expected. Thus when James Baldwin writes of the *Fire Next Time* one treats such expressions as forms of literary exaggeration. But nonradical white social scientists and journalists used similar titles to dramatize the situation of the late 1960s. We have Charles E. Silberman's *Crisis in Black and White*, Lewis Killian's *The Impossible Revolution?* and Masotti, Hadden, Seminatore, and Corsi's *A Time to Burn?* as illustrations.[1] Significantly, perhaps, the latter two titles end with question marks. Most of these books written by social scientists or their publicizers have been addressed primarily to the layman. Their theme was a consistent one, that white America had better wake up to the crisis in its midst. But at the same time, few if any of these authors held out any real hope that violence will result in constructive resolution.

The book by Masotti et al., *A Time to Burn?* traces the history of American racial violence, showing that the initiation of violent acts has gradually shifted from whites to blacks. Violent means of control by whites, such as lynchings, gave way to race riots in which blacks increasingly fought back. These, in turn, gave way to the urban riots of the 1960s that were primarily initiated by blacks against white property and only secondarily against the police. Other forms of black violence were also directed toward the police as the symbols of white control. As yet there has been no major violence directed toward the general white population, but the authors of *A Time to Burn?* clearly imply that this is a real possibility.

Obviously the major concern over "crime in the streets" reflects a similar fear on the part of the general public, black as well as white. It has been noted by many blacks that violence has always been an important ingredient of American race relations, but that it has not seemed to disturb the general white citizenry until they have been able to visualize themselves as the targets of aggression. Violence as a means of control of blacks has never seemed quite so repulsive to most whites, lipservice to the contrary notwithstanding.

At the time of this writing we seem to be in a period of relative calm. The long hot summers of the middle and late 1960s have all but disappeared. Student unrest has subsided as the Vietnam war has become history. During such lulls, given a proclivity to see violence and crises as abnormal and abhorrent, there is always the great temptation to believe that we have seen the last of the major urban riots, mass protests, or police-ghetto confrontations. Those who blame these recent crises on outside agitators and white liberals may now tend to believe that rather stern law-and-order approaches have brought the unruly under control. To these persons, the recent crises showed very clearly that certain elements of the population are not to be trusted, and that once these agitators and deviants are shown that they cannot get away with threats and violence they will be forced to behave themselves. But others argue that the underlying causes of the crises and racial violence have not been removed and that more serious crises are close at hand. Obviously one's working theories of social causation are again influencing the judgments of all concerned. Once more, these working theories are taken by each set of actors as being completely verified and valid, whereas in truth they are often only weakly supported empirically and therefore should be held much more tentatively.

The actors who are most immediately involved, however, are not going to evaluate the empirical evidence objectively. They will react according to their own biases and perceptions and will rationalize their behavior accordingly. Therefore we cannot count on rational analyses to influence the behavior of these persons directly, though perhaps a sufficiently strong and reasonably neutral third party can be so influenced. We shall return to possible roles of such third parties later. Here it is sufficient to emphasize that there will always be some actors who are motivated and influenced by rather simplistic conflict ideologies that support extremist and violent actions. These persons may successfully involve many more people into the action before they are through. Since minor violent confrontations have a way of accelerating into major ones—in spite of the fact that there are many more losers than winners in such struggles—it is important to face up to the danger as realistically as we can and to search for ways of dealing with crises before they get out of control. Those who are always attempting to minimize these risks, and who do not wish to look below the surface and correct minor faults before they become major ones, do us an extreme disservice in spite of their best intentions.

The ghetto riots of the 1960s apparently did not have any major payoffs for blacks in these urban settings. But this does not necessarily imply an end to widespread acts of violence. The magnitude of the spontaneous reaction on the part of blacks to the assassination of Martin Luther King, Jr. took practically all whites by surprise and indicated very clearly that other sparks could readily set off similar conflagrations in very short order, particularly since the mass media are capable of publicizing such reactions across the entire nation in a matter of hours.

There are other kinds of enduring problems that also seem likely to create more serious kinds of rebellions. One of these is a chronic high level of unemployment among ghetto youth, a topic that has already concerned us. A second is the return of black Vietnam veterans who have been trained in violence and who must also face this unemployment situation. A third is the gradual removal of moderate blacks from leadership roles through an aging process and a discrediting of their integrationist policies. Fourth is the growing awareness that guerrilla movements are often extremely difficult to counteract whenever a sufficiently large number of persons are basically in sympathy with their aims.

The gradual shift in approved black leadership tactics is of fundamental importance here, though white political leaders are seemingly unaware that their own policies are in many instances accelerating this change. Even without this help from white America in ousting an older generation of black leaders, the younger militants are of course aided by the passage of time. The black psychiatrists William H. Grier and Price M. Cobbs, in their book *Black Rage*, emphasize that one of the major functions of the black family has been to protect black children from an inner rage and rebelliousness.[2] Black children have had to be coerced into controlling themselves for the very reason that their survival literally depended upon it. The black boy, especially, has been taught from a very young age to control his aggression against whites.

These socialization patterns are changing radically, if only because of the greater freedom from white retaliation in the northern urban ghetto. In perhaps a decade or two we will be seeing a new generation of young black adults who have not been raised under the old repressive model and who will be much more inclined to teach their children to hit back and even to attack if slightly provoked. Leaders who stand up against whites and use aggressive language and gestures are much more likely to appeal to this new black generation than are the black moderates. It seems almost a foregone conclusion that militancy, if not the outright advocacy of violence, will increase with time unless important institutional changes are forthcoming.

Events in the outside world will also undoubtedly affect black thinking concerning the possibility of open guerrilla warfare. The fact that one of the two world superpowers was unable to deal effectively with what began as guerrilla tactics in South Vietnam will not have been lost on many black veterans. Although recent events in Northern Ireland do not seem to have produced much interest among blacks, the parallels between the situations of the Catholic minority and that of blacks in the United States are rather obvious. In Northern Ireland the seeds of discontent had been planted long ago, and both economic and political discrimination against Catholics were nothing new. Suddenly, however, the terrorist activities of the Irish Republican Army (I.R.A.) began to intensify along with more nonviolent protest.

In situations like those in Northern Ireland or the Middle East, once the hostilities have reached a point that retaliations begin to occur almost daily, each side can find ready justifications for its own behavior today on the basis of yesterday's brutality by the other side. Once the guerrilla forces become a well-disciplined army, with members operating in small cells, the identity of which is not known to other members, it becomes almost impossible to seek them out without at the same time playing into their hands through actions that further alienate members of the larger population from which they have been recruited.

Guerrilla warfare is not very likely as long as there are realistic signs that steady rates of progress are achievable by other means. The turmoil and hardship that such open conflict creates is simply too great for most normal citizens to take. But the potential is there particularly since guerrilla warfare can be conducted by a tiny fraction of a population. Unfortunately it is not always easy to assess very accurately just how close to an explosive situation we may be until it is too late.

We have already noted the tendency for most white Americans to underestimate the degree of black frustration, alienation, rage, and outright hatred that is being covered up in the normal day-to-day contacts between the races. There is the belief that crises are abnormal and due to outsiders or disturbed personalities. Nor can whites readily appreciate black impatience with very slow rates of change and with what appear to them to be very minor concessions offered grudgingly.

Nor do many members of the white middle class recognize the potential for violence among their own group or the degree to which they are willing to tolerate and even encourage violent behavior on the part of other members of their race, including the police.

The way things work out will partly depend on the kind of militant black leadership that develops, a factor that white liberals can only indirectly influence. There are of course many different forms of militant action, although there has been a tendency to lump practically all forms of protest together under the label. Not too long ago the NAACP was thought to be an extremist organization; now it is labeled conservative. Martin Luther King, Jr. seemed to represent black militancy at its extreme shortly before his assassination. When Stokely Carmichael and H. Rap Brown warned whites that there were many blacks whose extremism would make themselves appear as moderates, they were not taken seriously.

Joyce Ladner suggests that it is useful to distinguish between what she calls the "locals" among militants, namely those who stress very practical issues such as voter registration drives, jobs, housing, and police brutality, and the ideologically oriented.[3] The latter tend to be drawn from the intellectual classes and are much more revolutionary in orientation. Often, however, they are much less concerned with concrete local issues. Persons such as Malcolm X, Eldridge Cleaver, and Angela Davis immediately come to mind.

Apart from Martin Luther King, Jr., who was certainly not an extremist, there has been no single black leader on the national level who has been able to combine the two roles effectively. Had he lived, perhaps Malcolm X might have succeeded in uniting the ideological with the practical, though his skills in the latter direction seem to have been more in his ability to win new recruits to the Muslim movement than to come to grips with specific issues. But such a leader with a truly national following of black militants could arise at any time. A few dramatic successes, a devoted following, and later martyrdom might prove to be just enough to get a major radical movement among blacks under way, particularly if it were accompanied by a systematic effort on the part of whites to crush the movement. The Black Panther movement, which threatened to play this role and which had the potential leadership in Huey Newton and Eldridge Cleaver, has apparently been unable to cope with the kinds of internal crises that often accompany such movements and has drastically altered its approach in recent years. But it does not follow that other similar organizations, or perhaps even a revival of the Panthers under a more unified leadership, cannot develop as a truly revolutionary black social movement.

VIOLENCE CYCLES AND ESCALATION

Only a very small fraction of any population seems capable of extreme forms of behavior for prolonged periods of time, and so the usual result is that phenomena such as violence seem to come and go in cycles. This is at least true with respect to particular actors, though on a wider scale it is entirely possible that violence may wax and wane in particular localized areas but still have a more or less steady overall rate of increase over a prolonged period of time. There are many reasons for this cyclical kind of tendency. On the individual level there is of course sheer exhaustion plus the rather high probability of incarceration, banishment, or death. On the community level there is also a form of psychological exhaustion that comes from the gradual realization that, in the case of a stalemate, neither side is really gaining from the conflict. Resources and energies that might be applied to other objectives are being used up at what comes to be seen as a costly rate. Eventually, pride and anger give way to more utilitarian considerations and some sort of truce is reached. But "eventually" may be a long period of time and memories of the hostilities may take an even longer time to erase. Such memories, once the fatigue factor has worn off, may again set in motion another conflict situation. It may be a very long time before the hostilities really subside.

The obvious reason why such conflicts break out is that one or the other party believes that it has much more to gain than to lose by initiating hostilities. An objective outsider might dispute this belief, but even if one were in possession of all the information known to all of the parties at the time, and even if one were to make completely rational decisions on the basis of this knowledge, he or she would often find that there were too many unknowns in the picture to permit much more than an enlightened guess as to the outcome. Needless to say, the participants themselves are much more likely to distort the total picture, to misperceive the motivations and perceptions of their opponents, to exaggerate the magnitude of their own relative resources, and (unfortunately) to underestimate the intensity and duration of the conflict that will ensue and the nature and extent of the costs to both parties: In the cases of international conflicts and arms races this is a familiar story. But much the same kind of thing may occur in the case of minority relationships.

A major inhibiting factor in U.S. black-white relationships, of course, is the very unequal distribution of resources that is obvious to both parties. The potential black militant must therefore be either very desperate or suicidal before he or she considers overt conflict as a viable solution. There are a number of additional factors that we need to consider, however. First, a guerrilla-type movement only need contain a tiny fraction of the most desperate extremists among a population in order to create considerable conflict. Second, such persons may easily convince themselves that their actions will succeed in producing such an irrational counterreaction on the part of the police that others from the black community will be induced either to join their ranks or at least to provide tangible support.

Third, ideologically-oriented extremists readily tend to see themselves as part of a larger movement, believing that their own actions and martyrdom will stimulate massive worldwide rebellion. Furthermore they believe that a fear of such a mass movement will induce white Americans either to move in the direction of a right-wing totalitarian state, ultimately being defeated by third-world nations, or to make major concessions to the radical movement. Such an assessment of outcomes may be completely unrealistic, but it is the intensity with which these convictions are held—not their truth or accuracy—that will affect the initial actions of the believers. Particularly if they are able to isolate themselves from more realistic points of view, their behavior may be determined for a very long time by such an ideology of conflict. Once an extreme form of conflict is under way it becomes all the more difficult for third-party moderates to change these convictions. There will have been far too great an emotional investment in them and too much will already have been sacrificed to give them up.

There are always two or more sides to every conflict. As tensions increase everyone becomes increasingly hypersensitive and grievances mount. Interests that were previously taken for granted need to be emphasized and protected, overly simplistic resolutions are proposed and taken seriously, and those who advocate a showdown by force begin to predominate. Attempts are made to pull in third parties by exaggerating the nature of those incidents that can be blamed on the other side, while conveniently ignoring those for which one's own side has been responsible. Once the incidents become sufficiently serious, militant extremist groups may begin openly to take credit for at least those acts that have required a certain amount of bravado and that would not be decreed as outrageous by neutral third parties. Any crackdowns by the other side—especially if it is the dominant party—are then used as examples of the lengths to which it is willing to go in order to preserve its position. If innocent victims are killed in the process, so much the better from the standpoint of extremists on either side.

Accompanying the acceleration of hostilities is likely to be a shift in the requirements of leadership favoring those who are willing to take bold actions, who are less restrained by a concern for the rights and lives of relatively innocent third parties, and who are more likely to hold to simplistic ideological views. As more moderate individuals are displaced, the active participants come more and more to view neutrals or relatively inactive bystanders either as traitors to the cause or as members of the enemy camp. Extreme hostility and overt violence may be directed as much against the nonloyal members of the in-group as against the enemy.

Unless either party wins a clear-cut victory, exhaustion will eventually bring the conflict to a condition of uneasy truce or a tacit agreement to end the overt hostilities. If the conflict has been confined to a very small scale, exhaustion may mean literally just that, namely the need to recuperate from extreme levels of tension. But if it has been on a much broader scale no single individuals may be physiologically exhausted since there may have been a continual replacement of the most active participants by others. However, as the conflict spreads, the interests of third parties are also likely to be adversely affected, so that eventually they, too, become tired of the conflict and begin to exert pressure to bring the hostilities to a close. The more powerful these third parties, the more affected they are by the conflict, and the more truly neutral they are, the greater the likelihood that effective pressure will be brought to bear to cease the hostilities.

In many conflicts, however, third parties are not truly neutral and tend to lean in their sympathies more in the one direction than the other. This of course means that they will have vested interests in prolonging the conflict and supplying aid and comfort to one side, as long as there appears to be a reasonably high probability that the favored side will win and as long as they have relatively little to lose by a prolongation of the conflict. Such unneutral neutrals are therefore automatically suspect whenever they attempt to play a mediating role, particularly if they have previously given support to one or the other of the parties or are perceived as having done so.

There are also likely to be neutrals whose power is so weak that they are unable to bring effective pressure to bear on parties to the conflict, and who therefore attempt to stay as far away as possible from the arena of conflict. Obviously, the more widespread the conflict has become and the more powerful the combatants, the fewer the number of neutrals of any kind. Once conflict has been expanded sufficiently, there may not be any third parties with sufficient power to constrain the conflict, in which case only the exhaustion of one or both of the acting parties can bring the clash to a halt. The practical implication, here, is clear enough. Before an open conflict becomes too wide-spread, those neutrals or near-neutrals with any power at all must apply pressure to the combatants, sanctioning them as much as possible, so that exhaustion sets in early enough in the process that the conflict can be quickly brought under control.

As long as they are convinced they will win the struggle or that the enemy needs punishing, the combatants will of course resist activities of neutral parties. Their opponents may have set forth a list of demands stated as though they are nonnegotiable, and they will be reacted to as such. There can be no discussion of such demands while the hostilities are going on, so goes the argument. Then when the hostilities have ceased, attempts will be made to argue either that the demands are no longer relevant or that giving into them will merely represent a form of surrender and an open invitation to renewed demands of a more extreme sort and possibly renewed hostilities as well. Unless powerful third parties are able to impose compromise resolutions on both parties, the basic issues often never get resolved, and, once there has been a sufficient period of recuperation, the stage is set for later conflict.

An Example: Most of the examples of overt conflict that come to the attention of the general public are those that involve actual bloodshed or some rather unusual human interest twist. But there are undoubtedly many more that are brought under control and at least partly resolved before someone is killed or seriously injured. Let us consider one example that seems to involve many of the basic ingredients of many black-white confrontations—legitimate grievances that did not receive serious attention until too late, a series of demands and the rejection of these demands, a mobilization of forces and confrontations with the police, the drawing into the conflict of numerous third parties, a tentative resolution and a failure of this resolution, a resumption of the conflict on somewhat different grounds, pressure applied by outside groups, and a final resolution that left nearly everyone dissatisfied but that at least temporarily reduced the degree of overt conflict.

The setting was a large state university in the South. For a period of some four or five years prior to the incidents there had been a number of more or less isolated attempts to call the basic problems to the attention of the university administration. The specific issues were basically labor-relations problems involving black nonacademic personnel: janitors and maids, grounds personnel, hospital employees, and cafeteria workers. On two occasions actual complaints were filed with the U.S. Government, and both resulted in investigations of personnel practices at the university. The federal investigator for the second of these complaints told the writer that he could not actually pin-point discrimination against blacks, the reason being that personnel practices were so bad that for all practical purposes they would have to be considered totally nonexistent! He indicated that his report to the administration would say just this, and several sources close to the top administration indicated that this report had, in fact, been lying around for two years prior to the time of crisis—without any noticeable action having been taken.

As a result of the assassination of Martin Luther King, Jr., a group of faculty decided that they would take concrete steps to attempt to improve the status of black nonacademic employees. One group of senior professors prepared a list of questions for the personnel officer, receiving only rather vague answers in response. This group then met with top administration officials to emphasize the importance of the issue and to cite specific kinds of problems being confronted by the nonacademic labor force. There was no noticeable response. A second group of faculty simultaneously began raising funds for a union organizer, who worked closely with cafeteria workers and a group of black students, many of whom were leaders in the campus Black Student Union. After about three or four months of organizational work, as well as efforts by individual faculty members who attempted to call grievances to the attention of the personnel office, the cafeteria workers presented a list of specific demands to the administration. Some promises were made at the time to look into these matters, but again no noticeable changes were made.

At about the time that these demands were being made by the cafeteria workers, the Black Student Union was drawing up its own set of demands. Some of the latter included references to the treatment of black nonacademic employees, but in general they went much further. Although some were patently unreasonable, many were relatively mild as compared with those being made on other campuses. For example, this major state university had no blacks in administrative positions and only two black junior-level faculty. This in a state in which approximately 25 percent of the taxpayers were black! The demand was for a black dean or advisor who could serve as a kind of ombudsman for black students, and who could counsel black students in connection with peculiar problems they might face as members of a minority group on campus. The black students did not demand that blacks be hired as regular members of the faculty; instead, they urged that the university hire a number of visiting black scholars who could serve as models for black students without depriving the predominantly black colleges of their best faculty. They also demanded a black studies program, this being the only one of their specific demands that was later satisfied. Coupled with these demands was a rather general ultimatum and a deadline for response. The administration replied within the deadline but in effect rejected all of the demands and attempted to justify its stance with a series of pronouncements concerning the rate of progress that had already been achieved.

Knowing that there could very well be a rather serious reaction on the part of the black students to what they perceived as a basically negative response, a small group of faculty made a hurried effort to conciliate the two parties. For two days it appeared as though some sort of compromise might be reached. But the cafeteria workers had simultaneously decided to go on strike, with the support of the Black Student Union. Within a period of one or two days picket lines had been formed by sympathetic black and white students and faculty. There were also a few scuffles. In one of these, several conservative students physically attacked several white students who were obstructing the cafeteria lines. In another, several black students deliberately overturned a number of tables in the dining hall. The former incident was ignored, but the latter served as a justification for the governor to call in the state police. Members of the administration, at this point, made strong efforts to convince the governor to call off the troops but to no avail. The number of pickets was strictly limited by the police. There were numerous very minor incidents but no major ones and the conflict then settled down to a more or less normal labor union strike.

The strictly economic bargaining power of the cafeteria workers was of course virtually nonexistent, and both parties knew this only too well. For the black students and workers the aim had to be that of politicizing the issues and attempting to obtain campus support for the workers and general support from blacks elsewhere in the state. It soon became apparent, however, that donations and fund raising campaigns would not suffice and that the administration was bent on stalling tactics and a refusal to engage in direct negotiations. The fact that the black students had earlier presented a list of demands convinced administration officials that the workers were merely being used by students in their efforts to gain power. There was an out-and-out refusal even to consult with faculty members who were asked to represent the black students, and numerous informal attempts by faculty members to bring the two sides together produced no tangible results. In effect, these third parties had no real power. Had the entire faculty been mobilized on either side, the story might have been otherwise, but as is usual in such situations the vast majority were passive spectators whose sympathies lay slightly on the side of the workers but who were ambivalent about the Black Student Movement.

The major break that finally brought an end to the confrontation, and an apparent victory for the workers, came as a result of threatened legal suit against the state and university. Behind this threat, of course, lay the possibility that the federal government would withhold funds from the university. It was discovered that the official records definitely showed that workers had been cheated of approximately $180,000 in overtime pay. One university official admitted off the record that the situation was probably much worse. There were also known instances where white workers had actually been trained by black women to take over supervisory roles. Claims of sexual exploitation of these women by their white male supervisors also added an embarrassing note to the affair. The official state personnel office, working with a law firm representing the workers, in effect took the decision out of administration hands, and the workers were given their basic demands for a minimum wage, union recognition, and guarantees that seniority rules would be followed.

The two parties directly involved in the dispute thus reached agreement prior to an ultimate showdown primarily because outsiders representing the two parties were able to arrive at what was basically a political settlement of an economic issue. Had this not occurred at about that time, the tension on campus threatened to mount. The governor had ordered the state police to clear black students from a building they were occupying, and it was only through the efforts of the local police chief and a black organizer from a nearby city that these students were persuaded to leave prior to a possible campus confrontation. On the day on which the ousting was to take place, a long line of state police, with rifles and helmets, was confronting a rather angry group of white and black students. Suddenly, without any noticeable provocation, the police began to advance. One or two of the faculty supporters of the black students at this point directed the students away from the area by urging a march on an administration building in the opposite direction. Had this not been done, there might conceivably have been another Kent State incident.

As is often the case when issues are settled in the heat of controversy, the matter was not as quickly resolved as had been expected. Administration officials decided to turn the campus cafeterias over to a private firm and did not insist on iron-clad guarantees that the previous arrangements with the now-unionized workers would be met. For a time, all proceeded smoothly. During this breathing spell members of the faculty again urged the administration to take long-range steps to improve the overall personnel system. Those personnel officers who were most immediately involved soon resigned, and a committee was formed to find a new director and modify policies. At the urging of a committee of concerned faculty a black studies program was approved. But the other demands of the black students, including requests for a black dean and visiting black faculty, were ignored. There still were virtually no direct contacts between top administration officials and either the black students or workers.

During the next summer there were definite signs that all would not be well. The firm that had received the contract to run the cafeterias began very ambitiously, but soon discovered that the demand for services did not call for as many personnel as had been expected. They began firing certain of the workers according to convenience, rather than seniority, and charges of union busting were immediately raised. A number of faculty and white student leaders urged the university administration to intervene at this point, but once more there was no noticeable response. The argument had previously been that negotiations could not be conducted under the pressure of demands. Now that these demands had been relaxed—as in fact they had, out of sheer exhaustion on the part of the black students—there were other reasons given. In reality, of course, the administration now found that it had to deal with other pressing issues that had been neglected during the crisis period.

Mechanisms for dealing with crises were by now much better worked out, so that when a second strike began there were numerous committees established to attempt to work out compromise solutions and to keep the top administration posted on a daily basis. Had such mechanisms been available earlier perhaps the extreme tension could have been reduced. But the issues were now somewhat different since the university was no longer an immediate party to the dispute between union and management. The official stance taken was one of strict neutrality, but blacks were quick to point out that this amounted to a procompany position since all of the economic advantage rested with the employer. Slowly but surely, black workers were replaced either by food dispensing machines or by white students who were willing to work split shifts without normal worker benefits. The university claimed that it was powerless to enforce any previous agreements worked out with the union prior to the employment of the outside firm. Faculty and administration committees were created to play advisory roles, but the company remained adamant. It became clear to all concerned that they had no basic interest in renewing their one-year contract, but there was also no announcement by the university that such a contract would, in fact, not be offered.

Recognizing that time was running out, and that economic assistance from students, faculty, and union dues was much less substantial than in the previous year, black leaders again found it necessary to resort to noneconomic resources. In truth, not only were the students and faculty exhausted from the previous struggle but so were the black students and administration members. Outside leaders of the previous strike had been banned from the campus through a court injunction, which was only later ruled illegal, that also prohibited from the campus several hundred nameless John Does. Plans had been laid to keep out all outsiders. However, the injunction applied only to several hundred John Does, not to thousands. The state police had been wisely kept off the campus and had been replaced by a very tired group of local police. Tempers between the latter and a small group of black and white student picketers began to flare, and there was one major (unwitnessed) confrontation that resulted in the arrest of about twenty demonstrators, two of whom received blows on the head that required hospital treatment. According to many of those picketers who were not arrested, the police gave what the picketers defined to be unreasonable orders to back up and disperse and then almost immediately took after black picketers, with cries of "get those niggers." Fortunately no one was seriously injured, and most of the charges against the picketers were eventually dropped.

Meanwhile, black organizers throughout the state were making plans for "Black Monday," on which thousands of black students from other campuses would enter the community and attempt to join the picketers in support of the workers. Nerves again became jittery, though there were no known plans to call in the state police. Members of the top administration were strongly urged by at least one group of concerned faculty to intervene on behalf of the striking workers. Mysteriously enough, the strike was settled during the early morning hours of "Black Monday," and the planned confrontation never came off. Apparently the administration was finally moved to intervene and change its previously neutral stance. Technically the demands of the workers were met, and the university agreed to take positive steps to relocate and train all of the previous employees laid off by the company. Soon afterwards, however, the company's contract expired without renewal and a decision was made to close virtually all of the university's eating facilities, thereby reducing the number of these service personnel to a mere handful.

Charges were pressed by the university against several of the student leaders. In one case, a black student had been charged with being a leader of the student picket confrontation with the local police. However, he had witnesses who were in a position to know that he was not at the scene at the time. Nevertheless the university officials instigated proceedings against the student, dropping these at the very last minute when the single police "witness" refused to testify. Soon after this, the Cambodian invasion and the killings at Kent State and Jackson State turned campus attention to other issues, and the local dispute was "resolved."

SOME IMPLICATIONS FOR STRATEGY

What can we learn from this rather general discussion and this single example? Not much, if the illustration does not contain elements in common with many others and if the discussion of the way crises and violence tend to erupt does not apply to other instances. We should always be alert to possible differences as well as similarities between events, so that we do not proscribe an overly rigid program of response. There do seem to be a sufficient number of rather general implications that are definitely worth noting, however.

One of the most obvious points is that many crises can be prevented provided that those who are in positions of power and authority take the trouble to listen to the early warning signals and take steps to act on the basis of these warnings. Here there is an important role that the white liberal may play, though he or she must always be cautious not to usurp the role of black representatives who wish to take the initiative in this respect. In many instances it is important to publicize the state of affairs so as to mobilize support for reform movements prior to the necessity of taking a stand on more controversial approaches. In the case of the nonacademic personnel at this particular university there was a period of at least four years prior to the showdown during which pressure could have been applied on the administration. Instead, the very small number of liberals who took any interest in the matter attempted to rely on persuasion alone, and this did not work.

There are many rather impersonal economic trends that result in extreme hardship for persons who lack competitive resources. Those who are in a position to see these trends are often absorbed in other issues and activities. Those who are most immediately affected, however, are well aware of their own problems but are usually unable to articulate them or to suggest constructive solutions. Obviously, in the case of this university and perhaps many others, there had been a substantial effort to increase faculty salaries in order to compete with other major universities. Southern colleges were, at the time, in a difficult competitive position as compared with the nation as a whole, and administration officials had done a remarkable job of keeping faculty salaries at a competitive level. All administrators must cut corners somewhere, however. The result was that the lower-level nonacademic personnel, white as well as black, tended to suffer. Hurt most were those persons who were unable to bargain in any way for increased salaries. Black nonacademic personnel were generally the most disadvantaged in this respect.

The essential point is that, once their unfavorable employment conditions were pointed out, steps should have immediately been taken to correct for such inequities. Economic vested interests were at stake, however. Although the nearly all-white faculty might have supported higher wages for nonacademic personnel in theory, if this were to be at the expense of their own salaries it would have been quite another matter. In fact, practically all of them remained rather indifferent until the crisis actually developed. This is one more bit of evidence, perhaps, that blacks cannot count on the support of white liberals.

When the strikes themselves were underway it became obvious to all concerned that the economic bargaining power of such unskilled workers was extremely limited. Here, too, this bargaining power might have been effectively increased had there been a strong union movement within the region, or donations forthcoming from unions outside the area or from a vigorous campaign to raise funds in the local area. There was insufficient time and energy during the crises themselves to raise such funds. Had there been a national organization established with just such emergency funds available, the bargaining position of these workers could have been improved. Without the economic resources, blacks found it necessary to bargain in other ways. The fact is, however, that they tried the economic route first and failed. It is especially here that white liberals failed them, though without the organizational base and means to raise funds quickly this is not at all surprising.

The next moves in this particular drama, and in many other similar ones, were to obtain legal support. Here the strike leaders were very fortunate in receiving the services of an integrated law firm for a very nominal fee. Timing again turned out to be crucial. Had there not been definite word from the (white) lawyer involved, many graduate students were about to refuse to teach their courses and risk being fired. This would have precipitated an additional crisis that might have hurt the university considerably, and these students were well aware of this fact. This particular crisis, and perhaps others, was averted by a matter of a few hours. The point is that such legal services cannot be left up to chance where time is an essential factor. A national organization with roots in each state or region and financed well enough to take on such projects at nominal cost would be a definite asset.

In the case of the second strike against the private corporation there was basically no legal angle that could be worked, at least not during a short period of time. There was no real breach of contract and no illegal withholding of wages, as in the case of the university's actions. Furthermore there were many fewer picketers and more restrictions imposed on outsiders in the case of the second strike. Some of the previous faculty supporters had either left the campus or were exhausted from the previous year. The only recourse seemed to be that of direct action by large numbers of blacks, with the obvious possibility of a major confrontation with the police and, of course, bad publicity for the university. This last strategy happened to work, perhaps because it induced the university to intervene at the last minute, but also because the company involved did not really have a major economic investment in the issue.

Many liberals, such as the faculty in this particular case, tend to try to help out in these situations by entering the fray as individuals without any real influence or power except possibly the ability to help persuade others. But the time for persuasion is before the crisis, not during it. Even here, presuasion efforts may have little effect unless the parties involved can be convinced that their own best interests dictate a change in policy. The dilemma that applied in this particular example is as follows. A simple presentation of facts and appeals to fairness did not work in the face of the pressures on administration officials to deal with higher priority items. It is not that they were actively opposed to reform, but simply that they thought sufficient reforms could be accomplished by a few directives. They never could seem to find the necessary time to look into the matter first hand. They were then shocked when certain practices became public knowledge—though they had earlier received private communications indicating basically this same information.

If persuasion is coupled with veiled threats that there will be "trouble" if these matters are not dealt with promptly, the efforts to persuade in effect become a form of punishment power that almost immediately creates a defensive reaction. Furthermore, unless there have been other recent incidents that can serve as illustrations of the kind of trouble that may arise, the party concerned is not likely to take these threats seriously. There is always the convenient belief that "it can't happen here" or that the basic difficulties have been sufficiently resolved.

Thus the role of third-party mediators is a rather limited one unless these mediators also represent parties capable of exercising power in their own right or in calling upon others who may do so. State personnel officers and attorneys, in possession of evidence that legitimate wages had been withheld, were able to bring the dispute to a speedy conclusion, whereas faculty negotiators were not. The main lesson, then, is that organizations that have been set up in advance to deal with such crises and to apply pressure when needed will be of much more value than actions of isolated individuals. However, such individuals may play very necessary roles in helping to locate potential danger spots in advance, attempting negotiations at an early stage, and facilitating contacts between minority representatives and the appropriate branches of such an organization.

As always, there will be a number of dilemmas concerning the nature of the role that such an outside organization should play. Should it be strictly neutral, in the sense of being dead center on the average? I doubt very much that this is possible even assuming that it is desirable. As the workers' strike illustrates, there are likely to be many third parties that become involved, and most of these with any real power will probably be aligned with the so-called establishment. This is especially likely to be the case with respect to the police and those who control economic resources. Therefore it seems desirable for such an ombudsman organization to develop the reputation of generally siding with minorities, though making its own autonomous decisions. This implies that there may very well be instances in which the conclusion is that minority demands have been excessive or that their tactics cannot in any way be supported.

One very important function of such an organization may be that it can afford minorities with an opportunity to publicize their grievances in a favorable light. If, for example, a university administration or employer knew that a full public report of the incident might be forthcoming, this might serve as an inducement to correct certain abuses before they threatened to become major issues. Of course there are many situations that are sufficiently delicate that certain facts should not be brought to the attention of the public, and certainly not at the time of the crisis itself. But the threat of publicity, if properly restrained, can be an important instrument in the negotiating process, particularly if the organization wishes to develop a solid reputation among liberals and moderates for fair-handed practices and policies.

Another function of such an organization, provided that it had a sufficient number of local members, would be that of quickly finding groups of observers who would be willing to monitor locations at which tense encounters are expected to take place. In many instances, for example, there are confrontations between police and demonstrators that are never witnessed except by the parties themselves. Such incidents often become the focal-points of rumors and later disputes, and if they prove to be serious may exacerbate the tensions to the point at which a major explosion may occur. Witnesses with note pads may serve to inhibit violence on the part of demonstrators and police alike. Reporters and television cameras of course provide this important service, but they often arrive on the scene only after the major events have occurred. Around-the-clock witnesses are only feasible when likely scenes of violence are easily pinpointed, such as the picket lines in the case of the workers' strike. Also, these observers are not likely to be welcomed by the police and may be told to leave the scene because of the potential danger involved. If so, they may at least report that they were ordered by the police to leave, thus raising questions about police behavior in the event that disputes later arise as to the precipitating incidents.

In all of this, careful attention must be paid to the question of comparable roles that might be played by predominantly black organizations. Where the latter are capable of providing the necessary services, they should be encouraged to do so unless the policies of such groups are very much at odds with those of the liberal movement. The NAACP, for example, specializes in legal services and should be encouraged to provide these services whenever it is willing to do so. Often, however, it has defined its role as that of using its very limited resources to concentrate on test cases that have more general implications. Some sort of formal and informal division of labor would have to be worked out between the two organizations, both nationally and locally, so that in the case of particular crisis situations speedy action can be taken and the necessary funds made available without undue delay. Similarly, if there is already in existence an Urban League chapter or vigorous labor union having the confidence of the minority participants, these should be encouraged to play active roles. In effect, the proposed organization must be prepared to act quickly when called but not to take the initiative unless invited to do so.

There must also be a sensitivity to other problems that face black leaders. In spite of a rather natural tendency for white liberals to reject violence and to prefer to avoid crisis situations, it must be clearly recognized that the threat of such a possibility often becomes the only viable device to blacks who lack alternative means of achieving their objectives. For example, without the threat of keeping the university campus in a state of turmoil, and without the possibility of "Black Monday," it is entirely possible that the strikers would not have been able to achieve a resolution quickly enough in view of their highly unfavorable economic position. Especially where the law-and-order forces have been placed squarely on the side of the white establishment, and where legal action is either impossible or would result in interminable delays, more direct action will seem to be the only realistic response to many blacks. This will be true whether liberals favor this action or not, and regardless of one's assessment of the long-range alternatives.

This is, of course, why every effort must be made to help blacks achieve the kinds of economic and political resources that make threats of crises a much less attractive alternative. But until blacks have such resources, any attempts to block direct-action appeals will be rejected as hypocritical. The best strategy, in view of this, would seem to be to support those means that seem least likely to provoke a violent response on the part of whites, while assuring the minority of a basic support for those means of protest that stop short of extremism and unprovoked violence. At the same time, it must be made clear to those whites who have blocked alternative means to the minority that it is they who are in large part responsible for the consequences.

Liberal whites must also be sensitive to the fact that their ways of reacting to crisis situations may be very different from those whose lives are directly involved. Quite rightly, the liberal intellectual attempts to evaluate each issue, to gather as many facts as possible and to sort them out, and then to engage in numerous discussions before arriving at policy decisions. But during a crisis this often results in no action at all, since the issues will have been long since resolved before the debate has been ended. White radicals and black militants naturally see this inaction and deliberation as a stalling device that relieves the liberal of guilt while at the same time keeping one totally neutral with respect to the day-to-day events that are taking place. The larger the deliberating body and the wider the spectrum of viewpoints being represented, the slower the process and the more watered down the final action that is usually taken. This is as one would anticipate as a result of democratic processes and, in itself, is not unreasonable. It is, however, totally inadequate as a means of dealing with crisis situations.

Although there is probably no completely satisfactory way of resolving the dilemma of a joint need for deliberation and fact-finding, on the one hand, and speedy action, on the other, there are certain lessons to be learned from past experience on this matter. First, those liberals who find it necessary to deliberate in such a fashion can expect a hostile reaction on the part of the participants and should be psychologically prepared for this. Second, it is possible to set up mechanisms for dealing with crises before they occur. These include the formation of trouble-shooting committees that are authorized to go into action on a moment's notice, the appointment of ombudsmen who are in central enough positions to have close working relationships with all of the major parties, and the establishment of committees that will have the responsibility of providing daily reports of events to all parties. Such mechanisms were one positive outcome of the first of the two cafeteria workers' strikes, and they proved effective in reducing the overall amount of confusion if not overt conflict.

Prior to many crises there is often a rather lengthy period during which many charges and countercharges are made and where there are definite signs that all is not well. In the case of the cafeteria strike, for example, approximately three months elapsed between the time when specific demands by the workers were stated and the onset of the strike itself. For several years before that there had been other more general complaints and at least two official visits from Washington. Had reports from the latter visits been made public, for example, the administration might have been forced through embarrassment to take corrective actions that might have headed off the later dispute. But there were no organized groups that followed the matter up or made public recommendations. This was clearly the time for deliberative action, but it did not take place. In part, the problem was that no group of individuals had been authorized to engage in such a study, many thinking that an officially appointed "Mayor's Commission" was handling such responsibilities. An organization with local branches specifically encouraged to conduct such trouble-shooting investigations might have been of considerable help. If nothing else, it could have made available the pertinent facts at an early enough stage that the deliberative process could have been speeded up and organized support given to those demands that seemed compatible with the resulting recommendations. During a crisis itself, there is never sufficient time or energy for such deliberations, to say nothing of the fact that it will usually be much more difficult to obtain reasonably unbiased information at that time.

Finally, thought has to be given before an actual crisis to the nature of the local black leadership and how this might be affected by intervention of a particular sort. Often there are cleavages among blacks that may be aggravated by a crisis but that also may be resolved, depending on the nature of the tactics that are used and the outcomes of the struggle. If white liberals intervene in such a way as to support one faction rather than another, the outcome may be disastrous in terms of the consequences for future cooperation. The tendency, of course, will be to support the moderate and integrationist black leaders who are most likely to take a position similar to that of the white liberal. But if it has been determined that such blacks have, in effect, ignored the particular issue in question until forced by militants to take a stand, and if the basic initiative for the action has been taken by these militants, then a belated effort to reinforce the moderate elements is likely to backfire and create an even greater degree of distrust of whites among the younger generation of blacks.

It would seem much more wise, in such instances, to work more directly with the latter group even where there is somewhat less compatibility of means and objectives. Here a division of labor seems necessary. Those whites who are closer to the militant camp should be encouraged to work most directly with their black counterparts, whereas the generally older and less militant white liberals may attempt to work more closely with the moderate blacks. The aim should be to bring the two groups closer together, if possible, so as to strengthen the overall effort. This strategy can perhaps be best implemented by liberal organizations that contain a reasonably broad spectrum of members who agree on general principles but also see the need for such a division of labor.

During the crisis period third parties always face a number of difficult decisions concerning the role they should play during various stages of the conflict. One of the easiest and most tempting resolutions, of course, is to stay out of it altogether, or to intervene only when it appears that the side one most opposes is likely to win. This makes it difficult if not impossible to bring the conflict under control before it gets out of hand, however. We have just argued, in effect, that third parties that are in a position to apply sanctions to one or both parties may be able to play important roles. But if they actively intervene on one side, this will undoubtedly weaken their persuasive power with the other. After the immediate crisis is over, it becomes more difficult to persuade them to take the kinds of steps that appear necessary in order to prevent further crises. Thus those faculty who attempted to support the workers and black students in the campus crisis were unable to convince the administration to take corrective steps before the next one might occur.

Again a division of labor seems desirable. Those parties that have remained out of the fray may find themselves in the best position to exert influence at a later time, whereas the more active parties are likely to have used up their goodwill with one or even both of the parties through their participation. Provided that the two groups of neutrals are perceived as being distinct and yet are in reasonably close contact and can reach some sort of working compromise, perhaps both kinds of objectives can be achieved. Such a division of labor should not be left up to the workings of chance factors, however. In the final chapter we shall have more to say about the need for greater coordination of such efforts.

NOTES

1. Charles E. Silberman, *Crisis in Black and White* (New York: Vintage Books, 1964); Lewis M. Killian, *The Impossible Revolution?* (New York: Random House, 1968); and Louis H. Masotti, Jeffrey K. Hadden, Kenneth F. Seminatore, and Jerome R. Corsi, *A Time to Burn?* (Chicago: Rand McNally, 1969).

2. William H. Grier and Price M. Cobbs, *Black Rage* (New York: Bantam, 1968).

3. Joyce Ladner, "What 'Black Power' Means to Negroes in Mississippi," *Trans-action* 5 (November 1967): 7–15.

10

A Call for Organization

A NUMBER OF MAJOR THEMES HAVE BEEN STRESSED in the previous chapters, all of which point to the need for improved organization and coordination among liberals, including those with varying leanings toward the right or the left. The first of these themes has been that of urgency and the importance of timing. Given the fact that the patience of many blacks is running out, and that the outcome of internal cleavages and disagreements among blacks may very well depend upon how whites respond in the very near future, white liberals cannot afford to flounder much longer.

Many needed programs will require major funding that will necessitate a reordering of national priorities. There may be a number of crisis situations that could expand beyond control unless third parties are well enough organized to intervene in a constructive fashion. In the past, liberals have tended to rely too heavily on the federal and local governments to play such roles, but it is clear that there are many kinds of situations in which we cannot rely on such sources. Neither speed nor efficiency nor long-range planning are characteristic of governmental actions in America, except in instances where there is already a high degree of consensus or when a state of emergency exists. The present need is precisely that of acting quickly and decisively *before* major crises arise.

A second and obvious theme has been that we must develop policies that take into consideration that, at best, most white Americans are basically indifferent to what happens to blacks, except when it is apparent that there is extreme hardship or gross injustice, or when the situation is brought close to home through policies that affect the pocketbook or would imply actual contact with blacks. In the latter instances, unfortunately, the vested interests of many white Americans in maintaining economic and occupational privileges and in preserving racial segregation are likely to come out into the open. There do seem to be policies and types of behavior on the part of minorities that minimize the probabilities of conservative counterreactions, but these generally tend to involve processes that either require considerable restraint and conformist behavior or a prolonged period of waiting. In neither case, therefore, can these policies be expected to appeal to blacks.

We are thus faced with a very serious dilemma involving a power confrontation between a very impatient but weak minority, on the one hand, and a basically conservative and indifferent majority, on the other. Unless the latter can be induced to give ground at a pace that is deemed reasonable to most blacks, the internal dynamics of the situation within the black community are such that extremism stands a reasonable chance of winning out over moderation. This, in turn, will strengthen the hand of racial conservatives among whites and overt conflict may be unavoidable.

A third theme that has been stressed is that many of our policies should reflect the legitimate demand for greater black autonomy with respect to decision making. This has implied a number of basic dilemmas, the most important of which, for both black and white liberals, is the challenge to integrationist philosophy. It is difficult to see how we can force integration on blacks since, if we attempt to do so, those who oppose it can easily sabotage it through hostile reactions and a refusal to interact with whites on a friendly basis. On the other hand, we must attempt to see to it that those blacks who do wish to integrate will find this a viable solution.

A number of the specific proposals made in previous chapters have been aimed at strengthening the hand of those blacks who wish to increase their autonomy from whites. The problem is one of finding ways to accomplish this without, at the same time, undermining integration and those blacks who wish to pursue this goal. We must constantly assess such proposals, assuming that they are implemented, of course, from the standpoint of the degree to which they seem to be resulting in further separation and the possible growth of black racism. It is premature to make such an appraisal, particularly since we know too little about the processes that are internal to the black community. It has been noted, however, that the position of black integrationists was almost undermined by the tendency in the late 1960s and early 1970s to give major publicity to acts of violence and extremism and to those who used the most dramatic language and advocated the most outrageous policies.

A fourth theme—and the final one to be reviewed here—has stressed that there are several very different working theories of social causation. Even assuming a basic agreement on ultimate objectives, these working theories affect our specific priorities by providing alternative explanations for prejudice, discrimination and minority reactions. Such working theories are at least in part derived from vested interests and therefore not easily modified. But they also stem from the necessity of finding relatively simple explanations for a very complex reality. Our policies, if rational, should be based on the most adequate working theories, since grossly oversimplified policies are almost bound to fail.

Such policies must be based on certain pieces of factual information, as for example the stated priorities and goals of various segments of the population. For instance if it were found that blacks consistently listed certain goals as top priorities, while at the same time whites indicated that they would be least resistant to blacks' achieving these goals, then such information would be useful in formulating plans for projects that could be immediately implemented. It should be cautioned, however, that the relative priorities of both groups could be based on faulty working theories so that even if these objectives were totally met the overall situation might not be markedly improved.

The implicaton, of course, is that policy planning is highly dependent upon accurate knowledge, not only of factual information but also of the causal processes that are at work. Such knowledge cannot be attained rapidly, but it can be accumulated much more systematically than is presently the case. There are two aspects of this process: the collection of good data on a regularized basis and the careful integration of such data with theoretical explanations, that are considerably more sophisticated than the general working theories that most of us use. The processes of collecting data, conducting careful experimental evaluations of pilot projects, and constructing and modifying theories are also of real value in clarifying objectives, making hidden assumptions explicit, and anticipating consequences before programs are actually implemented.

These themes appear to imply certain basic incompatibilities. The need for swift and decisive action, on the one hand, and careful thought and research, on the other, do not seem consistent. Likewise, the argument that whites defer in many respects to judgments of blacks and that they learn to take a back seat with respect to many types of policies seems incompatible with the thesis that white liberals need to play a more positive and definitive role. Thus in addition to all of the problems and dilemmas previously noted, we have organizational difficulties as well. In the remainder of this chapter I shall attempt to specify in somewhat greater detail the nature and functions of two specific kinds of organizations that seem to be badly needed.

The first is a nation-wide action organization, based on liberal philosophy but not tied to either major political party, that is capable of proposing both short- and long-range policies, that serves to monitor governmental policies and programs and has an important lobbying function, and that is also capable of organizing local action programs and providing legal and other forms of assistance in crisis situations. The second is a major research foundation or organization, whose programs and recommendations are closely integrated with those of the action organization, but whose fundamental purpose is to provide the basic data and theoretical orientations that make it possible to formulate intelligent policies and continually reevaluate these policies in the light of new evidence and theories.

A POLICY AND ACTION-ORIENTED ORGANIZATION

For virtually every institution in America, race relations is a kind of side issue. This is true with respect to our economic and political organizations, but it is equally the case with respect to universities, churches, labor unions, and practically all voluntary associations. Each of these institutions has its own major functions or tasks, along with problems connected with fund raising, the recruitment of new personnel, and internal problems involving a division of labor and the motivation of its participants. In all of these instances, problems of race relations may create additional issues and difficulties to be resolved.

In each institution there may be specialists whose task it is to handle racial grievances and make policy recommendations concerning such matters. In certain federal agencies and departments of city governments, race relations may have actually become the dominant issue that tends to color most other decisions. Yet apart from the NAACP, the National Urban League, and a few other predominantly black organizations, nowhere do we have any major institutions or nationally-based organizations that have race relations as the primary responsibility, nor are there any important voluntary organizations or agencies of the government known to the writer that have assumed the responsibility of taking an overview perspective on policy.

In part this situation seems to have resulted because of the magnitude of the overall problem and the inability of any small group of persons to keep up to date on any but a tiny portion of the general situation. There are housing specialists in HUD, educational experts in government or on college campuses, labor specialists in unions and other organizations, political scientists with detailed knowledge of voting patterns and trends, and legal specialists who know about the most important judicial decisions. But we seem to have no efficient mechanism for putting the pieces of the puzzle together, so that we may see the picture both in detail and also in its entirety.

Likewise, we do not have systematic ways of transmitting knowledge and policy recommendations to the general public and to those persons who could apply this information on the local level. Nor are local action groups in effective contact with each other, in many instances even within the same community. Not only does this make for poor coordination but it also means that it is difficult for one group to benefit from the successes and failures of others. In effect, we have such an excess of miscellaneous and often faulty information that cannot be utilized because it has not been properly summarized and integrated.

It has perhaps been our working assumption that the federal government will take care of the big issues that require long-range planning and major funding, but that on the local level it is best to work at the grass-roots level so as to maximize participation and the input of new ideas. This has left several major gaps, however. One has been at the intermediate level of organization, at the state and regional levels. Another has been the lack of funding for activities, particularly in emergency situations, that are at a more ambitious level than those of which small community agencies are capable or that may be too controversial or pioneering to be sponsored by such groups.

Another gap has been the inability to provide experts, on relatively short notice, capable of assisting local groups with specialized programs or with resources for tackling problems. It is perhaps true that the existence of such larger organizations and the availability of such experts might tend to deenergize local groups of laymen by leading them to believe that most of the basic problems were automatically being handled by others. It therefore becomes important to consider ways in which a sensible division of labor can be worked out so as to minimize this particular risk while, at the same time, providing these specialized services.

What seems to be needed, then, is a national organization with multiple functions. One of these would be to help to coordinate activities of local branches, to finance small-scale projects that they may plan and to provide support in emergency situations. Presumably, specialists in major fields such as job opportunities, housing, education, and law could work out of regional offices, whereas more restricted specialized services and advice could be given to local units through a national office.

In order to provide improved communication among local groups, to stimulate them with new ideas, and to advise them concerning state and national programs and proposed legislation, the organization would need to sponsor a monthly or biweekly magazine or journal as part of its services to all members. Here would be an opportunity to describe apparently successful action programs and to evaluate the reasons why others may have failed. Latest research findings having policy implications could also be summarized in a nontechnical language appropriate for the layman. Bills currently before Congress could be explained in simple terms and scrutinized carefully in terms of possible unanticipated implications for race relations. Bills already passed could likewise be explained and their implications for the local level noted. The voting records and stances taken by particular legislators could also be analyzed, perhaps in supplementary issues designed for regional audiences. Major policy recommendations of the organization could be presented, criticized, and refined through the device of proposing preliminary versions in the journal, inviting specific responses and debate, and then formulating official policy at annual meetings.

Already implied is the necessity of having full-time staff specialists whose duties are to keep up with research developments, legislation, and executive practices in their area of concern; to offer technical advice to local and regional groups; and to help develop specific policy recommendations. These staff specialists should be in close working contact with their counterparts in the research organization to be proposed below, the aim being to coordinate policy-oriented research with the actual policy recommendations themselves. In some instances, for example, it may have been determined that there is already available sufficient data and adequate theories so that rather firm policy recommendations can be made. In other situations, probably the vast majority, policy recommendations will have to be much more tentative, pending the outcome of evaluations of pilot projects.

It is too much to expect that the same persons who are actually doing the research will have the time to study policy alternatives in great detail, but the two sets of personnel should be able to speak the same language and to coordinate their activities with the same goals in mind. In addition to these specialists, it will also be advisable to have a relatively smaller number of persons whose task it is to attempt to take an overview perspective, both in terms of integrating the diverse research findings and in recommending overall policy priorities that may cut across the several specialized areas.

The proposed organization should also have a political wing that would include a lobbying function having the specific purpose of attempting to influence both legislation and the implementation of policy by the executive branches of city, state, and federal governments. To the degree that intelligent policies have been formulated and dovetailed with a general program of applied research, such lobbyists will have the important advantage of being able to recommend a coherent package of programs to politicans who are nonspecialists in the area and whose time must be divided into many compartments, most of which have little or nothing to do with the field of race relations. One should not be overly optimistic or naive, however, concerning the potency of such a lobbying operation in the face of opposition from other quarters. To the degree that the organization can build up a large membership base and sell its general position to the American public, this lobbying function will of course be assisted. Aggressive lobbying in the absence of both a carefully planned program and an organizational base could very well backfire, however.

Finally, such a national organization must find ways of resolving the delicate problem of working out a division of labor with other major organizations, interest groups, and governmental agencies so as to minimize duplication of effort as well as inter-organizational rivalries. As any organization grows, its leaders naturally develop vested interests of their own, including wanting to maintain leadership positions within the organization itself and to expand the organization so as to take on more functions. I am not especially concerned, here, with rivalries between such a private organization and the federal government, since the latter seems entirely capable of expanding its own functions almost at will. As we have noted at numerous points, however, there is likely to be a problem in connection with the objective of stimulating the development of autonomous black leadership.

The proposed organization should of course be open to blacks as well as whites, and undoubtedly many of the staff specialists would be black. But another explicit aim would be to promote opportunities for organized effort on the part of liberal whites, who presently find themselves highly underorganized and poorly coordinated. Therefore it would be self-defeating if the organization were to become almost exclusively black, as has been the case with respect to organizations such as the NAACP, the National Urban League, the Southern Christian Leadership Conference, and CORE. The problem, then, is to create a truly integrated organization that is autonomous from these other groups, while at the time time not being their competitor. Although it is premature, here, to attempt to anticipate the nature of specific problems that might arise in this connection, it does seem necessary to sensitize white liberals to the advisability of taking such other organizations into consideration as policy is formulated and implemented.

We have also implied at several points that it is advisable to develop policy in such a way that both short- and long-term programs are instituted. If anything, it appears as though we have tended to neglect the kinds of short-term, bread-and-butter issues that are of primary concern to the black (and white) lower classes—matters such as unemployment, improved housing, and so-called quality education. Any newly formed organization may make a "splash" and gain adherents through a series of quick victories involving very tangible and concrete issues. This fact, plus the previous neglect of the black lower classes, would tend to favor a concentration on issues that have relatively immediate payoffs. Right now, liberals badly need these kinds of victories. But we also know that there are many long-range processes at work within the economy that, though they may have gone unnoticed by all except for a few specialists, may actually be of more fundamental importance. It would be foolish to neglect these questions or to leave them to others to resolve.

In connection with some of these larger and often more intractable problems, one of the first steps is that of publicizing their nature in terms that the layman can understand. A second step is to support the kinds of basic or apparently nonapplied research that often sheds light on such processes. And a third is to institute a series of experimental pilot programs designed to gain more insights into how these processes can be controlled in such a way that major priorities become attainable. One of the most important functions of the proposed national organization would be to devote sufficient energy and resources to such long-range questions that future problems can be anticipated before they loom as major crises on the horizon.

A FOUNDATION FOR RESEARCH IN RACE RELATIONS

The structure and financing of a major research foundation in race relations would of course vary over time, with the overall size and scope of the research being determined by the availability of funds, by developments within the social sciences, and by practical necessities. In view of the fact that funds allocated to social science research have been miniscule as compared with those devoted to military applications and the space program, the total outlay to such a foundation need not be large in any absolute sense in order to provide a substantial increment to existing funds devoted to research in the field. An annual budget of

3–5 million dollars would certainly be ample at the outset, with moderate increases becoming desirable once relatively ambitious long-range research projects were developed. Absolutely essential, however, would be the guarantee of steady sources of funds that are not earmarked for specific projects or conditional on immediate practical results.

Five important functions for such a foundation are as follows: (1) conducting basic research in race relations and developing systematic theories capable of being tested by means of the data so collected; (2) serving as a major data-collecting agency and databank making data available to social scientists at minimal cost; (3) conducting applied or action-oriented research designed to evaluate the effectiveness of pilot projects and to suggest modifications in these projects; (4) training of additional personnel, particularly blacks and other minorities, in the application of research methodology to applied problems in race relations; and (5) disseminating research results and practical recommendations based on these findings to the general public and, particularly, to the black community. Let me discuss each of these functions in some detail.

Basic Research

The term "basic" is obviously vague but is intended to convey the notion that certain research must be conducted without specific practical goals in mind. In the case of social research in general, there are many kinds of research that appear to have no immediate bearing on the field of race relations until someone extracts their implications. For example, psychologists have spent considerable energy studying the learning process and personality development. Results of these studies might (or might not) be found useful in analyzing the learning of black children in an integrated school setting or in studying the development of prejudice in the white child. Likewise, demographers' studies of migration processes may be used to form guidelines for a migration policy useful in encouraging the flow of black migrants away from our largest cities into smaller ones. Sociological studies of bureaucratic organizations may shed light on discriminatory hiring policies, and studies of urbanization in developing countries may suggest analogies useful in analyzing industrial processes and discrimination within the South.

Obviously a foundation for the study of race relations cannot afford to become involved with such basic research on all aspects of social life. Energies would be channeled in too many directions. Some of its scholars must be freed from other responsibilities, however, so that they may search for the implications of diverse research findings. They must also attempt to synthesize and boil down the findings of literally thousands of research reports bearing more directly on the field of race relations. A very common complaint among social scientists is that too few persons are really free to attempt this kind of synthesis. The result is a bewildering set of particular findings that are never added up and a field that contains very little real theoretical knowledge. Such theoretical syntheses of existing knowledge are absolutely essential in order to establish research priorities and to produce the kind of consensus on measuring instruments, basic concepts, and existing knowledge gaps that makes accumulation possible.

Also implied in the notion of basic research in the field of race relations is the conviction that comparative research must be encouraged, even where the immediate applications are not apparent. If we focus entirely on black-white relationships within the United States, we may lose valuable insights concerning alternative resolutions that may have been developed elsewhere. In order to construct realistic theories as to the causes of prejudice and discrimination we need to do research on other minority situations in which the intergroup relationships differ in specified ways. At present we have a number of such comparative pieces of research, but unfortunately they are not really comparable in a number of important respects, if only because they have been conducted by isolated scholars using different data-collection techniques and having very different foci of interest. There is a danger that we will become so totally absorbed with black-white relationships and other U.S. minority situations that such comparative studies will be neglected at the expense of valuable insights.

Data Collection and Measurement

Existing research is severely hampered by the lack of standardized data systematically collected at regular intervals. For purely practical purposes, a number of social scientists have argued that it will be useful to have available sets of social indicators, tapping various kinds of inequalities among blacks, other nonwhites, and whites, if only to make these public as measures of rates of progress or lack of progress and to sharpen our priorities. Such indicators may be highly misleading, however, unless accompanied by careful methodological studies of possible measurement errors and biases. Furthermore, for purposes of research it will be necessary to intercorrelate these indicators with each other and to attempt to link them with variables of greater theoretical and practical concern. This will require considerable technical knowledge as well as a much higher degree of coordination than we have at present. If such indicators are collected and reported by government agencies they will not only be automatically suspect (though perhaps improperly so) but they are less likely to be developed with basic research objectives in mind. If so, social scientists will have a much harder time relating the indicators to their theoretical variables. This is a problem that has plagued users of the U.S. Census and other federal data-collecting agencies and should be anticipated in advance.

A coordinated effort by a single agency can, in many respects, be much more economical than activities by several. Well-designed samples can take advantage of the fact that not all respondents need be asked the same questions, that some but not all may be interviewed more than once, and that in many instances selected samples of opinion leaders or other elites may be desirable. Data collected in several different ways may be coordinated and methodological studies conducted which will yield insights as to possible biases and the relative advantages of each procedure. Some variables may be measured in exactly the same way over a period of time, whereas others may be measured in two or three different ways, perhaps only one of which remains fixed over time. Many of the points being raised in this connection are technical, but the essential point is this: we badly need standardized data that can only be collected through a coordinated effort. I would like to see this effort begin as soon as possible and to be sponsored independently of government agencies, which of course are collecting certain selected kinds of information with other purposes in mind.

There are also a growing number of opinion polls and other sources of data that need to be coordinated and made readily available to users at a minimal cost. There is a trend favoring so-called databanks, the purpose of which is to provide data to individual social scientists. The danger in the uncritical use of such databanks, however, is that the user is seldom in a position to evaluate the adequacy of the data and may have only a very vague notion as to how they have been collected, the nature of the sample that has been selected, or the social conditions existing at the time. Clearly, users must be warned about possible biases and be given a realistic assessment of the data's quality. Only data meeting reasonably high minimum-level standards should be made available. Otherwise, the findings may be highly misleading.

Applied Research

The distinction between basic and applied research is overdrawn. Research that is not motivated by any particular application may, at some later time, be found to be much more useful and practical than most so-called applied research; in fact, this is often used as a justification for basic research. Likewise, applied research may generate ideas that contribute to major theoretical developments in a field. Nevertheless, some research is much more action-oriented than theoretical. And most sponsoring agencies pay for research that is directed toward solving some concrete problem of practical interest.

A distinction can conveniently be made between two kinds of applied research in the field of race relations. The first, which is by far the most common, is fact-finding. What is the local demand for housing within a certain price range? What are the opinions of whites and blacks concerning school busing? The second kind of applied research is much more difficult but potentially more important, namely evaluation research. This involves an attempt to assess the effects of some particular action program, to use this appraisal to suggest modifications or to predict certain outcomes, and then to study the results of the modifications or to assess the degree to which the predictions have proven accurate.

With respect to fact-finding, there are a number of very good opinion polls and other types of agencies capable of conducting such research. However, on a relatively smaller scale it will be necessary to train research personnel, especially blacks, or other minorities, who are capable of conducting relatively inexpensive fact-finding studies for local agencies. The proposed foundation may be able to assist in such training programs, as I shall discuss below, but should not get into the fact-finding business except, possibly, in the case of extremely important national surveys. It should develop a close working relationship with the major public-opinion polling organizations, however.

Evaluation research is much more difficult because it requires the assessment of the effects of specific programs, which means that accurate measures of change must be made under carefully controlled conditions. If such research is not to be highly misleading, it must be carefully conducted by persons who have a sound knowledge of the principles of experimental design and applied statistics as well as detailed familiarity with the research literature in the relevant fields. Such research is relatively more expensive and requires a higher degree of objectivity on the part of the investigator, if only because there are fewer standardized procedures available for the analysis of one's data.

Important as it is, really careful evaluation research has been much more rare than one would expect in view of the number of action projects and pilot programs that have been instituted. In part this lack of research has been due to a shortage of trained personnel. But it has also been owing to the operation of vested interests, to a fear that impartial research will only emphasize negative results or downright failures, and also to a genuine ignorance of the advantages of good evaluation research in the planning process. Too often, for example, investigators have been asked to evaluate a program after it has been underway, at which time it is impossible to obtain measures of the previous state of affairs or to plan for adequate controls.

Given the complexity of race relations and our ignorance of the specific means by which to produce changes most efficiently, the obvious strategy is to try out a large number of alternative pilot programs, gradually weeding out the least effective and investing increasing resources in the remainder. At the same time, innovations must be encouraged and features of the more successful programs put together in various combinations in a search for optimal packages. This strategy obviously depends on one's ability to evaluate programs objectively, to assign priorities on the basis of tentative findings, to replicate on somewhat larger scales, and to communicate concerning the most and least successful features of each program. Without such evaluations, the result will be an endless proliferation of programs, each of which is jealously sponsored by competing agencies. This seems to be precisely the state of affairs that now exists within the federal government and that has led to a major disillusionment with liberal-sponsored remedial programs.

Research Training

Although the supply of social scientists now appears to be catching up with the demand, there is still a scarcity of persons adequately trained in the basic research skills of data collection and analysis. Of course most of this training must be accomplished through ordinary university programs, but a foundation specifically oriented to research in the field of race relations can play a supporting role in a number of respects. It can offer special summer seminars and provide experience in ongoing projects. And it can assess the overall manpower situation and attempt to correct for temporary shortages of various kinds.

As indicated earlier, fact-finding research is relatively simple to conduct, and there is available a rather large potential pool of researchers with A.B. or B.S. degrees in the social sciences. Relatively short training programs can be set up to provide supplemental practical research experience for these persons. If a visible job market develops, undergraduate and M.A. level training programs could easily be geared to careers in research, which would appeal to a large number of high-ability students who wish to engage in relevant research, rather than pursuing more advanced degrees in the social sciences.

At present, and probably for the next several decades, there is an extreme shortage of qualified minority social scientists. There are a number of reasons for this in addition to the fact that the percentage of minority college graduates is, of course, much lower than that of whites. First, in the case of blacks, a relatively higher proportion of college graduates are women who are somewhat more likely than men to drop out of the labor force to raise families. A concerted effort to coordinate research in the field of race relations could undoubtedly utilize much of this potential as part-time help as interviewers, observers, coders, and as statistical analysts for relatively routine fact-finding research. Secondly, black college graduates with social science backgrounds are in such heavy demand in other professions that the shortage is further aggravated. Black intellectuals are under great pressure to play the role of spokespersons for their race, and this means that professions such as law or social work become more suitable than that of social scientists. Hopefully, a well-established program of applied action research would attract many such persons.

Evaluation research ideally requires training at the doctoral level plus a good deal of practical experience. Since this type of research is generally not emphasized in conventional Ph.D. training programs in social science, it will be advisable to accept a number of postdoctoral trainees who already have substantial methodological backgrounds and to utilize these persons as advanced-level assistants on ongoing projects and as instructors for less-advanced personnel. Ideally, as many minority social scientists as possible should be recruited, but given the present shortage the majority of trainees at this advanced level will undoubtedly have to be white.

Publicizing Findings and Implications

One of the major reasons for the poor communication between social scientists and laymen is that there is no systematic effort being made to disseminate information about research results and their practical implications. To be sure, there are popularizers and there are a small number of social scientists who have taken upon themselves this responsibility. But the result is a rather erratic and miscellaneous set of reports that reflect the biases of the reporters and that do not convey accurately the nature of our most important findings. Those social scientists who are most likely to come to the public attention are those who have a special axe to grind or who are willing to dramatize in order to publicize. The result is often a series of exaggerated claims that gloss over necessary qualifications and possible alternative explanations.

It would be far better if the communication were more carefully guided by the sponsorship of an organization devoted to research and put on a regularized basis. For example, a quarterly bulletin of research findings might be published and an annual summary of the most important findings, implications, and research gaps circulated more widely. There must in addition be a genuine effort to reach the lower-class population, both black and white. At present, social scientists are not rewarded for such writing and are encouraged to publish primarily in the professional journals. Nor are most of them capable of writing with more than one audience in mind. What is obviously needed are persons with journalistic skills who are both motivated and sufficiently trained to translate rather dull statistical tables and numerical results into understandable and provocative reports. Since this must be done without distorting the findings and without either belittling the research or exaggerating its implications, it is obvious that the proper personnel must be carefully selected and kept well informed about the research operation.

CONCLUSION

We may conclude very briefly. To some readers it may seem anticlimactic to end a book that has dealt with tensions, conflict, and discrimination with a call for better organization, planning, and research. Yet I have tried to emphasize throughout that this is precisely what we need if we are to achieve any real gains and maintain a sense of direction. It is a kind of sustained effort involving very mundane kinds of tasks by large numbers of persons that we have generally lacked but that now seems absolutely essential. Furthermore, these efforts will have to be much more carefully coordinated if the cumulative effect is to be realized within the relatively brief time span that we seem to have remaining.

In the world of fiction, a dramatic effect is produced by finding some unusual or unexpected solution that very quickly results either in a happy ending or in deep tragedy. Most Americans have come to expect the happy rather than the tragic endings, there being a kind of fairy-tale or dreamlike quality to our expectations. But in the case of black-white relationships we had better be prepared for the tragic ending unless we are willing to become active participants in the unfolding drama. There will, however, probably be no single climax and no specific event that one can point to as determining the outcome.

The real world is much more complex than this and is not filled with a few heroes and villains and a large and completely passive audience. We are all actors, of a sort, but the drama is so complex that we all perceive ourselves as playing such minor roles that no one will ever notice. This is perhaps true. But meanwhile the tragedy unfolds. It is urgent for us to realize that the "other persons" we are counting on could very well be ourselves and that the proper time for acting is now. Black citizens of America have every right to demand that we begin to act in a constructive and coordinated fashion, to reexamine our priorities, and to give them a greater voice concerning their own destinies. Not only do white Americans owe this to blacks and other minorities, but we can be assured that we will all pay a terrible price if we fail.

About the Author

Hubert M. Blalock, Jr. is currently Professor of Sociology and Adjunct Professor of Political Science at the University of Washington. He received his B.A. at Dartmouth College, his M.A. at Brown University, and his Ph.D. at the University of North Carolina. He has previously taught at the University of Michigan, Yale University, and the University of North Carolina at Chapel Hill.

A specialist in applied statistics and research methods, as well as race and ethnic relations, his books include *Social Statistics*, *Causal Inferences in Nonexperimental Research*, *Toward a Theory of Minority Group Relations*, *Theory Building: From Verbal to Mathematical Reasoning*, *An Introduction to Social Research*, *Applied Multivariate Analysis and Experimental Designs* (with N. K. Namboodiri and L. F. Carter), and *Intergroup Processes: A Micro-Macro Approach* (with P. H. Wilken).

Dr. Blalock is currently serving as President of the American Sociological Association and has been elected a Fellow of the American Statistical Association. He has also been elected to the National Academy of Sciences and the American Academy of Arts and Sciences. His interest in applied race relations dates back to the early 1950s and includes experience relating to the Civil Rights movement in the South during the 1960s. More recently he has served as Chair of the University of Washington's Human Rights Commission.